Existential Wellness Coaching

This comprehensive guide merges existential philosophy with wellness coaching strategies, equipping coaches with powerful tools to help clients meet their existential challenges and lead lives of authentic purpose, deeper meaning, and sustainable well-being.

Dr. Eric Maisel introduces existential wellness coaching as a holistic approach that recognizes how physical and psychological well-being are intrinsically connected to our sense of purpose, meaning, and authenticity. Grounded in concepts from existential philosophy, this practical guide helps coaches, therapists, and other mental health practitioners deepen their work with clients to address existential challenges and to help clients develop the resilience to maintain existential well-being in challenging times. Unlike traditional coaching that focuses solely on goals or conventional therapy that treats symptoms, existential wellness coaching empowers clients to confront life's fundamental questions while developing concrete strategies for living with greater intention. Each chapter systematically addresses core existential concerns, including self-relationship, value identification, purpose creation, meaning-making, authenticity, and developing a personal life philosophy.

Offering new ways of thinking about common existential issues, this book contains tools that will help coaches enable their clients to make life-changing shifts and necessary mental reframes.

Eric Maisel, PhD, is the author of 60+ books, including *The Coach's Way*, *Rethinking Depression*, *Brave New Mind*, *Night Brilliance*, *Coaching the Artist Within*, and *The Van Gogh Blues*. He writes the "Rethinking Mental Health" blog for *Psychology Today*, with 3.5 million views, and is the lead editor for the Ethics International Press Critical Psychology and Critical Psychiatry Series.

"As an experienced psychotherapist, couples' counselor, and existential life coach, I've been waiting for a book that moves us beyond the frame of 'existential coaching' to the contemporary and highly useful idea of 'existential wellness coaching.' In these difficult times, this book is needed now more than ever. Highly recommended!"

Don Laird, *Psychotherapist, Adjunct Professor, Carlow University, co-editor,* Existential Wellness

"I've seen Eric Maisel in action training coaches and the level of professionalism and humanity he brings to the task is unparalleled. We see it again in *Existential Wellness Coaching*, a breakthrough book that joins his books for coaches (like *The Coach's Way* and *Coaching the Artist Within*) as an essential guide for helpers in all of the healing and helping professions."

Lynda Monk, *MSW, RSW, CPCC, Director, International Association for Journal Writing*

"Eric Maisel created our Existential Wellness Coach Certificate Program, which students love. His new book, *Existential Wellness Coaching*, will become the text for that training; and I highly recommend that if you teach in the areas of existential coaching or existential therapy, that you consider adopting *Existential Wellness Coaching* as a text for your class. Your students will relish it!"

Gerard O'Donovan, *CEO and Founder, Noble Manhattan Coaching*

*"Existential Wellness Coachi*ng is a stunning work. Besides being a tutorial on a specific kind of coaching, it is also a treatise on how to live in today's chaotic world. It is a must read, not only for people interested in coaching and/or existentialism, but for everyone. The book, and its author, should be remembered in the history books as the first twenty-first century addition to the earlier works of existentialism and their creators, Soren Kierkegaard, Jean Paul Sartre, Albert Camus, et al."

Denise Beck-Clark, *author,* Thirty Years Hence *and* Concurrent Sentences

"When I first discovered Dr. Eric Maisel's work several years ago, I was a professional creative seeking to deepen my path. Now, as a creativity coach, educator, and filmmaker, I continue to find his books both inspiring and intellectually rigorous. *Existential Wellness Coaching* offers profound insights into addressing life's and clients' challenges. Not to be missed!"

Nefeli Soteriou, *independent filmmaker and creativity coach*

"*Existential Wellness Coaching* is a masterful menu of ideas, tactics, and coaching vignettes to support clients with the 'project of their life.' Eric Maisel's ability to weave existential practices into accessible and powerful coaching tools is evident in every page. His personal vision of existential wellness confronts big topics such as freedom, authenticity, creativity, absurdity, and rebellion, while delivering a compelling coaching model for clients who are struggling with the complexities of human nature and existence. I highly recommend this book as a valuable addition to your coaching toolkit."

Sharon Stratford, *Career and Creativity Coach, New Zealand*

"We are grateful to have Eric Maisel, the United States' most sought-after Master Creativity Coach and Existential Wellness Coach, supporting our international community of coaches with CPD masterclasses. For many years, he's brought a wealth of practical life and business experience to these sessions; he's also demonstrated a genuine love, and feel for existential issues. Added to which, he has a pragmatic and a light approach that makes his teachings accessible, which is much appreciated. *Existential Wellness Coaching* brings these qualities together in a single much-needed volume. Highly recommended for coaches, therapists, and anyone interested in meaning, purpose, and existential well-being."

Aurora Dawn Campbell, *Accredited Fellow Coach and Mentor, Business Director, International Authority for Professional Coaching & Mentoring (IAPC&M)*

Existential Wellness Coaching

A Guide to Helping Clients Make Meaning and Live Authentically

Eric Maisel

Routledge
Taylor & Francis Group
NEW YORK AND LONDON

Designed cover image: © Getty Images gremlin

First published 2026
by Routledge
605 Third Avenue, New York, NY 10158

and by Routledge
4 Park Square, Milton Park, Abingdon, Oxon, OX14 4RN

Routledge is an imprint of the Taylor & Francis Group, an informa business

ISBN: 978-1-041-20950-8 (hbk)
ISBN: 978-1-041-20927-0 (pbk)
ISBN: 978-1-003-72497-1 (ebk)

DOI: 10.4324/9781003724971

Typeset in Times New Roman
by Apex CoVantage, LLC

For Ann, 49 years into this adventure

Contents

1 From existential thought to existential wellness 1

2 The history of a concept 10

3 On existential wellness coaching 20

4 Existential wellness coaching tactics 32

5 The weight of individuality 47

6 The story of life purposes 59

7 Coaching meaning 71

8 The pain of meaning crises 81

9 On existential sadness 92

10 On existential anxiety 104

11 Dealing with ambiguity and uncertainty 116

12 The problem of work 130

13 Freedom, resistance, and rebellion 142

14 On authenticity 154

15 Creativity's place in the puzzle 166

16 The possibility of existential joy 180

Postscript 190

References *192*
Index *194*

Chapter 1

From existential thought to existential wellness

In this book, I want to present my personal vision of what existential wellness coaching looks like and means. This is not a comprehensive overview of a field or a scholarly examination of a concept. Rather, it is one person's view. This is in itself very existential—can we imagine the religious Soren Kierkegaard and the atheist Jean-Paul Sartre or the religious Fyodor Dostoevsky and the atheist Simone de Beauvoir, except that we indubitably and uncomfortably exist?

So you will be receiving my idiosyncratic understanding of meaning (that it is merely a feeling), of life purpose (that "life purposes" are the better and truer idea), and of other ideas personal to me that amount to my version of what existentialism, existential wellness, and existential wellness signify. You will naturally have your own ideas. That, after all, is the existential imperative! But I do hope that my ideas will at least interest you and get you thinking.

Let's begin!

1.1 An ambitious philosophy

Existentialism is an ambitious philosophy that demands that each human being try his or her darnedest. It begs the individual to make use of the measure of freedom he possesses that he look life in the eye and deal with reality and that he stand tall as an advocate for human dignity.

It argues that life, by pairing tremendous ordinariness with tremendous difficulty and by leading to nothing but death, is a kind of cheat, and that human beings must nevertheless cheat the cheater by adopting an indomitable attitude, making the meaning, and choosing the purposes they require. This agenda sets the bar very high and doesn't suit most people.

Existentialism failed to become a truly widespread philosophy because it is not really to most people's taste. It makes work for them; it pesters them to be moral; it demands that they articulate their life purposes and live them; it alerts them to the likely complete purposelessness of the universe; and it announces that a kind of perpetual rebellion is necessary.

DOI: 10.4324/9781003724971-1

It trumpets that fitting in will not do and that all those easy pleasures and vices, while nobody's business but your own, still must be judged by you—and, very often, found too easy and too unethical. It keeps asserting that you must be a hero—an absurd hero, to be sure, heroically keeping meaning afloat in the face of the void and working hard at the project of your life when life itself cares nothing about your efforts—but a hero nonetheless. It sets the bar extremely high—too high for the vast majority of people, most existentialists included.

Existentialists themselves usually failed at living with the bar set that awesomely high. They could articulate why the bar ought to be set that high, at the place of personal responsibility and ethical action that they called authentic living, but they found it inconveniently difficult to live that mindful, measured, and pure a life.

They proved in the living that our foibles defeat our resolutions much of the time. They proved it by womanizing. They proved it by gambling. They proved it by succumbing to addiction. They proved it by giving in to despair and taking to the sofa. They proved it by rejecting real work and choosing second-rate projects. They saw clearly where they had placed the bar—apparently much too far above them.

It was simply too hard to live as carefully, ethically, and authentically as the tenets of existentialism demanded. The tenets were lovely, albeit in an ice-water sort of way, but the reality was daunting. Therefore, existentialism never really caught on. For a while after World War II, millions of young people read about it, nodded in agreement with its premises, but drifted away from it because of its rigors. Jobs called; sex called; vision quests called; soccer on Saturday called; and stock portfolios called. It was fine to read a little Nietzsche, Sartre, and Camus in college—but seemingly very sensible to then put that behind you and get on with your daily commute and your evening drinking.

Existentialism didn't allow for an array of things that human beings actually wanted, like permission to be petty and permission to waste vast amounts of time. It didn't condone silent acquiescence or slogan-sized commandments. It frowned on group allegiances and social frivolity. Existential philosophy acknowledged these desires perhaps more clearly than any other philosophy, but it then asked people not to indulge them—and people passed on the invitation. Many remained nostalgic for those high ideals and sometimes did a little looking back, maybe rereading *Nausea* or *The Stranger* in the bathroom. But, essentially, they passed on the invitation, any nostalgia notwithstanding.

People passed for other reasons, too. Not only did existentialism demand that they live an ethically vigilant life where each action was the culmination of an important internal moral debate, but they were also supposed to "transcend" personality and the facts of existence and escape the net into which every human being is entangled. This was not only a lot to ask—but it was also perhaps unfair and impossible. How were you supposed to not be the person you had developed into? How were you supposed to shrug off illness, war, disaster, and every manner of calamity and constraint and stand tall? How was any of that really doable?

To take one example, people were supposed to transcend pride. But our smartest, most talented people have rarely been able to come close to such maturity. In their relations with each other, Dostoevsky and Tolstoy couldn't. Camus and Sartre couldn't. Freud and Jung couldn't. Picasso and Matisse couldn't. Elton John and Tina Turner couldn't. Scientists haven't, businesspeople haven't, and parents attending a Little League game or a PTA meeting haven't. It turns out that ego, pride, and wounded pride aren't snaps to transcend. Where did we ever get the idea that they were?

Or take the matter of appetite. People with large, undeniable, and maybe unquenchable appetites—for sex, for peanuts, for experience, for seduction, for fast rides, for competition, and for the rush of adrenaline—were supposed to put their appetites in their back pocket and approach life with the measured restraint of an ascetic. Authenticity required that you avoid gluttony, promiscuity, and all the other faces of appetite. Who wanted to give up any of that? Could it even *be* given up?

Or take human energy itself. The existential vision pictures a human being in control of herself. But what if you are flying along in a manic way in pursuit of some impossible dream and really don't want to stop and take a measured reckoning? What if you want to act impulsively—intuitively, if you like—and take a pass on some stolid calm that seriously slows you down? It seemed like a choice had to be made between a snail's pace rationality and our very life force—and people choose pulsation over calculation.

Many existentialists understood all this. They understood it very well. Each danced the poignant dance of demanding much from human beings while doubting that the effort was possible or even plausible. They doubted and wondered. Why make such a Herculean effort at authenticity when personality hung like a lead weight around your neck and the facts of existence ruined many of your plans? All that wondering and doubting lead to those trademarks of existential thought: fear and trembling, nausea, existential anxiety, existential dread, and, of course, absurdity.

1.2 Why existentialism remains needed

For thousands of years, human beings suffered from one sort of unhappiness as we lived at the mercy of storms, tigers, germs, and tyrants. Then, starting in the seventeenth century, we experienced 400 years of the celebration—and inflation—of the individual.

Certain amazing ideas bloomed, and some even more amazing realities followed. We got individual rights. We got the rise of science and technology. We got the sense that man might get to know himself and his world through the application of self-awareness and the scientific method. We got progress on all fronts. A wild, strange euphoria arose: man mattered!

But disaster was brewing.

Existential writers as far back as the pre-Socratic Greeks warned that the better we got to know our situation, the closer we would come to a psychological disaster. We would, by pushing back the curtain and looking reality in the eye, stand face-to-face with a reality so cold that the space between the stars would seem warm by comparison.

We would get nothing from science except what science could provide. We would get nothing from civil society except what civil society could provide. We would get nothing from the truth except hard truths. Existentialists understood that we would keep losing hope as each new mighty idea, including and especially that a given human being mattered, came up against its startling limitations.

The more we announced that man mattered, the more we saw that he really didn't. The better we understood that the dinosaurs could be extinguished in the blink of an eye by an asteroid strike or some other natural disaster, the better we understood that we could suffer a similar fate. The better we understood the power of microbes, and even as we worked hard and pretty well to fight them, the better we understood that something functionally invisible and endlessly prevalent could end our personal journey on any given afternoon. The more science taught us, the more we shrank in size—and shrank back in horror. You could build the largest particle accelerator the world had ever seen and recreate the Big Bang, and psychologically speaking, you would end up with only more of nothing—*even* more of nothing, if that were possible.

Certain enormous twentieth-century earthquakes cemented this psychological disaster. Hundreds of millions of human beings had been slaughtered before the Nazis' efforts at extermination, but never before had towering piles of bones appeared in darkened movie theaters as newsreel footage. Never before Hiroshima could our species picture with such spectacular clarity the possibility, verging on something like a certainty, that our species might vanish—and even in our own lifetime. These two events, Hiroshima and the Holocaust, were special. They were something like the last straws and shattered our belief that individual human life mattered.

It is this apprehension of cosmic indifference that existentialists faced squarely and demanded that you face, too. But who wants that daily dose of despair? We had all somehow wagered that well-stocked supermarkets and guaranteed elections would do the trick and protect us from the void. But they didn't. This now hundred-year-long *certainty* that we are throwaways has made life look completely unfunny. We can laugh together over a bottle of wine and make small talk about this and that, adding a kind of cultural laugh track to a very unfunny situation comedy. But, in most of our private seconds, there is not much laughter. Rather, there is a deep, wide, abiding "Why bother?" And who wanted existentialists reminding us of *that*?

Well, today, many people do. They have "come back around" to facing their meaning challenges and life purpose challenges. More and more often, they are saying out loud, "I do not want to work a meaningless job sixty hours a week," and "I need more to life than a new phone or a new side hustle." They are coming around to realizing that the existential ideals are the right ones.

They are beginning to embrace the following ideas and ideals:

You take as much control as possible of your thoughts, your attitudes, your moods, your behaviors, and your very orientation toward life, and you marshal your innate freedom in the service of your intentions. You stand up, you tell truth to power, you name and then take responsibility for your life purpose choices, you deal with meaninglessness by making new meaning investments and seizing new meaning opportunities, and you dismiss absurdity as true but irrelevant. This may still be as hard as it ever was to do, but now it makes deeper sense. People are primed to embrace this way of looking at life and this way of living.

What does embracing an existential way of life or an existential orientation toward life look like? Here's one report, from a student of mine. Mary explained:

> As a young college student, I came to the conclusion that existentialism meant hanging out in cafes drinking coffee and wine, arguing philosophy, politics, and imminent nuclear annihilation, rounded out by sex and sly jokes. "Hell is other people!" declared Sartre in my professor's voice, and we all giggled nervously, because that already seemed true. But I was eager for my chance to prove an exception, sure I could create my life as I wished it to be.
>
> Cue the years to roll past, with a banner by Beckett: "I can't go on. I'll go on." What I learned at seventeen and eighteen, accepting futility and trying anyway, is newly useful now that I'm in my sixties, dealing with cancer and mortality, aloneness, and life on the edges. I see life as insistent, persistent, no matter what or where. And my little individual existence is all right, all of it. I'm here. It's enough.

Here's a second report. Sarah shared:

> For me, "existential" has a feeling of heavy responsibility. When I look around, I often feel envious of other people who seem to be okay with having someone or something (church, religious figures, parents, capitalism, cultural norms, etc.) tell them what the point of it all is. Especially in the past few years, when I look around and see how easily people seem to fall into divisive factions, it appears that people are often only too happy to have someone else tell them what to believe in.
>
> Being existential, by contrast, is looking around and realizing with a sinking feeling that there is no one truth, no single way of living, no one belief system that will make sense of this life. On days when I feel overwhelmed and exhausted, I really wish there was something I could believe in and a set of

rules I could follow to know I was doing the right thing and to just be happy. But . . . I know better.

And lastly, from Helen:

My overriding concern throughout my life has been how I and other people have been limited in their expectations for themselves because of the expectations of the cultures and societies in which we are raised. As a white, female farm kid, I learned that I and my sisters were disappointments for not being a male to take over the farm. I was given the impression that higher education would be wasted on us. We could be farmers' wives but not farmers ourselves. We could finish high school but college was laughable (the adults literally laughed when I said I intended to go to college).

My work as an artist and educator has always been tied to using the creative process to overcome the injustice and violence of limited expectations based on stereotypes. I used my art to think about this, to unlearn limiting norms, and to figure out how to find my own creative voice and share it. I desired to decide for myself what I believed, what I was capable of, and what subjects and materials I could use to create art and who I really respected for what they brought to the world. I have been thinking about this—and living this—my whole life.

1.3 A fanciful visit to an existential wellness coach

For a long time, the existential ideal fell flat in the real world, but it only went dormant. As a species, we may not be as courageous or capable as existential thinkers hoped that we would be or wished that we would be. But it looks like millions upon millions of people are opening up to existential ideas again.

We may not be able to do an even adequate job of transcending the pitfalls of personality, negotiating the facts of existence, or living fully authentically. But many people are being called to try. That is where existential wellness help and existential wellness helpers come in.

As a result, because many human beings have come to realize that they require help at the existential level, people who call themselves existential therapists, existential coaches, and existential wellness coaches have popped up to fill that need.

What does that help look like? The following is a fanciful depiction of an existential wellness coaching session. It is meant to make you smile, not to represent a real session. Real sessions would not sound like this. Rather, I want to communicate the kinds of ideas and themes that can and will come up in an existential wellness coaching session. This, then, is a fanciful look at how "existential ideas" can inhabit the coaching space.

A fellow we'll call Bob has cycled through all of society's helpers: he's been to a psychiatrist, a psychologist, a Jungian therapist, a cognitive-behavioral therapist, a spiritual coach, a clinical social worker, a life coach, and even a shaman and an astrologer. To each of them, he has presented the "hole" he is experiencing, the hole in his life that he can't fill. Each has given him their sort of answer—but, so far, he has not been impressed.

That hole is still coldly and insistently in place, and Bob suspects that he has probably exhausted the cadre of helpers his society is able to provide him. He fears that he is obliged to go it alone again. Then, he stumbles upon someone calling himself an existential wellness coach. After a while, figuring that he doesn't have much to lose, he decides that he might as well try a Zoom session with this person. And so, he schedules a session, and the session commences.

He describes his hole as best as he can. The existential wellness coach listens and calmly replies:

Bob: The hole is natural. It is the feeling that comes with an absence of meaning. Since meaning is a subjective psychological experience—a feeling, really—that sometimes visits us but that is also apt to vanish, you will continue to experience this hole until you begin making meaning for yourself. You can't get rid of the hole by looking for meaning or seeking meaning, as that only occasionally generates the experience you crave. Rather, you will be better off trying to coax meaning into existence. Should I elaborate?

Coach: Yes, please!

Bob: The hole is caused by the fact that we understand a lot about ourselves and a lot about the universe and we have inadvertently extrapolated from that knowledge the belief that we do not matter and that our efforts do not matter. We have made ourselves sad and ineffectual by virtue of taking in several centuries' worth of the deconstruction of everything. But that belief, that we do not matter and that our efforts do not matter, is a mental mistake. It is that exact mental mistake that makes the hole. Once you understand that the meaninglessness you are experiencing is an artifact of wishful thinking about a universe you think ought to exist and instead accept the reality of this precise natural world, created as a result of natural forces and without the sort of purposefulness or fairness you want for it, you can get on with life.

Therefore, you will need to change your mind about what you need life to be—objectively purposeful, part of a cosmic plan, watched over by unseen eyes or guided by some unseen hand, and so on—and hold instead to a new, clear vision, that you do not need to be happy, that you do not need to move mountains, but that you do need to make yourself proud of your own efforts by engaging in what I call value-based meaning-making. Are you following?

Coach: I am!

Coach: You make yourself proud of your efforts by donning the mantle of meaning-maker and engaging in value-based meaning-making and then the hole shrinks to a manageable size. It becomes a pinprick—maybe still a constant one, but only a pinprick—rather than the gaping, unmanageable, painful thing that it is now. Is that clear?

Bob: Yes!

Coach: Existentialism posits that there are certain core issues facing human beings, issues like existential anxiety, suffering and dread. It reminds us that we have evolved into a certain sort of creature and it is that creature that must deal with these issues. We are creatures without an adequate off switch for our brain; and therefore, racing brain issues like mania afflict us. We are creatures with contradictory impulses, with the wish to destroy the world and the wish to save the world, often depending on nothing more than our mood. Most poignantly, we are creatures with a persistent but nevertheless still only intermittent need for the subjective psychological experience of meaning. We are very particular and specific creatures, maybe not like our distant ancestors were and maybe not like our far future descendants will be, but exactly as we are right now; and we are obliged to take that into account.

We do not argue philosophical questions like whether existence precedes essence or vice versa. Rather, we assert that we are creatures who have evolved into exactly the creature that we are, with a psychological and biological reality that can't be ignored. This creature can make meaning, but only exactly and precisely as a human being can make meaning: that is, with the knowledge that it is doing the making, that it has made a decision about life, and that nothing out there is monitoring that decision, smiling or frowning about that decision, or caring about that decision. Maybe you wanted life to mean something more than that or different from that: that desire, which is the exact equivalent of a negative evaluation of life as it is, helps maintain the hole.

And by the way, we have a vision of personality! We take you to be a member of a species that comes with a personality. We have a way of honoring the logic and reality of original personality, that genetic inheritance that includes your baseline intelligence, sadness, anxiety, and even core mindset; the intractability of your formed personality, that personality that accretes over time with its built-in loss of freedom; and all the remaining freedom of your available personality. Our model of original personality, formed personality and available personality helps us not only better discuss your emotional distress but paints a picture that includes necessary emotional distress, the distress that arises as you engage in value-based meaning-making. And so, we explain that there are varieties of emotional health, including a variety where you experience emotional distress and emotional health at the same time! That is liberating information.

Oh, and we also have tactics, strategies, and techniques. We float the idea of a morning life purposes check-in where you make your life purpose choices for the day and organize your day around those choices. We float the dual ideas of a life purpose statement and a life purpose icon, the latter a personalized visual representation of your life purpose vision that can work for you nicely, as nicely as a cross works for a Christian or a Star of David works for a Jew. We have our bag of tricks and we think that bag helps!

But enough about what we have on offer. There's certainly more to say; but it's past time that we got to you!

The session continues with Bob announcing what life purpose choices and meaning investments he thinks he would like to make and what upgrades to his personality he thinks are needed if he is to pull off the feat of living an authentic life. He finds himself with new tasks, a new vision, and new hope. Finally, he thinks to himself that the lovely word "authentic" has some flesh on its bones! It does not mean living in alignment with anything "out there." It is now a simple-to-say thing: living a life aligned with his life purpose choices. For a split second, he feels happy.

Of course, this wasn't anything like a real session. But I think that it may provide you with a glimpse of how existential ideas, ideas that have repeated themselves for thousands of years, can be dressed in modern clothes and can serve a contemporary person looking for help with the very basics of life.

FOOD FOR THOUGHT

1. What thoughts, feelings, and pictures does the word "existential" conjure up for you?
2. Do you sense a difference between "existential" and "existentialism"? What do those differences feel like?
3. What does the phrase "existential wellness" signify to you?
4. If you are already a coach, can you imagine adding "existential wellness coaching" to what you already do?
5. If you aren't yet a coach, what about existential wellness coaching might attract you? Does it strike you as an interesting, rewarding path?

Chapter 2

The history of a concept

In this chapter, I want to start out by reminding us of psychiatry's indifference to the idea of "existential wellness" and then provide a brief history of the concept.

2.1 Psychiatry and existential wellness

Psychiatry, as the dominant discipline for understanding and treating mental suffering, has no doubt made some contributions to human well-being—and also failed in many profound ways. One of its many failures is that it has largely ignored the idea of *existential wellness*—that is, the idea that we are obliged to cultivate meaning, purpose, authenticity, freedom, and resilience in the face of life's inescapable conditions of uncertainty, mortality, and responsibility.

Instead of embracing the existential dimension of human life, psychiatry has tended to reduce suffering to neurochemical imbalances, symptoms to be managed, or maladaptive behaviors to be corrected. In this way, psychiatry has marginalized some of the deepest questions of the human condition, leaving them to philosophy, literature, and the occasional existentially minded therapist or coach.

2.2 The narrow-frame medical model

The cornerstone of psychiatry since the mid-twentieth century has been the *medical model*, which assumes that mental disorders can be understood, classified, and treated much like physical illnesses. While this model provides a naming system and chemical remedies, it has two significant limitations when it comes to existential wellness.

First, it treats *suffering as pathology*. For psychiatry, persistent sadness may be labeled "major depressive disorder," even if that sadness emerges from a loss of meaning, an existential crisis, or a confrontation with mortality. The emphasis is on eliminating symptoms rather than exploring their human significance. The

DOI: 10.4324/9781003724971-2

client's despair is framed as a disease to be cured, not as a possible sign of an authentic reckoning with life's difficulties.

Second, the medical model seeks *standardization and universality,* whereas existential wellness is inherently subjective, personal, and context-dependent. What constitutes authenticity or purpose varies widely across individuals and cultures. Psychiatry's preference for measurable and reproducible outcomes systematically excludes dimensions of life that cannot be easily quantified—such as courage in the face of nothingness.

2.3 The DSM and the disappearance of meaning

The *DSM* is psychiatry's central text, a taxonomy of symptoms and disorders. While useful for communication and insurance reimbursement, the DSM has been criticized for *over-pathologizing normal human struggles* and for neglecting existential concerns.

For example, grief has been increasingly medicalized, with bereavement-related sadness being distinguished from "major depression" by only subtle criteria. Yet grief, as philosophers and existentialists have long argued, is not merely a symptom but an existential confrontation with finitude and attachment. To reduce grief to a disorder strips it of meaning and flattens its existential dimension.

Similarly, the DSM has no category for "loss of meaning" or "crisis of authenticity." These experiences, central to existential wellness, appear nowhere in the psychiatric nosology. They may be recast as depression, adjustment disorder, or anxiety disorder, but this framing eliminates their existential depth. The very questions of who we are, how to live authentically, and how to make peace with mortality vanish in the clinical translation.

2.4 The dominance of pharmacology

In recent decades, psychiatry has become increasingly identified with *psychopharmacology*. Antidepressants, antipsychotics, mood stabilizers, and anxiolytics dominate psychiatric practice, often overshadowing psychotherapy or holistic approaches. While medication can relieve suffering and enable functioning, it also narrows the conversation about what wellness means.

A patient who reports emptiness, lack of purpose, or existential dread may receive a prescription for an SSRI. The implicit message is that their distress stems from a serotonin imbalance rather than from the human condition itself. This approach risks trivializing existential suffering, suggesting that it can be chemically neutralized rather than meaningfully engaged.

Moreover, pharmacological approaches focus on relief, not growth. Existential wellness, by contrast, acknowledges that suffering is not only inevitable but can also be a source of insight, transformation, and authenticity. Kierkegaard called despair not only the *sickness unto death* but also saw in it the possibility of a deeper relation to the self and, in his view, the divine. Psychiatry, through its pharmacological lens, misses this potential.

2.5 The marginalization of existential reality

Within psychotherapy, there exists a lineage of approaches explicitly concerned with existential wellness: for example, logotherapy (Frankl, 1967), existential analysis (Boss, 1963, 1963/1983), and existential–humanistic therapy (May, 1953; Yalom, 1980, 2008). These modalities take our human need for meaning, our confrontations with mortality, and our understanding of the responsibilities of freedom seriously.

Yet, in mainstream psychiatry, such therapies remain marginal and marginalized. They are rarely taught in psychiatric training, rarely reimbursed by insurance, and rarely prioritized in clinical guidelines. Instead, cognitive-behavioral therapy (CBT) and pharmacotherapy dominate.

This neglect is not accidental. Psychiatry prizes empirical validation—randomized controlled trials, meta-analyses, and measurable outcomes. Existential therapies, with their emphasis on unique subjective experience, resist such quantification. As a result, they are dismissed as less scientific or rigorous, even though they directly address dimensions of life that patients consistently describe as central to their suffering.

2.6 Existential suffering in modern life

The irony is that psychiatry's neglect of existential wellness comes at a moment when existential suffering is increasingly visible. Secularization has diminished traditional sources of meaning; globalization and technology have fragmented identities; and climate change and geopolitical instability amplify anxiety about the future. Patients come to psychiatrists not only with panic attacks or insomnia but also with questions of purpose, identity, and despair over the state of the world.

Psychiatry's current tool kit is poorly suited to these challenges. A person who reports despair at the lack of meaning in their career may be diagnosed with "generalized anxiety disorder." A young adult overwhelmed by climate anxiety may be prescribed medication rather than supported in their search for agency and purpose. Such interventions may (and only may) reduce symptoms but do nothing to cultivate existential wellness.

2.7 Toward a broader vision of wellness

If psychiatry were to take existential wellness seriously, it would need to expand its paradigm. Such an expanded approach might include

- Asking patients about sources of meaning, purpose, and authenticity alongside symptom checklists.

- Recognizing existential crises (grief, identity loss, and confrontation with mortality) as normal, meaningful struggles rather than pathologies.
- Valuing therapies that cultivate existential resilience—such as logotherapy, narrative therapy, meaning-centered psychotherapy, or existential wellness coaching—alongside CBT and medication.
- Training psychiatrists to engage with philosophical, existential, and spiritual questions, or at least to collaborate with professionals who do.

Such a shift would allow psychiatry to move from a narrow focus on symptom elimination to a richer vision of wellness—one that includes existential flourishing as well as clinical stability.

2.8 The concept of existential wellness

"Existential wellness" refers to a cluster of concerns—meaning, freedom, responsibility, authenticity, purpose, belonging, and finitude—that originally entered modern discourse through European existential philosophy and phenomenology. Later, it migrated into psychiatry, psychotherapy, counseling, coaching, education, and public conversations about well-being.

While the phrase itself is relatively recent, its elements are centuries old: for example, the anxiety of freedom (Kierkegaard, 1843/1983a), the demand to "become who you are" (Nietzsche, 1967, 2003, 2006), authenticity under the threat of mortality (Heidegger, 1927/1962), the burden of choice (Sartre, 1944), and the ethics of relational freedom (de Beauvoir, 1949/2011).

In psychology and counseling, these themes emerge as logotherapy (Frankl, 1967), existential analysis (Binswanger, 1963; Boss, 1963, 1963/1983), American existential–humanistic therapy (May, 1953; Bugental, 1965, 1987), the encounter group and human potential movements (Rogers, 1957, 1961; Perls; Maslow, 1968, 1971), and contemporary integrative and positive psychology approaches (Yalom, 1980, 2008; Wong, 2016a, 2016b, 2021; Seligman; Kashdan & McKnight). The history of existential wellness is a story of translation and transition—how questions about the meaning of existence became questions about living well.

Let's take a brief look at five arcs: (1) pre-existential forerunners, (2) classical existential–phenomenological sources, (3) the entry of the concept into psychiatry and psychotherapy, plus humanistic and experiential expansions after World War II, (4) late-twentieth-century critiques and integrations (including postmodern, feminist, and multicultural perspectives), and (5) twenty-first-century convergences with well-being science and public health.

2.8.1 Forerunners: spiritual care, moral philosophy, and classical therapies of the self

Long before "existential" became a label, Western and non-Western traditions developed practices aimed at "soul care" and meaning-making. Stoicism

(Epictetus and Marcus Aurelius) trained attention to what is within our control and cultivated equanimity in the face of fate, anticipating modern themes of agency, appraisal, and death awareness.

Early Christian and medieval spiritual direction, with its exercises of self-examination and conscientious choice, foreshadowed the later emphasis on personal responsibility and conscience. In modern moral philosophy, Rousseau's valorization of authenticity and Kant's respect for rational agency contribute important strands to the conversation.

Nineteenth-century "talking cures," including Romantic self-cultivation and moral treatment in asylums, already pivoted around meaning and dignity; here, the person was addressed not only as a patient but also as a moral agent. These prehistories supply existential wellness with three durable intuitions: that clarity about what ultimately matters protects the self, that practices of reflection can reorganize experience, and that freedom entails both risk and responsibility.

2.8.2 *Classical sources: the existential–phenomenological turn*

2.8.2.1 *Kierkegaard: anxiety, despair, and choosing the self*

Søren Kierkegaard placed subjective passion at the center of truth and framed anxiety as the "dizziness of freedom." Despair, for him, amounted to a failure to be oneself, a despair overcome not by information but by decision and commitment. Existential wellness inherits from Kierkegaard the norm that well-being is inseparable from self-relation—how one stands to one's freedom, faith, and responsibility.

2.8.2.2 *Nietzsche: life affirmation and self-creation*

Friedrich Nietzsche dismantled received moralities and called for creative self-overcoming: "become who you are." His vision of wellness is not comfort but vitality—an honest, courageous style of existence that says "yes" to life, suffering included. In contemporary terms, existential wellness bears this stamp whenever it privileges value creation, courage, and artistic or ethical self-authorship.

2.8.2.3 *Heidegger: authenticity under the threat of mortality*

In *Being and Time*, Martin Heidegger analyzes everyday inauthentic absorption in "the They" (*das Man*) and contrasts it with authenticity, a resolute owning of one's finite possibilities in the face of death. Wellness here is not hedonic balance but existential lucidity and responsiveness—living deliberately under finitude. This then becomes a cornerstone for therapeutic work having to do with making meaning, experiencing the passage of time, and dealing with anxiety.

2.8.2.4 *Sartre and de Beauvoir: freedom, bad faith, and the ethics of ambiguity*

Jean-Paul Sartre recasts pathology as *mauvaise foi* (bad faith): the evasion of freedom by pretending to be an inert thing. Simone de Beauvoir radicalizes this by insisting that my personal wellness is bound up with the other's freedom; authentic existence is an "ethics of ambiguity" that refuses domination or self-erasure. Existential wellness thus acquires a relational and political horizon—well-being cannot be privatized without distortion.

Phenomenology enters clinical life with Ludwig Binswanger's Daseinsanalysis and Medard Boss's work with Heidegger, rethinking suffering as ways of "being-in-the-world" rather than as mere symptom clusters. The clinic then becomes a place to clarify existence and make a personal sense of the vagaries of living.

2.8.3 *From philosophy to therapy: logotherapy, existential analysis, and American existential–humanistic therapy*

2.8.3.1 *Frankl and logotherapy: meaning as a vital need*

After surviving the concentration camps, Viktor Frankl argued that "will to meaning" is a primary human motivation; suffering becomes bearable when it is meaningfully borne. Techniques such as dereflection and Socratic dialog can help clients discern their values and their life purposes. Frankl's work gave existential wellness a crisp, practice-ready thesis: meaning protects life.

2.8.3.2 *Rollo May, Bugental, and the existential–humanistic turn*

In the United States, Rollo May introduced European existential ideas into a humanistic framework, emphasizing courage, creativity, and the encounter with anxiety. James Bugental developed a nuanced method for presence, subjective depth, and responsibility in session—"the art of the psychotherapist." Here, the wellness ideal shifts from symptom reduction to deepened aliveness and personal agency.

2.8.3.3 *Rogers, Maslow, and the human potential movement*

Carl Rogers's person-centered therapy, with its core conditions of empathy, unconditional positive regard, and congruence, overlaps strongly with existential wellness. In this view, psychological health is the increasing alignment between lived experience and self-expression. Abraham Maslow's hierarchy culminates in self-actualization and later self-transcendence. This era relocates existential care into education, organizations, and group work, expanding the wellness horizon beyond the therapy room.

2.8.3.4 *Yalom: existential psychotherapy for clinical practice*

Irvin Yalom identified death, freedom, isolation, and meaninglessness as four "ultimate concerns," offering a clinically tractable map that clinicians still use. In effect, he provided the field its most widely adopted grammar for existential wellness: anxiety as a signal, relationship as a laboratory for authenticity, and meaning as a daily construction.

2.8.4 After the 1960s: pluralization, critique, and cross-cultural dialogs

2.8.4.1 *Feminist, multicultural, and critical interventions*

Existential language risks becoming hyper-individualistic if it ignores social power. Feminist philosophers and therapists, building on de Beauvoir, critiqued a "heroic" freedom that overlooks structural constraint, trauma, and care.

Multicultural and liberation psychologies pressed the point that well-being is coauthored by communities, histories, and institutions. These critiques rebalance existential wellness by incorporating notions of solidarity, justice, and belonging.

2.8.4.2 *Dialogs with Buddhism, Confucian, and Indigenous traditions*

Cross-cultural dialogs enriched existential practice. Buddhist mindfulness reframed anxiety and attachment, offering practices for non-grasping awareness that harmonize with existential presence while disagreeing about the status of self, creating a tension that continues to exist between the idea of "self" as instrumentality and "self" as illusion.

Confucian role ethics and Indigenous relational ontologies underscore interdependence and the importance of time and place, correcting Western individualism and extending the "relational" dimension of well-being.

2.8.4.3 *Medicalization and the DSM era*

From the 1980s onward, diagnostic manuals and randomized trials standardized care. CBT's ascendancy risked marginalizing existential formulations; yet, "third-wave" therapies (ACT and mindfulness-based approaches) reintroduced existential themes "by another name." Existential wellness survived by integrating with evidence-based methods while keeping a longer view of what counts as "health."

2.8.5 The twenty-first-century scene: meaning, belonging, and well-being science

2.8.5.1 Positive psychology and the return of meaning

Positive psychology's shift from pathology to flourishing made conceptual room for existential wellness, especially via research on "meaning in life." Wong's *positive psychology 2.0* explicitly centers suffering, virtue, and meaning, aligning tightly with existential thought. Empirical literature now consistently links meaning, purpose, and coherence to lower mortality risk, better health behaviors, resilience, and life satisfaction.

2.8.5.2 Death awareness and "good enough" authenticity

Studies in the areas of terror management theory and palliative care echo Heidegger and Frankl: they argue that a calibrated awareness of finitude can clarify values and strengthen prosocial motives. Contemporary practice tends to reframe authenticity not as radical self-assertion but as "good-enough" congruence, negotiated ethically within relationships and roles.

2.8.5.3 Digital life, loneliness, and social meaning

The social determinants of wellness—a lack of decently paid, meaningful work, political and social polarization, digital fragmentation, and epidemic loneliness, among them—push existential questions into the arena of public health. Loneliness, for example, is now treated as a population-level risk comparable to smoking, showing that belonging and meaning are as somatic as they are philosophical. Existential wellness thus broadens from individual therapy to community design, education, and policy.

2.8.5.4 Measurement and practice

New measures—the Meaning in Life Questionnaire, the Purpose in Life test, and the Valued Living Questionnaire—operationalize existential constructs for research and program evaluation. Coaching services and organizational development programs adapt existential exercises (value audits, mortality reflections, and narrative identity work) for leadership, ethics, and burnout prevention. The field has moved from "Do we need meaning?" to "How do we cultivate and sustain it responsibly?"

2.9 Core dimensions of existential wellness

Across eras, five dimensions recur; together, they do a decent job of defining the concept:

1. *Meaning and Purpose.* A focus not just on goals but on the felt sense that life "makes sense" (coherence), that it matters (significance), and that one is oriented toward valued aims (purpose).
2. *Freedom and Responsibility.* The capacity and willingness to choose, accept consequences, and revise life projects.
3. *Authenticity and Integrity.* Aligned self-presence and behavior within constraints; neither self-abandonment nor narcissistic self-assertion.
4. *Relational Belonging and Ethical Recognition.* Wellness as coauthored; my flourishing implicates and affects the others' freedom.
5. *Finitude and Transcendence.* Life projects owned under the threat of death; transcendence not necessarily religious but value-anchored and other-regarding.

These concerns and interests are not seen as boxes to be ticked off but as tensions to be lived—hence the language of "practice" rather than "achievement."

2.10 Persistent critiques and live debates

2.10.1 Individualism versus social structure and constraint

Does existential wellness overemphasize choice and underestimate constraint? Contemporary practice answers by holding both: agency is real but scaffolded by social conditions. Programs that ignore poverty, discrimination, and other social and political realities risk moralizing distress.

2.10.2 Authenticity as a commodity

When "be yourself" becomes a market slogan, authenticity can slide into performance and consumerism. The corrective is ethical authenticity oriented to shared goods and the other's freedom.

2.10.3 Evidence and integration

A frequent challenge is whether existential methods are "evidence-based." The research base is now substantial for meaning, purpose, values-based action, and mortality preparedness; newer work integrates existential themes with CBT/ACT, compassion approaches, and palliative care.

2.11 Where the concept stands now

Today, existential wellness is less a niche therapy and more a transdisciplinary lens:

- In *health care,* dignity therapy, meaning-centered interventions, and serious illness communication embody existential care.
- In *education,* purpose learning and character education tackle meaning, agency, and belonging.
- In *organizations,* leadership identity work and values-driven cultures aim at congruence and ethical responsibility.
- In *public health,* loneliness, polarization, and ecological grief are framed as existential ailments needing social and symbolic repair.
- In the *helping professions*, to include psychotherapy, counseling, and coaching, existential wellness themes are gaining significant ground and a new cachet.

2.12 The durable promise of an uncomfortable ideal

Existential wellness keeps uncomfortable company: with anxiety, ambiguity, despair, finitude, and death, on the one hand, and with the demands of self-proclaimed personal responsibility and ethical action, on the other hand. From Kierkegaard's inwardness and Nietzsche's self-creation through Heidegger's finitude and de Beauvoir's ethics to Frankl's logotherapy and Yalom's clinical synthesis, the tradition repeatedly insists: to live well is to choose, to answer, and to belong—under limits.

That insistence is precisely why the concept endures. It refuses easy optimism yet refuses despair, seeking a style of living that can carry tragedy without collapsing the possibility of joy, community, and meaning. As the twenty-first century confronts loneliness, ecological threat, and technological dislocation, existential wellness offers neither a panacea nor a posture—but a practice: lucid, value-anchored, relational, and brave.

FOOD FOR THOUGHT

1. If you're familiar with a particular tradition (like Stoicism, Buddhism, and Judaism), how does your tradition align with (or maybe dismiss) the idea of existential wellness?
2. How would you personally define "existential wellness"?
3. Imagine sharing the concept of existential wellness with someone (maybe a coaching client). How might you present it simply, in a brisk sentence or two?
4. To what extent are they "existentially well"? How would you describe your own situation?
5. Is there one change you would like to make that you believe would aid your own existential wellness?

Chapter 3

On existential wellness coaching

Existential wellness is at once a simple idea and an elusive idea. At its most simple, it means that you have entered into a personally acceptable relationship with life. The details of this will always be purely personal, but that is the essence of the matter.

For one person, it might mean an easygoing surrender to the facts of existence, with a cessation of striving and an eye on inner peace. For another person, it might mean active rebellion in the service of the true, the beautiful, and the good, with no particular concern for either ease or happiness.

Existential wellness is about alignment and agreement. You internally nod when you think about how you are living your life. Your life may be hard, but you have "risen above" that hardness and can honestly say, "I am fine with the universe, I am fine with life, I am living authentically and I will die that way, too."

That is the simple version. Scratch that surface, and you will find yourself in the wilds of what it means to be human: why the mind and the human organism seem to require (and often misunderstand) meaning and purpose, how it looks to be possible to feel like one matters one moment and feel like one doesn't matter the next, and everything else peculiarly and poignantly human.

Given that these are life's basics—that this alignment and agreement matter more than anything else—they should interest and concern every coach, whether she's a life coach, a spiritual coach, a wellness coach, or a business coach, for that matter. Because a business coach, too, will be less helpful and less successful in her work with clients if clients achieve goals that don't actually matter to them and don't actually promote self-alignment. Existential wellness should be on every coach's mind.

But few coaches are trained in these matters. They typically don't have a working "existential" vocabulary. They typically haven't thought through their own understanding of meaning and purpose. They typically haven't considered that clients who don't possess a "working philosophy of life" court despair and are less likely to be motivated to do the work. Indeed, it may not even cross their mind to fish in these waters.

DOI: 10.4324/9781003724971-3

Coaches aren't alone in not fishing in these waters. Psychiatry maintains a firm hands-off policy when it comes to existential matters, preferring to collect and combine symptoms into symptom pictures that are then offered up with handy labels like ADHD or clinical depression—this is called "diagnosis." Psychiatry then delivers up a second helping called "treatment," in the form of chemicals called "medication." Nothing at all is existential there.

As to psychotherapy, that is a wild mixed bag of ideas, intentions, and practices. What do a positive psychologist, a Freudian analyst, a cognitive-behavioral therapist, a Jungian depth psychologist, a transpersonal psychotherapist, and a therapist who sees himself as helping clients deal with life's challenges have in common, apart from the fact that they help by talking? And how often (or rarely) is that talking about existential wellness?

Let's leap ahead. Let's imagine that you're a coach of some stripe or other and that you agree that you would like your clients to experience existential wellness because you understand that its absence is painful and a problem for the coaching. You understand that it is unlikely, bordering on impossible, for a person who finds her job subjectively meaningless, say, or for a person who doesn't think that the novel she is writing matters, to feel well or to be much inclined to do the work of coaching.

You understand that a person in this position is going to be vague about goals, that he is going to procrastinate, that he is going to miss coaching sessions, and that he will in other ways play out his existential difficulties.

You understand that coaching a person experiencing existential difficulties is going to feel on the superficial side, unless and until those existential matters appear on the table. So you decide that you are going to add existential investigating to the repertoire of things that you do. But what does that mean, and what does that look like?

First of all, it means a very simple thing. It means asking questions that put existential realities on the table. What sorts of questions? Here are 12.

1. A creativity coach might ask, "Does writing your novel still matter to you?"
2. A relationship coach might ask, "Have the two of you settled on whether or not you are trying for children?"
3. A life coach might ask, "What are the pros and cons of moving back to Greece, apart from the practical considerations?"
4. A business coach might ask, "So, it sounds like your high-paying job feels meaningless to you?"
5. A mindfulness coach might ask, "How might you keep your life purposes in mind as you live your life?"
6. A sleep coach might ask, "Do you think you might sleep better if your days were filled with more meaningful activities?"
7. A spiritual coach might ask, "How do your spiritual beliefs and your ideas about personal freedom connect?"

8. A health and wellness coach might ask, "What might it feel like to elevate minding your nutrition and exercise goals to the level of life purposes?"
9. A leadership coach might ask, "Is it hard to lead your group, given that they don't seem to have much investment in the company's product?"
10. A public speaking coach might ask, "Given that you find public speaking both scary and meaningful, what does that suggest about the plan we might create?"
11. A parenting coach might ask, "How do you think you might go about communicating your values to your children?"
12. A dating coach might ask, "What do you think an 'authentic relationship' might look like?"

How would an "existentially minded" coach then proceed? Let's say that you're a creativity coach and that your client's ostensive issue is that she's been blocked for six months and gotten no work done on her novel during that time.

You inquire, and you learn that she's been in pain from an auto accident, that her first novel has gone out of print, that her husband out of the blue called her a parasite for not contributing to the family income, that she's not sure about the viability of her current novel idea, and that a friend of hers recently had a bestseller.

All of these seem important to you and seem like likely contributors to her blockage. You have other thoughts as well, having to do with what she's shared about her childhood and having to do with how she presents as a scattered, distracted, and apologetic person. All of this feels relevant. Indeed, this might feel like enough or more than enough. But, because you have decided to keep an eye on existential matters, you decide to inquire about the following.

You inquire if she feels "existentially wounded" by the remaindering of her first novel. You wonder if writing, or maybe publishing but not writing, has lost its meaning for her. You likewise inquire if her identity has been reduced, harmed, or altered by recent events, such that she no longer thinks of herself as a writer but now as a former writer, a shadow artist, or a failed writer.

Some of her pain points, like her husband calling her a parasite and her friend having a bestseller, feel more psychological than existential. Others, like perhaps no longer experiencing writing as meaningful or perhaps no longer believing that she or her efforts matter, feel clearly existential. But these lines are not easy—or maybe even possible—to draw with real accuracy. The psychological and the existential naturally blend, inform one another, and trip over one another.

That tripping might prove a thorny theoretical problem, but, in practice, it is no particular problem at all. If you keep reminding yourself that existential matters matter, then you can proceed whether or not a given issue is exactly more psychological or more existential. You can just consider them both and train yourself to keep one eye on the one and another eye on the other.

Really, what in life isn't tangled up with questions of meaning and purpose, on the one hand, and subjective psychological experiencing, on the other hand?

Even if you aren't a trained existential wellness coach, you can add paying attention to existential wellness to your current coaching practice simply by having it on your radar. You can do this by asking existentially oriented questions, by finding your own personal language for speaking about meaning, purpose, suffering, anxiety, freedom, authenticity, and other existential ideas, and by being existentially aware yourself.

Or you might go "all the way" and become an existential wellness coach and formally add existential wellness coaching to your current practice. Whether or not you go down the formal route of training in existential wellness coaching, it will serve you and your client to make sure that you keep an eye on your client's existential realities.

3.1 Twelve pillars of wellness

Where does an existential wellness coach focus as she works with clients? Well, fundamentally, where the client wants to focus: on getting his novel written, on coming to some new conclusions about how life ought to be lived, on creating a new, more meaningful career, on living with less worry, on achieving life balance, and on . . . just about anything under the sun.

That is a very broad and large mandate, and exactly as it ought to be. For the sake of convenience, we can refine this huge broadness into some categories that can help organize our understanding of wellness and that can serve as a kind of template for action.

One way to think about what we are doing in our work with clients is that we are helping them in the following 12 areas of life, 12 areas that together amount to "a picture of wellness":

- Life philosophy
- Peaceful mind
- Healthy body
- Positive outlook
- Helpful thoughts
- Safe environment
- Integrated personality
- Purposeful occupation
- Sustainable meaning
- Valuable relationships
- Daily steadiness
- Purposeful living

Let's look at each one of these.

1. *Life philosophy:* There is profound value in having a life philosophy that supports your aims and intentions, one rich enough to satisfy you and simple enough to be memorable. For example, a single life purpose statement like "I do the next right thing" can usefully and even beautifully organize a whole life.
2. *Peaceful mind:* It is hard to live well if the "room that is our mind" is an uncongenial place, a place where we don't like to be. If it is a place of chaos, noise, worries, doubts, and other self-pestering energy, how well can we feel? We can invite clients to "redesign their mind" so that it is a more peaceful and more congenial place to be.
3. *Healthy body:* We are not doing anything like medicine as existential wellness coaches, but we are certainly helping clients think about their physical wellness. This might mean supporting their efforts to lose weight or exercise regularly, supporting them as they create their personal plan for dealing with a chronic illness, etc. We know for sure that we are embodied creatures for whom physical wellness matters.
4. *Positive outlook:* We want our clients to experience more hopefulness, more positivity, and a growing sense that life can and does have its joys and rewards. It is hard for a client to boldly live her life purposes if she has given life a thumbs-down. We want her to understand why giving life a new thumbs-up reduces her sadness and supports her intentions to live well.
5. *Helpful thoughts:* Our clients are unlikely to fully understand the extent to which what they think determines and controls how they feel and what they can get accomplished. An existential wellness coach can provide simple, useful cognitive ideas, like, for example, "thinking thoughts that serve us," that, despite their simplicity, can transform lives.
6. *Safe environment:* If your client is being bullied by her parents, her partner, or her boss, how well can she feel, and how good a job can she do attending to her life purposes? We want to help clients understand the extent to which their circumstances matter, we want to help them identify which circumstances they want to change, and we want to support them in their efforts to make those changes.
7. *Integrated personality:* All clients—all human beings—can use a little personality upgrading. You might employ a simple but robust "theory of personality" that personality is made up of three parts—original personality, formed personality, and available personality—to help clients achieve needed personality integration.
8. *Purposeful occupation:* Given how many hours it consumes us and how connected it is to our basic survival needs, we have the important existential and practical challenges of finding or creating work that feels meaningful

to us and that brings in the income we need. Existential wellness coaches pay attention to "the problem of work," one that virtually all of our clients will present as a pressing issue.

9. *Sustainable meaning:* Existential wellness coaches are comfortable chatting about the subject of meaning: what meaning is and isn't, why it naturally comes and goes, and how a life can be lived that feels meaningful given the precise nature of meaning as a feeling and a subjective psychological experience. Can meaning really be sustained over time? Existential wellness coaches look that question straight in the eye.
10. *Valuable relationships:* It is hard to feel emotionally and existentially well going it completely alone in life. We are obliged to take charge of our lives and manifest our individuality, but that isn't the same as living in isolation, alienated from all of our fellow creatures. Relationships that we experience as valuable contribute greatly to our wellness.
11. *Daily steadiness:* Can your client live her life in the way that she wants to live it, every day, steadily, without life feeling like a roller coaster to her? Wouldn't that amount to the epitome of emotional and existential wellness? Therefore, existential wellness coaches focus on the idea of daily practice and how wellness is a function of the steady daily practices that we put into place.
12. *Purposeful living:* Foundational to the idea of existential wellness is the notion that we are obliged to decide what is important to us and that we are likewise obliged to live in light of those choices and decisions. "Waiting for purpose to arrive" and "not having purpose" do not work and do not support wellness. Purposeful living is a key to existential wellness.

Would you formally "go over" these 12 areas with each client? You might. You might prepare a questionnaire that invites clients to describe "where they are" in each of these categories. Those questionnaire answers might provide you with a wealth of information and might prove a really useful exercise for your client, one that provides her with new insights and that paints a picture of how to think about her life. You may find that you really like using these "twelve pillars" in that way.

But, even if you don't use them in a routine or formal way, they are there to help guide your thinking and your understanding of what "a complete picture of existential wellness" might look like. And, of course, this is just one scheme: you might like to try your hand at creating your own scheme, picture, or vision. You get to decide what you believe "wellness" looks like. I think that these 12 pillars amount to a sturdy construct, but that is for you to decide.

3.2 Four questions and three paths

To use traditional existential language, as an existential wellness coach, you are helping clients with "the project of their life."

Existential thinkers have conceptualized life as a certain sort of task demanding personal responsibility, a philosophical attitude toward life's absurdities, and great fortitude. Like every high-minded version of how life ought to be lived, this version has only appealed to a small percentage of our species. But it will appeal to your clients.

That small fraction keeps civilization afloat. They keep it alive—as investigative reporters, as documentary filmmakers, as progressive politicians, as performance artists, and as outspoken voices—while necessarily feeling sad, alienated, outnumbered, and overwhelmed. Your clients are likely among that small percentage, and they have come to you for help.

Part of their tragedy is that they must live life, which is hard, while at the same time trying to save the world, which is absurd. What a job! No one is really equal to this job. How could a person be equal to such a task? This job of holding your life as a project and the world as your charge is so taxing and preposterous that virtually everyone who would love to set the bar that high is reduced to living a pale version of that high-bar ideal. How could that not be the case?

As a result, people go off on tangents and lose two years here and five years there. They enter a profession, soon stop liking it, but remain there because that is now their identity and their source of income. Or they bounce from path to path, moving from graphic artist to project manager to stay-at-home mom to personal assistant to podcaster to jewelry maker, all the while stewing about life and feeling that the project of their life is rather unmanageable.

One thing that can help, and that you can offer clients, is a simple way of conceptualizing her "life as a project."

Your client can do a better job of living an existentially solid life by trying to answer the following four questions while taking the real complexities of life into account as she tries to answer them. She then, with your coaching help, endeavors to live her answers in an integrated, coordinated fashion.

The four questions are

1. Why be?
2. How to be?
3. How to be with myself?
4. How to be, given the world?

As to "how to be," contemporary members of our species tend to provide themselves with one or the other of two main (and poor) answers. One is "You tell me." This is what might be called the traditional path in life, one that posits a universe guided by the hand of unseen powers, forces, or gods. A person following this path is likely to become a lifelong seeker, someone looking for the secret to life or the answer to life. She is likely to cycle through religions, to fall in love with occult forms of guidance, and to take workshops that invite her to embrace mystery and unravel mystery, as if life were a certain sort of detective story.

A person on the first path does not see himself as making meaning. External forces construct meaning, human meaning included, and the individual's job is either to obey the laws of the supreme meaning-maker (the Judeo-Christian-Islamic model) or to stand open to meaning and to flow with it (the Taoist model). A multitude of variations on this theme grew up over the millennia, each rooted in the idea that meaning already exists "out there" and that the individual was limited and bound by the agendas of gods, spirits, karmic or astrological determinism, and other powerful forces that put (and kept) an individual in his or her place. Even as a person lost his free will ("the stars made me do it!"), he grew ever more narcissistic because this belief system allowed him to do whatever he chose to do, under the cover of the notion that forces out of his control ruled the universe.

The other main answer is, "There is no answer. It's all arbitrary, meaningless, and silly." This is the nihilistic path that so many of your clients will find themselves plying. This path is defined by the felt sense that there are only cultural conventions, biological necessities, and contrivances of one sort or another to get us from birth to the grave. A person on this second path does not see meaning or purpose as being genuinely available.

Whether he has studied it or not, he has modern history in his bones and his blood, a history of mass destruction, genocides on television, the worldwide rise of crass materialism, and the discrediting of superstitious religions, accompanied by linguistic analysis "proving" that talk about meaning is meaningless. This person became a nihilist simply by virtue of looking around.

As an existential wellness coach, you are providing a third answer, one that your client likely craves and that she likely already believes but that she hasn't quite encountered embodied in a helper like you. This third path is a path that an existential wellness coach can fully support. It is the revolutionary path of the meaning-maker, the person who says "No!" to the constraints of tradition and "No!" to the idea that his time on earth is empty and pointless.

This person makes a new wager with the universe: "You may remain mysterious—I don't care. I will rise to the occasion. I will do this because I intend to matter, in my own way, as is my birthright." You decide to live an ethical, personally meaningful life, and you live with your decision. That is the height of nobility.

This third path may not sound so radical, but it is. It is a radical departure from the traditional path because it blasts all received knowing out of the water. Its central tenet that you must decide for yourself is exactly the following announcement: that you create your universe of intention from scratch and from your best understanding of what is right, what is good, and what is valuable, and that no one gets to arbitrate meaning for you.

No book orders you about, not even one penned by gods. No leader orders you about. No cultural, corporate, or community pressure prevents you from deciding what values you intend to manifest and how your righteousness and heroism will play themselves out. You decide.

This third way is also a radical departure from the forlorn postmodern position, which moves from what may be a fact that the universe is not run by an unseen mind or unseen forces and that we are simply throwaway creatures who delude ourselves when we feel self-righteously self-important to the unwarranted conclusion that life is not worth taking seriously. The conclusion is unwarranted because it takes a thought, that the universe is patently meaningless, and a feeling, one of despair, and elevates them above an equally valid thought, that life can be lived seriously, and an equally available feeling, one of engagement.

You are helping your client learn to mark time with her personal stamp and accept that her activities must rise to the level of personal conviction. If she can't accept how she is spending her time on earth, she is obliged to do something to change her activities or to change her relationship to her activities.

To use "meaning language," she must invest meaning in this, divest meaning from that, shore up meaning leaks when they occur, handle inevitable meaning crises, and become adamant about and expert at making and maintaining the meaning in her life. This is the job that no one discusses and that no one has trained her for, and you get to help her understand this point of view and to see it not only as necessary but also as beautiful.

You are encouraging your client to see that addressing these four questions is an important task and a beautiful thing and that, indeed, she is the beauty in life. She, living the project of her life to the best of her ability, is the beauty in life. A marble kitchen counter is not the beauty in life. The ceiling of the Sistine Chapel is not the beauty in life. A red sunset over a pristine beach is not the beauty in life. Your client is, when she does the next right thing, supports the ideals encapsulated in the phrase "truth, beauty and goodness," makes herself proud by her efforts, and can say, "I am attending to life." Encouraging her in this way is the epitome of existential wellness coaching.

From my point of view, an existential wellness coach works with individuals struggling with life purpose, life meaning, and life choice issues; individuals endeavoring to identify their values and principles in order to make better life and career choices; individuals who suspect that their emotional problems, like depression, anxiety, and addiction, may be related to their meaning issues; and institutions and businesses wanting to clarify their mission and purpose.

Existential wellness coaches work with many sorts of clients, from individuals looking to make personal sense of meaning to organizations concerned about their mission. Clients are likely to be experiencing the following sorts of challenges:

- They have the feeling that they are spending their days just going through the motions.

- They are unsure about where to invest their time and energy.
- They have the feeling that they are not really following their path or making use of their talents.
- They have trouble believing that their efforts matter.
- They spend a lot of their day feeling empty and listless.
- They're concerned that they need to make important changes but don't know how to make them.
- They have a career change or retirement looming.
- Meaning and purpose have always been issues and challenges for them.
- They frequently second-guess their choices and keep switching from one path to another.
- They are frequently bored, anxious, or existentially blue.

Millions of people feel listless, dispirited, and unfulfilled. What do they do to change their mood and their outlook? They play another computer game, take an antidepressant, keep very busy, and so on. At the same time, they likely try their hand at one or another of those time-honored practices meant to give life meaning, like volunteerism, creativity, or religion. For most, though, the listlessness and sadness remain. Why?

The listlessness and sadness remain because they haven't fully understood where our species has moved in the last century, and they haven't embraced the fundamental change required of human beings today. It is no longer possible for a smart, sensible person to seek meaning and purpose. In her heart, she knows that there is no meaning or purpose "out there" to seek and that her pursuit of meaning and purpose is bound to fail. This makes her deeply sad.

What she doesn't realize is that an alternative approach is available to her—an approach that you can teach and support. You can help her understand that she can make powerful life purpose choices, coax into existence all the meaning she needs, and find personal fulfillment as a genuine, self-directing, and empowered individual.

This is the fundamental change required of human beings today and the beautiful help that an existential wellness coach can provide. This fundamental change can be expressed as a path or program with nine steps. There are many ways to conceptualize your aims as an existential wellness coach, but one way is to suppose that you are helping clients understand and follow the following path.

1. *You decide to matter:* The universe is not built to care about you. You must care about yourself. You must announce that you are opting to matter. You must announce that you are making the startling, eye-opening decision to take responsibility for your thoughts and your actions and live life instrumentally.
2. *You accept that you must make meaning:* You finally let go of the demoralizing wish that meaning would rain down on you from some golden universal shower and accept that the only meaning that exists is the meaning

that you make. You announce once and for all that you are the final arbiter of meaning.

3. *You identify your life purposes:* If you are going to actively make meaning in accordance with your life purposes, you had better know what your life purpose choices are, articulate them, prioritize them, and make sure that you really believe in them.
4. *You articulate a life purpose statement:* You list your life purposes, maybe rank order your life purposes, and as part of the process create a single phrase or sentence that represents a clear understanding of how you intend to live your life and represent yourself in the universe. My personal life purpose statement is "Do the next right thing."
5. *You hold the intention to fulfill your life purposes:* You must be able to remember your life purposes even when you are tired, bothered, distracted, upset, and otherwise not in your best frame of mind. When life resumes its habitual busyness, you are still able to firmly hold your intentions and manifest them.
6. *You passionately act to fulfill your life purposes:* Every day you make some meaning in accordance with your life purposes. Maybe eight hours of your day are robbed by activities that do not align with your life purposes and that you must attend to for all the usual reasons. But some hours remain—and you must use them.
7. *You navigate the world and the facts of existence:* The world is not built to accommodate you. Your favorite bakery may close, or war may break out—from the smallest to the largest, the facts of existence are exactly what they are. They include pain and pleasure, loyalty and betrayal, and life and death. All this you must navigate, right up until the final moment.
8. *You create yourself in your own best image:* You have indubitable strengths and every manner of shadow. If you live in those shadows, you will never quite respect yourself. Do better by manifesting your strengths and becoming the person you know you want to become. Surrender to the truth that you would prefer to be your best self.
9. *You live the life of a passionate meaning-maker:* You don't idly chat about meaning, brood about meaning, look for meaning, complain about meaning, buy a book about meaning, or take a workshop on meaning: you make meaning. You live a life where, day in and day out, you make meaning by living your life purpose choices. You make those choices, you make daily decisions, and you make an effort. You wait on nothing: you live.

This is one vision of life and one "program" that an existential wellness coach might present to clients. This is not the only vision and only program, but it is also one worth thinking about and, if you find it congenial, embracing for both you and your clients. This, then, is one person's view of what existential wellness coaching can look like and mean.

FOOD FOR THOUGHT

1. What comes up for you when you hear the phrase "existential wellness coaching"?
2. Can you see yourself engaging in existential wellness coaching? If not, is there one particular objection?
3. Does the idea of "twelve pillars of wellness" resonate with you? Might you add or subtract pillars, or tweak the ones I've presented?
4. If you are already a coach, how might you keep an eye on existential matters as you coach? Are there perhaps a couple of quality questions you might ask every client to check in on their existential health?
5. Leap ahead to being an existential wellness coach. How might you describe your practice?

Chapter 4

Existential wellness coaching tactics

An existential wellness coach is first of all a coach and uses all of the tactics that coaches use: listening, reflecting, questioning, wondering, suggesting, cocreating goals, monitoring progress, and so on. For more on general coaching, I invite you to take a look at my book *The Coach's Way* and at the many other resources available to you.

Second, existential wellness coaches are familiar with the ideas of existentialism, including the extent to which their clients are troubled by challenges around meaning, purpose, freedom, individuality, mortality, core anxiety, and the facts of existence. They create strategies and tactics that flow from their understanding of what helps human beings meet these challenges.

Third, if they're inclined to use the model of wellness I described previously—the "twelve pillars of wellness" model—then they might create tactics and strategies connected to each pillar: tactics that support the creation of a life philosophy, the maintenance of physical health, and so on.

Fourth, existential wellness coaches, as independent and individualistic human beings with their own ideas about authentic helping, dream up their own tactics. These might include creating and providing journal prompts, guided visualizations, calming rituals, and anything and everything they have come to believe helps clients heal and flourish.

Imagine a client who presents the following issues: she does not feel fulfilled as a housewife and homemaker; she thinks that she would like to write a mystery but doesn't know where to begin; she feels some hole or void that she usually calls depression but suspects that it is some kind of existential crisis; she feels isolated and would like more friends, but she also doesn't feel all that social; she is worried about not contributing financially to the household; and more.

This sounds like a lot and is a lot, but it is exactly the sort of issue picture that a real-life client might present. She has already "bought into" the idea that some existential problem must be implicated here: remember, she has sought you out. But she isn't sure what to do, and she isn't sure how you might be able to help.

She is probably intrigued by the idea of receiving some existential wellness coaching, but she also probably believes that her issues are as much practical,

DOI: 10.4324/9781003724971-4

psychological, and relational as existential and is likely wondering how something as "abstract" as existential wellness coaching might translate into action. To put it simply, she is probably both hopeful and doubtful.

You begin by listening; you start to conjure thoughts and responses; you ask questions for clarification, if you do not understand; and at some point, you decide where you want to focus and how you want to reply. In essence, all coaches do the same thing: they provide the help a client is seeking by listening to the client and responding to the client. Coaching is exactly that simple—and exactly that complicated.

4.1 Struggling with purpose

When Daniel, a 45-year-old marketing executive, first sat down in Emily's coaching office, his opening statement was blunt.

"I don't see the point of anything anymore," he said. "I get up, I do my job, I go home, I watch some shows, and then I do it all over again. It's not depression, exactly. I'm functioning fine. It's more like . . . the emptiness is showing through."

Emily, an existential wellness coach, recognized the sound of a meaning crisis. She knew that Daniel's pain was real, even if invisible to others. Over the course of several months, she used a range of tactics to help Daniel wrestle with and reshape his experience of purpose.

4.1.1 Tactic 1: normalizing the crisis of meaning

Early in their work, Emily assured Daniel that what he was experiencing was not a personal failure but a deeply human condition.

"Many people," she explained, "reach a point where the surface structures of life—career, routines, even relationships—stop supplying meaning automatically. It doesn't mean life has no meaning. It means you are being called to create meaning more deliberately."

For Daniel, this normalization eased his shame. He had secretly feared that he was uniquely flawed for feeling purposeless. Instead, he came to see himself as engaged in a classic existential struggle, one shared by philosophers, artists, and ordinary people alike.

4.1.2 Tactic 2: clarifying values through stories

To uncover what mattered most to him, Emily asked Daniel to recall moments in his past when he had felt most alive.

He told her about his college years, when he had been part of a student theater group. He described late nights building sets, the camaraderie of shared creative effort, and the thrill of opening night.

Emily highlighted the values embedded in this story: creativity, collaboration, expression, and community. Together, they listed these as possible cornerstones of meaning.

Daniel looked at the list and said, "None of that shows up in my life now." The realization was painful but clarifying. It suggested a direction for rebuilding purpose.

4.1.3 *Tactic 3: confronting avoidance and fear*

When Emily encouraged Daniel to reintroduce creativity into his life, he hesitated. "I don't have the talent anymore. I'd embarrass myself."

Emily recognized avoidance disguised as realism. She gently challenged him: "Is the fear of embarrassment worth trading away the joy of creating?"

This confrontation wasn't harsh but compassionate. It named the cost of avoidance: by protecting himself from imagined shame, Daniel was also cutting himself off from vitality. He agreed to experiment with small creative acts—sketching, journaling, and even attending a community theater production.

4.1.4 *Tactic 4: reframing work as a platform for purpose*

Daniel's job in marketing felt like a treadmill. Yet quitting wasn't feasible—he had financial obligations and a family. Rather than urging a drastic career change, Emily asked, "What if you thought of your work not as your primary source of meaning, but as a platform that funds and supports meaning?"

This reframing reduced Daniel's resentment. He began to see his job less as a prison and more as a scaffold. By detaching meaning from work, he freed himself from the unrealistic expectation that his career alone should provide him with a sense of purpose. Work could be a means, not the meaning.

4.1.5 *Tactic 5: encouraging purpose through service*

Emily introduced the idea that meaning often grows through contribution. "When we help others, we step outside the closed circle of our own emptiness," she said.

Intrigued, Daniel began mentoring a younger colleague at work, guiding her through career decisions. To his surprise, he found this deeply rewarding. "It feels different than chasing metrics," he told Emily. "It feels . . . real."

Emily noted that service, whether small or large, often provides a direct line to the feeling of meaning. She encouraged him to notice how this form of contribution affected his sense of vitality.

4.1.6 Tactic 6: creating a personal philosophy of life

Over time, Emily encouraged Daniel to articulate his own philosophy of life. Through journaling, Daniel drafted a statement:

"Life does not hand me meaning. I must create it. I create meaning by expressing myself creatively, by nurturing genuine connections, and by leaving others better than I found them."

The act of writing this down proved powerful. It gave Daniel a compass. Whenever the old emptiness returned, he could ask, "Am I engaging my values of creativity, connection, and contribution?"

4.1.7 Tactic 7: practicing small, daily acts of meaning-making

Emily emphasized the importance of practice. "Purpose isn't just discovered in big projects," she said. "It's cultivated in daily choices."

Daniel began a ritual of morning journaling, where he set one intention each day to align with his values. Some days, it was calling an old friend. Other days, it was sketching for ten minutes. Sometimes, it was simply mentoring with full attention.

Over many weeks, these small acts accumulated into a felt sense of purpose. Daniel no longer waited for a grand revelation. He experienced meaning as something woven into the fabric of daily life.

4.1.8 Breakthrough: from emptiness to engagement

After six months, Daniel reported feeling different, not euphoric but anchored. "The emptiness isn't gone," he said, "but it doesn't scare me anymore. I see it as a space I get to fill."

He had joined a community art class, continued mentoring, and was even planning a small local theater project with friends. His job remained the same, but he carried it with lighter shoulders.

Emily reflected back to him: "You've shifted from seeing life as meaningless to seeing yourself as a meaning-maker. That is the heart of existential wellness."

4.2 20 client scenarios

Here are 20 client mini-scenarios demonstrating various existential wellness tactics—each mini-scenario featuring a fictional client with a particular existential theme or challenge.

1. *Client: Rachel, 38—Lost Sense of Meaning*
   Theme: Meaning-Making
   Tactic: Explore meaningful past experiences for patterns

Scenario: Rachel is a mid-career nonprofit professional who recently left her job, feeling burned out and disconnected from her original sense of purpose. In coaching, she engages with the "life timeline" exercise, plotting moments that felt most alive or meaningful. Together, you help her uncover a pattern: she's most fulfilled when mentoring others and building community. This becomes a thread for reimagining her next chapter—not only a job but also a life in alignment with her strengths and values.

2. *Client: Marcus, 52—Haunted by* "Wasted Time"
   Theme: Mortality Awareness
   Tactic: "5 Years Left" scenario
   Scenario: Marcus, a tech executive, admits he feels like time is running out. You ask, "What if you had five years left—how would you live differently?" He's startled to realize how much of his energy goes into impressing others. He begins to experiment with shifting his focus to being more present with his teenage kids and starting a personal photography project he's put off for years.
3. *Client: Janelle, 30—Overwhelmed by Choice*
   Theme: Freedom and Responsibility
   Tactic: Reframe "I have to" into "I choose to"
   Scenario: Janelle, a talented artist, is paralyzed by career indecision—should she stay in her stable teaching job or pursue her art full time? She often says, "I have to pay the bills" or "I can't risk it." You introduce the concept of radical ownership and work together to reframe her internal language. By owning her choices, she feels more empowered and eventually opts for a hybrid path: part-time teaching and part-time art-making.
4. *Client: Samir, 44—Identity Crisis After Divorce*
   Theme: Authenticity and Identity
   Tactic: Explore who the client is without their roles
   Scenario: Samir's identity was deeply tied to being a husband and father. After a divorce, he feels like "no one." In coaching, he uses journaling to explore his values outside of those roles and eventually rediscovers old passions—reading philosophy, cooking, and volunteering. This sense of inner identity becomes a new anchor for his life.
5. *Client: Olivia, 61—Facing Mortality*
   Theme: Mortality Awareness
   Tactic: Legacy journaling
   Scenario: Olivia is undergoing treatment for cancer. She's working with you not just on coping but also on legacy—how to live fully and leave something behind. She begins writing letters to her grandchildren, creating a "wisdom book" of family stories, values, and insights. It gives her a sense of peace and generativity.
6. *Client: Leo, 29—High Anxiety About the Future*
   Theme: Existential Anxiety

Tactic: Reframe anxiety as "energy of becoming"
Scenario: Leo is a law student plagued by constant dread about making the "wrong" life choices. You introduce the idea that anxiety is part of the human condition and can be a signal that he's awake and evolving. By learning to sit with uncertainty rather than fix it, Leo finds new resilience and even excitement about the unknown.

7. *Client: Carmen, 47—Needs a Creativity Reboot*
   Theme: Creativity and Meaningful Action
   Tactic: "Create anyway"
   Scenario: Carmen used to be a poet but hasn't written in years. She says, "What's the point? No one reads poetry any longer." You invite her to "create anyway," just for herself, just for now. She takes on a daily ten-minute poetry ritual, which begins to feed her soul again and unlocks ideas for a creative retreat she might host.
8. *Client: Daniel, 35—Struggling with Isolation*
   Theme: Existential Relationship
   Tactic: Journal about "What can never be fully shared?"
   Scenario: Daniel feels isolated in his relationships, like "no one really sees me." You give him a journaling prompt on existential isolation. Through this, he realizes he's been expecting perfect understanding, rather than intimacy. This shift helps him open up more with his partner and deepen his friendships with fewer idealized expectations.
9. *Client: Theresa, 50—Facing an Empty Nest*
   Theme: Time and Temporality
   Tactic: Ask, "What season of life are you in?"
   Scenario: Theresa's youngest child just left for college. She feels purposeless. You ask her to reflect on what season of life she's entering and what this season might invite. She decides it's a season of "deepening and discovery." She enrolls in a literature course and joins a hiking group, embracing the richness of this transition.
10. *Client: Andre, 41—Wrestling with Meaningless Work*
    Theme: Meaning-Making
    Tactic: Normalize absurdity and invite creative response
    Scenario: Andre works a corporate job that he finds meaningless but doesn't see a way out. You introduce Camus's idea of the absurd and ask, "What if life *is* absurd—how might you respond?" He laughs, then says, "Maybe I paint something every morning, as an act of rebellion." This tiny ritual becomes a gateway to joy—and eventually to a new side business making surrealist art.
11. *Client: Nina, 33—Caught in Approval-Seeking*
    Theme: Authenticity
    Tactic: Explore authenticity versus approval
    Scenario: Nina's stuck in her creative business, constantly second-guessing her choices. You explore how much her actions are driven by seeking

approval—from clients, family, and social media. In coaching, she experiments with a "week of radical authenticity," making decisions solely based on what aligns with her inner compass. She's surprised to find new energy and clarity.

12. *Client: Gabriel, 39—Avoiding Big Decisions*
    Theme: Freedom and Responsibility
    Tactic: "Three Doors" exercise
    Scenario: Gabriel's miserable in his job but says he's "not ready to leave." You guide him through the "Three Doors" exercise:

    - Door 1: Quit in three months.
    - Door 2: Stay and make peace.
    - Door 3: Take a sabbatical and explore.

    Through engaging with this exercise, he realizes he's not stuck—he's afraid. The visual metaphor helps him see his options as invitations, not traps.
13. *Client: Carol, 58—Struggling with Aging*
    Theme: Time and Mortality
    Tactic: Use seasonal metaphors for life stages
    Scenario: Carol feels invisible and anxious about aging. You explore the metaphor of seasons: what gifts does autumn bring? What wisdom, shedding, or harvest? Carol connects with her longing to mentor others and begins volunteering as a writing coach for young women, reframing this life stage as generative and powerful.
14. *Client: Jason, 27—Fear of Commitment*
    Theme: Existential Relationship
    Tactic: Explore love as choice versus fate
    Scenario: Jason's in what appears to be a great relationship but won't commit—he's worried he'll make the "wrong" choice. You explore Sartre's idea of love as a daily act of freedom and responsibility. Over time, Jason begins to see love not as something that *happens to him* but as something he *builds*. That mindset shift opens the door to deeper commitment.
15. *Client: Amelia, 43—Paralyzed by Perfectionism*
    Theme: Existential Anxiety
    Tactic: Practice shadow journaling
    Scenario: Amelia's writing project is stalled. She says she's "lazy," but deeper probing reveals a fear of failure and ridicule. You guide her through shadow journaling—writing from the voice of her inner critic. She discovers a familiar childhood voice and, with compassion, begins separating her current self from those old stories.
16. *Client: Brian, 46—Struggling with Faith Transition*
    Theme: Spiritual and Transcendent
    Tactic: Explore awe, transcendence, and mystery
    Scenario: Brian is leaving a conservative faith community and feeling untethered. You don't try to fill the spiritual void but instead explore

experiences of awe—under a night sky, listening to music, and witnessing birth. These moments become a new source of spiritual connection that doesn't require dogma.

17. *Client: Denise, 50—Longing to Start Something New*
    Theme: Creativity and Becoming
    Tactic: Write a one-act existential play
    Scenario: Denise is at a crossroads: retire early and start a passion project, or play it safe. You suggest she write a one-act play starring her two inner voices—security and adventure. In the process, she sees that security is tired and adventure is knocking loudly. She decides to launch a coaching practice for midlife reinvention.
18. *Client: Max, 36—Feels Emotionally Numb*
    Theme: Meaning and Aliveness
    Tactic: Encourage micro-moments of meaning
    Scenario: Max doesn't feel depressed, but life feels flat. You invite him to track small daily sparks—anything that gives a flicker of joy, awe, or interest. Over weeks, a pattern emerges: nature, music, and mentoring younger colleagues. These become anchors for designing a life that feels more alive.
19. *Client: Sofia, 31—Grieving a Miscarriage*
    Theme: Mortality and Suffering
    Tactic: Explore the meaning of suffering in the client's narrative
    Scenario: Sofia is not only grieving deeply but also questioning everything—her beliefs, her body, her future. You don't rush to reframe her pain. Instead, you hold space for existential questions and gradually explore how this loss might shift her worldview, deepen her empathy, or alter her sense of time. She begins to write letters to her unborn child, integrating the experience into her story.
20. *Client: Calvin, 40—Burned Out Entrepreneur*
    Theme: Identity and Renewal
    Tactic: Construct a "life metaphor"
    Scenario: Calvin is successful on paper but feels spiritually depleted. You invite him to find a metaphor for his life. He lands on: "I'm a river dammed up." That metaphor shifts everything. He sees where he's blocked, and together, you identify what needs to flow again: music, solitude, and spontaneity. That clarity reignites his sense of direction.

4.2.1 Troubled in Paris

Étienne sat in the coach's small office in Montparnasse, his shoulders hunched forward as if the weight of a laboratory hood still pressed down on them. His voice was soft but tense, a scientist's voice trained to precision but now fractured with anguish.

"I can't remain there," he said.

> They are producing things—compounds—meant for uses that I can't support. Cosmetic enhancers, yes, but also substances to be used in ways . . . I don't wish to describe them. It's not what I imagined when I became a biochemist. And yet if I leave, I leave with nothing.

His existential wellness coach, Marianne, listened carefully. Étienne had been referred by a friend, a psychologist who believed that Étienne's problem was less a matter of pathology and more a matter of meaning, freedom, choice, and the consequences of authentic action. Marianne nodded.

"Let's begin," she said. "We'll go slowly. Tell me—what matters most to you?"

4.2.2 *Values clarification*

Étienne frowned, then exhaled. "Truth. And usefulness. I wanted to create things that helped: medicines, nutritional advances. I grew up in Lyon, surrounded by illness in my family. I wanted science to serve life. But this—" He gestured vaguely, as if the company's entire pipeline floated before him. "This serves markets. Not lives."

Marianne leaned forward. "So, your core values are life, truth, and usefulness. And you feel you are betraying them by remaining in your current role?"

"Yes," Étienne said. "Exactly."

Naming these values was not only painful but also clarifying. His despair had felt amorphous, but now, it was tethered to specific values that were being violated.

4.2.3 *Meaning-centered reframing*

Marianne asked,

> Could you see your current crisis not only as a loss, but also as a signal—a sign that you still care deeply? Many people drift, become numb, accept compromises. You are feeling anguish because you remain loyal to your values.

Étienne blinked. The thought startled him. He had considered his distress as weakness, even failure. But Marianne reframed it as evidence of vitality.

"So . . . my despair proves my integrity?"

"Yes. It hurts because you haven't lost yourself," Marianne replied.

Étienne sat a little straighter. The crisis began to feel less like a collapse and more like a reckoning.

4.2.4 Emotional acknowledgment

Then he whispered, "Still, I'm afraid. Without work, without income—Paris is expensive. And they will not give me a recommendation. I will leave with nothing. Nothing." His eyes welled.

Marianne did not rush to fix it. She let silence rest, then said,

> Of course you're afraid. And, of course, you're going to have to grieve this situation. This is the rupture: your past self, loyal to the company, is dying. And you don't yet know who you will be next. Let the grief come. It is part of the passage.

Étienne's tears spilled, quiet and unguarded. For once, he did not analyze his emotions but simply allowed them. The acknowledgment created space for his humanity, beyond the cold rationality of the lab.

4.2.5 Narrative reconstruction

After the silence, Marianne asked, "Tell me the story of Étienne the biochemist. Start from the beginning. What brought you to science?"

Étienne described his father's long illness with kidney disease, his fascination with molecules, and his belief that research could bring healing. He remembered his first experiments at university, the exhilaration of discovery.

"But somewhere along the way," he said, "the story shifted. It became about funding, patents, markets. And I lost the plot."

Marianne smiled gently. "That phrase—you lost the plot. Perhaps this coaching is about reclaiming the authorship of your story. You're not only the subject inside the company's narrative. You're also the writer of your own narrative."

Étienne considered this. His life could be rewritten and redirected. He was not condemned to remain inside a chapter that had betrayed him.

4.2.6 Decision ownership

Still, he hesitated. "But how can I know if leaving is the right choice? What if I regret it?"

Marianne said,

> You can't outsource this decision to me, or to your employer, or even to fortune. Existential freedom is heavy—it means you must choose, and you must own the choice. Not because it guarantees comfort or security, but because it is your life. Do you want to remain and betray your values, or leave and face uncertainty? Both are hard. Which hardness will you choose?

Étienne sat silently. Then, he said, "To remain is impossible. My values would rot. I will leave."

The words were final, not tentative. By owning the decision, he reclaimed agency.

4.2.7 *Tolerance of uncertainty*

But the moment after deciding, fear returned. "What will I do next? There are no offers. I have no prospects."

Marianne responded,

> You are entering uncertainty. That is unavoidable. The question is: can you bear it? Can you cultivate the patience to let the next possibility emerge? Many people flee uncertainty by running back to what betrays them. You must learn to tolerate not knowing.

She offered a practice: each morning, instead of catastrophizing, Étienne would journal a single line beginning with, "Though I don't know what comes, I can." He might find himself writing: Though I do not know what comes, I can breathe. I can walk along the Seine. I can send an email to a colleague. I can rest.

The exercise grounded him in small certainties, easing the terror of the void.

4.2.8 *Future visioning*

Finally, Marianne asked, "If you imagine five years from now—Étienne living by his values, contributing through science—what do you see?"

Étienne closed his eyes. "I see myself in a research institute, a small one, perhaps linked to medicine. I see collaboration, not commerce. I see students, teaching them not only techniques but ethics. I see myself lighter, with laughter."

"Good," Marianne said. "That vision is not yet a plan, but it is a beacon. It can orient your steps."

4.2.8.1 The aftermath

Over the next weeks, Étienne resigned. As predicted, his company withheld a recommendation. He walked away with no guarantees. Yet, instead of collapsing, he carried Marianne's tactics with him:

- He returned to his values whenever doubt gnawed.
- He used meaning-centered reframing to remind himself that anguish was proof of integrity.

- He allowed emotional acknowledgment, weeping when fear swelled.
- He practiced narrative reconstruction, rewriting his story as one of courage, not failure.
- He reaffirmed his decision ownership each time he second-guessed himself.

He journaled daily, cultivating tolerance of uncertainty.

And he held fast to his future vision, using it to guide inquiries and applications.

Within months, he connected with a university laboratory in Marseille interested in sustainable biochemical research. The position paid less, but it aligned with his values. Étienne stepped into it without illusions—science was never pure—but with renewed authorship of his life.

For Marianne, the coaching journey affirmed a central existential truth: that wellness is not the absence of pain but the alignment of living with one's chosen values, even when it requires rupture. And for Étienne, the rupture became not an ending but the start of a more authentic chapter of his life.

Leaving her order.

Sister Margaret sat opposite her coach in the quiet counseling room of a London convent guesthouse.

Her hands twisted the rosary she no longer used for prayer. Her voice was both clipped and weary, the voice of someone who had lived in obedience for decades and suddenly found that the anchor of her life no longer held.

"I cannot say the words anymore," she confessed. "At Mass, in the chapel, even alone at night. I mouth them, but they fall dead. It is as if my faith evaporated, and I am left with nothing but habit."

Her existential wellness coach, Hannah, did not rush. She had met seekers who lost their belief before, but for a nun who had given her entire adult life to the Church, the rupture was seismic.

"Let's begin," Hannah said softly. "We'll work step by step. You're not alone in this passage."

4.2.9 *Existential questioning*

Hannah leaned forward. "What does it mean for you that you can no longer believe? Not in doctrine, but in your own life?"

Margaret hesitated. "It means . . . the ground is gone. For fifty years I thought I knew the meaning of my existence. To serve God, to serve the poor. Now I ask: What is the point?"

"Good," Hannah said gently. "That is the right question. Not to look at this as a failure but as an opening. Life never comes with a prewritten point. We are invited to create it. What do you imagine your point might be now?"

The question unsettled Margaret but began to liberate her. For the first time, she considered that the purpose was not handed down but chosen.

4.2.10 *Taking a life inventory*

Next, Hannah suggested, “Let’s take an inventory. Not of your faults or sins or missteps, but of your lived life. What have you done that mattered, separate from your spiritual beliefs?”

Margaret began listing: teaching children in East London, visiting prisoners, tending the convent garden, and sitting with the dying. As she spoke, her posture lifted.

“You see?” Hannah said. “Meaning is not erased because faith has shifted. Your acts, your kindness, your presence—they remain.”

Margaret nodded slowly. “So, I have not wasted my life?”

“No! You lived fully within a certain story. Now a new story begins.”

4.2.11 *Paradox exploration*

Soon despair returned. “How can I be both grateful for my past and yet reject it? How can I love my sisters here but know I cannot stay?”

Hannah introduced a third tactic.

> That is the paradox: to hold two truths at once. You loved and you served, and now you must leave. Both are valid. Life is full of contradictions. The mistake is thinking you must resolve them neatly. I know you have it in you to live with paradox, contradictions, and complexity.

Margaret exhaled deeply. She had been raised to think contradictions were errors. Now, she saw them as part of human existence. She could honor her past devotion even as she walked away from it.

4.2.12 *Silence and presence*

At their next session, Margaret arrived trembling. “I told the prioress I could not remain. She was kind but sad. I feel as though I have killed something.”

Hannah said nothing. She simply sat with her, breathing slowly. They shared long minutes of silence. Margaret wept softly, her tears falling onto the unused rosary.

Finally, Hannah said, “Not every wound needs to be met with words. Sometimes what heals is presence. Notice: you are not alone in this room. I am here. Your grief has a witness.”

Margaret later said those minutes of silence were more healing than any advice that Hannah might have given her.

4.2.13 *Boundary clarification*

As the weeks passed, practical questions emerged. Where would she live? What would she do with her days? “I feel guilty,” Margaret said. “The sisters will think I abandoned them. Should I still visit every week? Should I continue wearing my habit until I find other clothes?”

Hannah guided her into a boundary clarification exercise. "Ask yourself: what belongs to you now, and what belongs to them? You cannot carry both sets of responsibilities. Draw a line."

Together, they wrote two lists: Mine and Theirs. On Mine: her time, her new choices, and her search for community. On Theirs: the convent's routines, their expectations, and their judgments.

Margaret studied the lists. "I see. I can love them, but I do not owe them my life anymore."

4.2.14 *Ritual creation*

Still, Margaret felt unmoored. She missed the rhythm of bells, prayers, and vespers. "Without ritual, my days unravel."

Hannah introduced the tactic of ritual creation. "Ritual need not be religious. It can be human, personal. What small practice could mark your mornings and evenings?"

They experimented. Margaret began walking to the Thames each dawn, throwing a pebble into the water as a symbol of release. At night, she lit a candle and wrote a single sentence about the day's meaning.

These simple rituals steadied her. "I am inventing my own liturgy," she said with a shy smile.

4.2.15 *Community mapping*

Eventually, Margaret admitted, "I'm lonely. I can't live only in my own head. Where will I belong?"

Hannah offered a seventh tactic: community mapping. Together, they sketched a chart of possible circles: former teaching colleagues, volunteer groups, and seaside towns where she might find openness. Brighton, with its mix of artists, retirees, and seekers, caught Margaret's imagination.

"Could I really?" she asked. "Live in Brighton?"

"Why not?" Hannah said. "Circle it. Let it be a destination, not just a dream."

4.2.15.1 *The passage*

Within months, Margaret left the convent. She packed two suitcases, said farewell to the sisters, and boarded a train south. In Brighton, she rented a small flat near the sea. The first weeks were bewildering—shopping in ordinary clothes, making tea in her own kettle, and choosing her own hours.

But the tactics carried her:

- *Existential questioning* reminded her that she could create meaning.
- Her *life inventory* assured her she had lived with value.
- *Paradox exploration* allowed her to carry gratitude and grief simultaneously.
- *Silence and presence* had taught her to trust stillness.

- *Boundary clarification* freed her from old obligations.
- *Ritual creation* gave her mornings and evenings shape.
- *Community mapping* led her to a circle of volunteers who helped refugees at the pier.

Soon, she found herself surrounded by new friends: artists, activists, elderly widows, and young mothers. They laughed together in seaside cafés. They argued and sang and comforted one another. Margaret felt community, not bound by vows but chosen in freedom.

One evening, she stood on Brighton's pebbled beach, the tide washing close. She thought of the convent, the decades of devotion, and the rupture of leaving. She whispered, "I am still a servant, but now of life itself."

4.3 Tactics for the hardest questions

As existential wellness coaches, we don't hand our clients easy answers. Instead, we walk beside them as they ask the hardest questions: who am I? What matters most? How do I live authentically when life is uncertain and when time is limited?

The tactics we've just explored—whether legacy journaling, role-playing courageous conversations, creating rituals, or mapping meaning—are simply invitations. Each is a way to help clients pause, reflect, and step toward a life that feels more genuine and alive.

Some clients will find resonance in art-making, others will find it in philosophy, and others will find it in storytelling or courageous action. What matters most is not the tool itself but the spirit with which we offer it: with respect, with curiosity, and with a willingness to sit with what is difficult.

Our role is to remind clients that meaning is not handed down from outside but can be created, moment by moment, choice by choice. In this way, coaching becomes a shared act of courage—two people cocreating space for authenticity, purpose, and the possibility of joy.

FOOD FOR THOUGHT

1. What are your thoughts about the idea of "coaching tactics"? Does that resonate as an idea?
2. Do you have your own personal existential wellness tactics? What are they?
3. How might you introduce a given tactic? What sort of language might you use?
4. Do a couple of existential wellness tactics stand out for you? What are they?
5. Try your hand at creating an existential wellness tactic of your own. What might it be?

Chapter 5

The weight of individuality

Clients do not come in to see an existential wellness coach and say, "I want to be an individual." And yet, that is why they are there. They want the opportunity to be themselves, to be allowed to act according to their nature, and to be as unfettered by society's conventions and their personal circumstances as is humanly possible.

As an existential wellness coach, you understand that this is why they have come to see you. They arrive fully in the existential tradition—whether or not they are employing existential language—a tradition where "individuality" stands at the center of the human project.

5.1 The existential theme of individuality

Existentialism has always placed individuality at the center of its concerns. From Kierkegaard's early formulations of the individual before God to Nietzsche's proclamation that one must "become who you are" to Sartre's and Camus' mid-twentieth-century explorations of freedom, responsibility, and authenticity, the existential tradition has consistently affirmed the primacy of the individual over systems, abstractions, and collectives.

To speak of the existential theme of individuality is to examine what it means to live as a singular being in a clumsy, unforgiving, and often absurd world—as a being who must make meaning rather than receive it, who must decide rather than defer, and who must bear the consequences of those decisions.

The existential theme of individuality begins with Søren Kierkegaard, who resisted the abstract systems of Hegel and insisted instead that truth is "subjectivity." For Kierkegaard, the individual is always situated, finite, and confronted with choices that cannot be dissolved into rational systems.

The Hegelian dialectic might claim to grasp the movement of history or the unfolding of spirit, but for Kierkegaard, that grand vision neglected the living, breathing human being who must face despair, dread, and faith (or a lack of

DOI: 10.4324/9781003724971-5

faith). Individuality, for Kierkegaard, is the confrontation with one's own existence and the decision to relate oneself rightly to it.

Nietzsche advanced the theme of individuality by rejecting inherited religious and moral frameworks. He warned against "herd morality," the tendency of individuals to conform to values imposed by the majority. For Nietzsche, individuality demanded self-overcoming, the creation of values rather than the passive reception of them. His famous exhortation—"Become who you are"—is both a challenge and a paradox, for it suggests that individuality is not given but must be wrestled into being through acts of will and courage.

The twentieth-century existentialists, especially Sartre and Camus, radicalized individuality further. Sartre declared that "existence precedes essence," meaning that human beings are not born with a predetermined nature but must define themselves through choices. Camus, in turn, highlighted the absurd—the tension between our longing for meaning and the silence of the universe. For Camus, individuality emerges in the confrontation with the absurd, when one refuses resignation or false consolations and instead affirms life on its own terms.

The existentialists agreed that individuality entails freedom. To be an individual is to recognize oneself as free to choose, free to create, and free to act. But this freedom is never a simple blessing. It is also a burden. Sartre famously described human beings as "condemned to be free," meaning that we cannot avoid the responsibility that comes with freedom. Even refusing to choose is itself a choice, and therefore, we are always accountable for our existence. We examine the themes of freedom, resistance, and absurd rebellion in Chapter 13.

For Kierkegaard, responsibility was understood in religious terms: the individual before God, accountable in faith. For Nietzsche, responsibility meant the ability to bear the weight of creating values in a godless world. For Sartre, responsibility was the inescapable fact of human freedom. In each case, individuality is inseparable from this double-edged reality: the exhilaration of freedom and the anxiety of responsibility.

If freedom and responsibility are the conditions of individuality, authenticity is its aim. To live authentically is to live in accordance with one's chosen values, rather than in conformity with external pressures or internal evasions. Existentialists insist that individuality can only be genuine if it is lived authentically, without self-deception or bad faith. We examine the theme of authenticity more closely in Chapter 14.

Individuality is not only a source of freedom and authenticity, but it also courts alienation. To affirm oneself as an individual is to separate oneself from the crowd, from traditions, and from easy comforts. Kierkegaard described the individual as "the single one," set apart from the group and called to stand in solitude before God. Nietzsche warned that the path of self-overcoming would isolate the creator from the herd. Sartre and Camus likewise highlighted the loneliness that comes with individuality. To live as an individual is to confront the indifference of the universe, the skepticism of society, and the fragility of one's projects.

The existentialists consistently warned of the forces that threaten individuality. Chief among them are conformity and bad faith. Conformity is the tendency to adopt the values, beliefs, and behaviors of the group without reflection. It is easier to go along with the crowd than to assert one's freedom and easier to accept ready-made answers than to create one's own. Conformity allows one to escape the anxiety of individuality, but only at the cost of authenticity. Heidegger's "they," Nietzsche's "herd," and Kierkegaard's "crowd" all point to this danger.

Bad faith, as Sartre articulated it, is subtler. It is the internal evasion of freedom, the self-deception that allows one to believe that one is not responsible. The individual convinces himself that he is determined by his role, his past, or his circumstances, thereby avoiding the anguish of freedom. Yet, in doing so, he forfeits authenticity and betrays his individuality.

Modern society presents additional dangers: mass media, consumer culture, bureaucratic systems, and digital networks can all erode individuality by promoting passive consumption and uniformity. The existential call to individuality is therefore not only a philosophical position but also a call to resist the pressures of modern life.

If individuality is threatened by conformity and bad faith, how can it be affirmed? The existentialists propose creativity as one possibility. To affirm individuality is to create values, projects, works of art, and ways of life that express one's freedom. Creativity is not limited to artists; it is the fundamental act of shaping one's existence. We look at this idea more closely in Chapter 16.

Nietzsche emphasized the aesthetic dimension of individuality: one must "give style to one's character" and live as an artist of existence. Sartre likewise saw artistic creation as a paradigm of freedom, but he also emphasized that every choice is a kind of creation: to choose is to project oneself into the future and to constitute oneself as an individual.

5.2 Retaining individuality in a conformist world: a coaching vignette

Michael was 38 and a software engineer living in a mid-sized city. His career was stable, his primary relationship was harmonious, and his social circle was respectable. Yet he arrived at his first coaching session with an air of quiet desperation.

His words were measured but heavy:

> I feel like I'm slowly disappearing. Every choice I make seems like the choice that everyone else is making. It's as if I'm on autopilot, following the script. And I hate the idea that I might live my entire life without ever truly being myself.

His existential wellness coach, Sarah, had heard similar sentiments before but recognized and acknowledged the uniqueness of Michael's struggle. She knew that while the desire for belonging is universal, the fear of losing individuality to conformity is deeply existential. Her role was not to provide easy answers but to create a space where Michael could examine the tension between self and society.

Sarah began by inviting Michael to describe concretely the pressures he felt. He spoke of colleagues who all seemed to buy the same houses in the suburbs, send their children to the same private schools, and post the same sorts of vacation photos on social media. He described workplace expectations of dressing in near-uniform attire, of keeping conversations safely in the realm of sports and weather, and of stifling any unusual opinions.

As Michael spoke, Sarah reframed his experience in existential terms:

> What you're feeling is the clash between authenticity and conformity. Society sets out patterns—acceptable ways of being—and the existential task is to ask, "Which patterns, if any, fit me? Which ones do I want to resist?" The very fact that you're noticing this pressure suggests you still have a strong core of individuality. You wouldn't feel the loss if there wasn't something real at stake.

This reframing gave Michael a sense of relief. His discomfort wasn't pathological or trivial. It was the natural friction of a person trying to live authentically in a conformist world.

To help Michael reconnect with his individuality, Sarah guided him through a values clarification exercise. Instead of abstract words, she asked for lived memories.

"When have you felt most yourself?", she asked.

Michael recalled a summer in college when he had bicycled through rural France alone. He carried little more than a backpack, a tent, and a notebook. "Every decision was mine," he said. "Where to stop, what to eat, whether to talk to someone or stay silent. I wasn't following anyone else's plan. I was improvising, and I felt alive."

Together, they named the values implicit in that memory: freedom, spontaneity, simplicity, and independence. Michael contrasted those with his current life, where routines and collective expectations dominated. Sarah didn't suggest that he abandon his job or his primary relationship, but she did highlight the possibility of weaving those values back into his daily existence.

Michael admitted that much of his conformity was motivated by fear: fear of being judged as odd, fear of losing career opportunities, and fear of alienating friends. "It's easier to go along," he confessed.

Sarah nodded. "Yes, conformity reduces friction. But it also reduces you. The existential question is: do you want a smoother, smaller life, or a bumpier, fuller one?"

Michael paused, visibly moved. "I want the fuller one. But how?"

Sarah explained that authenticity often requires tolerating the anxiety of difference. "You can't erase that fear. You can only decide whether the expression of your individuality is worth bearing it." She reminded him that every authentic act, no matter how small, is a reclaiming of self.

Rather than urging radical change, Sarah suggested "experiments in individuality." These were low-risk actions that tested his willingness to resist conformity.

Michael decided that at work, he would start by voicing genuine opinions in meetings instead of echoing the majority.

He also resolved to dress slightly differently—not outrageously but in ways that expressed his taste rather than corporate blandness. Socially, he would decline some group outings that felt obligatory and instead pursue solo activities that brought him joy, like sketching in the park.

Sarah emphasized that these experiments weren't about rebellion for rebellion's sake. They were about alignment: acting in accordance with his own values rather than defaulting to external expectations.

In a later session, Sarah introduced the idea of narrative identity. "Each of us tells ourselves a story about who we are. Conformity pressures can rewrite that story without our noticing."

Michael realized that his internal narrative had become "I am a responsible professional who does what's expected." While not false, it was incomplete. He remembered earlier identities: the traveler, the musician, and the dreamer. He saw how he had gradually let those characters fade from his story.

With Sarah's encouragement, he began writing a more expansive narrative: "I am a creator, an explorer, a partner, and a professional. I value independence, beauty, and truth. I walk some common paths but also carve my own." This act of writing became a declaration of individuality.

One pivotal session occurred after Michael experimented with dressing more distinctively at work. A colleague had made a teasing remark, and Michael had felt the sting of embarrassment. Yet, afterward, he noticed something surprising: a younger coworker approached him privately and said, "I really admire that you don't just blend in."

Michael shared this story with Sarah, who highlighted the paradox: "When you show your individuality, yes, you risk criticism. But you also inspire others. You become a model of authenticity."

This insight shifted Michael's frame of reference. Individuality wasn't only self-serving; it could also serve as a beacon in a conformist environment.

As the coaching process continued, Sarah helped Michael develop practices to sustain his individuality. These included (1) weekly reflection journaling, where he assessed whether his week's actions had aligned with his values; (2) creative expression, through returning to guitar playing, which reconnected him to his imaginative self; (3) micro-adventures, such as day trips without an agenda, to revive his sense of freedom and spontaneity; and (4) boundary-setting, politely declining social events that drained him and prioritizing those that nourished him.

Sarah also reminded Michael that individuality didn't mean rejecting all social norms. "Existential wellness lies in the dance—sometimes joining, sometimes resisting, but always consciously choosing."

After several months, Michael reported feeling less invisible. He was speaking up more at work, carving out more creative time, and cultivating friendships with people who appreciated his uniqueness. "I don't feel like I've escaped society's pressure," he told Sarah, "but I feel like I'm negotiating with it rather than surrendering to it. I'm in dialogue with the world instead of letting it dictate who I am."

Sarah recognized this as the essence of existential wellness: not the elimination of tension but the capacity to live deliberately within it.

5.3 Individuality, rebellion, and the creative personality

What about self-identified creatives and their particular relationship to individuality? You'll likely see many such clients: clients who self-identify as creative and who struggle either with asserting their individuality, retaining their individuality, or dealing with the consequences of manifesting their individuality.

It is a creative person's individuality that defines them. Most people are conventional and prize conformity; creatives tend to prize their individuality. Even if they train themselves to hold their tongue, individuals will already know as young children that they can't conform and that they weren't built to conform.

Looking around, unable to understand why people are acting so conventionally, starting to feel alienated, out of place, and like a "stranger in a strange land," they find themselves burdened by this pulsing energy: the fierce need to be themselves. This need produces lifelong emotional, practical, and existential consequences.

If you are born an individual and find yourself presented with some arbitrary, odd-sounding rule—that you can only play with one of your toys at a time or that God will be offended if you don't wear a hat—you will immediately ask, "Why?" If the answer makes no sense to you or if you get your ears boxed, you will cry "No!" and begin to grow oppositional.

A certain oppositional attitude naturally and inevitably flows from an individual's adamant effort to reject humbug and to make personal sense of the world. What does this feel like, emotionally? It feels like a combination of sorrow and anger, tangled together to form a root ball of despair.

This oppositional attitude, perhaps suppressed in childhood, begins to announce itself and assert itself in adolescence and to grow as an individual's interactions with the conventional world increase. It grows as their ability to "do their own thing" is directly or indirectly restricted by the machinery of society.

They find themselves in an odd kind of fight, not necessarily with any particular person or group of people but with everyone and everything meant to constrain them and reduce them to a cipher. They find themselves in a fight to the death and a fight to retain their individuality.

One proof that this dynamic actually takes place is the frequency with which we see it in the lives of creative people. Arnold Ludwig, in his study of "1000 extraordinary men and women" called *The Price of Greatness*, explained,

> These individuals often have an attitude set that is oppositional in nature. These are not people who just see that the emperor has no clothes; they offer their own brand of attire for him to wear. When dominant ideologies challenge reason, they feel obliged to speak out, do what they believe is right, and pursue their own goals, even when they may be punished for doing so.

Popping out of the womb as individuals, needing to experiment and to risk as part of their individuality, and feeling thwarted and frustrated by the oh-so-conventional universe into which they have been plopped at birth, the world's individuals rush headlong like a ski jumper down a ramp toward reckless ways of dealing with their feelings of alienation and frustration. They are not only individual, but they are also driven to *be* individual, a drive that sets them apart and sends them racing through life.

Nature is not stupid. Nature makes the calculation that, for an individual to truly be individual, it had better invest them with enough power, passion, energy, and appetite to manifest that individuality. Otherwise, individuality would be a cosmic joke, and nature doesn't joke that way. So it regularly invests this individual with extra drive. Just as it makes no sense to produce a creature that enjoys the leaves at the tops of trees without also providing it with a long neck, it makes no sense to produce creatures that are built to assert their individuality without providing them with the energy of assertion. This nature regularly does.

Thus, these individuals likely have more energy, more charisma, bigger appetites, stronger needs, greater passion, more aliveness, and more avidity than the next person. This is all the same idea and flows from the same wellspring. It is nature's way of fueling individuals so that they can *be* individuals. It should also be clear how this extra energy and fuller appetite lead to conditions like addiction, mania, and insatiability.

How can you have an outsized sex drive and not become obsessed with sex? How can you have a ton of energy and not court mania? How can you have a full measure of extra adrenaline course through your system and not need to drive a hundred miles an hour or have several drinks in order to "take the edge off"? Nature, by fitting the individual with sufficient energy to write complex novels and penetrate the mysteries of the universe, inadvertently creates a driven, insatiable, addiction-prone creature.

Nature does not joke, but it does produce unintended consequences. One of the major unfortunate consequences of this extra drive—this extra ambition, this extra egotism, and this extra appetite—is that the individual is hard-pressed, and often completely unable, to feel satisfied. They eat a hundred peanuts—not satisfying enough. They write a good book—not satisfying enough. They have a shot of excellent Scotch—not satisfying enough. They win the Nobel Prize—not satisfying enough.

This inability to get satisfied produces constant background unhappiness and makes them want some experience that will mask this feeling or make it go away. So they have another hundred peanuts or another Scotch without, however, coming any closer to satisfying themselves.

It is as if nature turbocharged some of its creatures and then failed to give them a decent braking system. It provided extra energy—and with it a susceptibility to mania. It provided extra ambition—and with it a susceptibility to grandiosity. It provided extra appetite—and with it a susceptibility to promiscuity, obesity, and alcoholism. It provided extra adrenaline—and with it a susceptibility to car wrecks. If all of these "extras" could be channeled and regulated, we might thank nature for its largesse. As it is, these extras make the individual's life unruly and fraught with danger.

Nature, which doesn't joke, nevertheless has its little joke and creates individuals who must know for themselves, follow their own path, and be themselves; puts it in their mind that they are born to do earth-shattering and life-saving work; gives them the energy to pursue this work and the courage to stand in opposition even to the whole world; and then turns around and tortures them. First of all, it heightens their core anxiety by giving them an existential outlook, making sure that nothing will satisfy them, pouring adrenaline through their system, and swelling their head so that they are primed to tip over, top-heavy, into self-centeredness.

This mandate to individuality forces creative individuals to wonder about life's large questions—pesters them with those questions—and demands that they respond to what they see going on in the universe. It forces them to write a mournful poem, craft a subversive novel, and walk the earth from one end to the other on some unnamable quest. Each of these is an existential response; that is, a response arising from their plaintive, poignant questioning of the world into which nature has dropped them. On top of everything else, nature tells them that they are responsible for looking out for the world—nothing less is expected of them.

Of course, we aren't equal to all of this, or even much of this. As individual as we are, as magnificent as we are, we are also quite puny. We may be large, but we are also small. Even if we do manage to persevere—to write our poems and to battle our windmills—it is not without a thousand ups and downs, frustrations and disappointments, and rages and dirges. Is this your emotional landscape? Then, you are probably a born-creative individual.

Individuality produces all sorts of consequences. Nature may have designated you as one of her individuals, but she has not provided you with a blueprint to follow. You (and your clients) will have to work that out, even while nursing a pain in your heart and a pain in your head. Our creative clients are like this. And it can pay dividends to invite them to think about, and maybe journal about, prompts like the following ones.

- How does the issue of individuality relate to you?
- Have you grown oppositional as you fight to retain your individuality?
- What kind of 'balance' are you able to achieve between retaining your individuality and successfully relating to others and to the world?

5.4 Helping clients regain and retain their individuality

Many clients visit an existential wellness coach precisely because they feel that they have lost this sense of individuality: they find themselves conforming to outside expectations, playing roles that no longer fit, or drowning in the noise of other people's needs and voices. Here are eight tips to help you as you engage with this essential client work.

5.4.1 Help clients recognize the forces of conformity

Individuality is often eroded by conformity—the subtle or overt pressures to fit into family expectations, cultural norms, workplace demands, or social media trends. Many clients do not realize how much of their life is shaped by external forces. They may believe their choices are freely made when in fact they are complying with scripts handed down by others. Coaches can help clients identify these forces by asking questions such as

- Whose voice are you listening to when you say you "must" do this?
- Who benefits when you act this way?
- What would you do if nobody were watching?

5.4.2 Normalize the anxiety of individuality

Choosing individuality may sometimes feel exhilarating, but it is also anxiety-producing. Sartre and Kierkegaard both emphasized that freedom comes with dread: when I realize that I alone am responsible for my choices, I confront the vertigo of possibility. Clients may resist individuality not because they lack courage but because the weight of freedom feels unbearable.

An existential wellness coach can help normalize this anxiety. Instead of trying to "eliminate" it, the coach frames it as a sign that the client is touching something vital. Anxiety is the price of freedom; it is also a compass pointing toward authenticity. By learning to tolerate and even befriend this anxiety, clients strengthen their capacity to live as individuals rather than retreat into conformity or bad faith.

Coaches can help clients understand this dynamic by asking questions such as:

- Does the idea of freedom make you feel anxious?
- How does exerting your individuality affect you?
- If you've gotten oppositional while trying to retain your individuality, do those conflicts make you anxious?

5.4.3 Support clients in value creation

Individuality is sustained by living in alignment with one's own values and not borrowed or inherited values. Many clients struggle because they have adopted the values of their culture, parents, or peer group without reflection. An existential wellness coach guides clients in clarifying, testing, and creating their own values.

This may involve journaling exercises, dialogs about what matters most, or experiments in living where your client focuses on one particular value like compassion, courage, or service. For example, a client may discover that "independence" is less central than they thought and that "connectedness" actually feels more authentic, or vice versa. The goal is not to hand clients a ready-made list of values but to help them engage in the ongoing, creative process of value formation.

5.4.4 Encourage authentic decision-making

Existentialists emphasize that individuality is forged in decisions. Every choice reflects and shapes who we are. Yet clients often avoid decisions, waiting for clarity or certainty that never comes. Others make decisions reactively, without aligning them with their deeper commitments. An existential wellness coach helps clients see that indecision is itself a decision and that authenticity requires stepping into the responsibility of choice.

By practicing decision-making that is congruent with their values, clients reinforce their individuality. A coach might employ reflective questions like: *does this choice express who you most want to be?* Or *what are you avoiding by not deciding?* Through this process, clients learn to act as the authors of their lives rather than passive recipients of circumstances.

5.4.5 Address the role of relationships

Individuality is not the same as isolation. Clients often fear that reclaiming their individuality will alienate them from loved ones or communities. An existential wellness coach helps clients see that healthy individuality and healthy relationships can coexist.

This may involve boundary work—teaching clients how to assert their needs and protect themselves from harmful interactions. It may involve communication skills—for example, how to express one's individuality without anger, irritation, or resentment. It may involve grief work—acknowledging that some relationships may not survive a client's movement toward authenticity.

5.4.6 Teach strategies for resisting "bad faith"

Sartre's concept of *bad faith*—the evasion of freedom by pretending one is determined by external forces—is central to helping clients retain individuality. Many clients unconsciously fall into bad faith: "I have no choice but to stay in this job," "I can't help being this way," or "My past defines me."

An existential wellness coach gently challenges these statements, pointing out where freedom is being denied. This certainly doesn't mean announcing to clients that they can control everything—we recognize real limits—but it does mean highlighting where responsibility lies. Even within constraints, choices remain. By consistently calling clients back to their freedom, coaches help them resist the slide into bad faith that undermines individuality.

5.4.7 Cultivate creative expression

Existentialists such as Nietzsche and Camus saw creativity as essential to individuality. To create—whether through art, writing, music, or simply the shaping of one's daily life—is to affirm one's uniqueness. Clients often lose touch with their creative nature and their imaginative faculties, opting instead for dull routine. An existential wellness coach encourages clients to find creative outlets, not for the sake of productivity or external success but rather for the sake of self-expression and manifesting potential.

5.4.8 Emphasize retention through ongoing reflection

Finally, individuality is not something "achieved once and for all." It is an ongoing project. Life's pressures—new jobs, relationships, aging, and crises—constantly threaten the pursuit of individuality. An existential wellness coach prepares clients not only to regain individuality but also to retain it over time. By regularly asking: *am I living authentically? Have I slipped into conformity? Am I honoring my values?* Clients sustain individuality against the drift of everyday life. Retention requires vigilance, but it is also rewarding: it keeps life vibrant, self-directed, and genuinely one's own.

5.5 Conclusion

The existential theme of individuality runs like a red thread through the works of Kierkegaard, Nietzsche, Sartre, Camus, and others. It is the recognition that human beings are singular, free, responsible, and capable of authenticity. It is also the recognition that individuality is difficult and that it entails alienation, anxiety, and resistance to conformity.

Camus' figure of Sisyphus, endlessly pushing his boulder up that hill yet affirming his life, is itself a creative image of individuality in the face of absurdity. To affirm individuality is not to retreat into solipsism but to engage the world on one's own terms. It is to act, decide, and create without guarantees, to shoulder responsibility without excuses, and to live authentically in a world that offers no ultimate justification. This is both the burden and the gift of individuality.

The existential theme of individuality is both timeless and urgently contemporary. In a world of mass culture, algorithmic nudges, and overwhelming social pressures, many people feel their individuality slipping away. Existential wellness coaches are uniquely positioned to help clients regain and retain this essential dimension of life.

Retaining individuality in today's world is both difficult and essential. It requires vigilance against conformity, courage to face the anxiety of freedom, and commitment to living authentically. By practicing reflection, clarifying values, making conscious choices, setting boundaries, nurturing creativity, choosing supportive relationships, resisting labels, and embracing growth, clients can safeguard their uniqueness.

Individuality cannot be given to clients—it must be claimed. But coaches can offer the guidance, presence, and encouragement that make this claiming possible. In doing so, they help clients live not as shadows of external expectations but as luminous individuals, responsible for and reconciled with their freedom.

FOOD FOR THOUGHT

1. Is "individuality" an issue for you? If so, how does that issue manifest?
2. Have you personally grown oppositional as you endeavor to claim and maintain your individuality?
3. What are your thoughts on the connections between creativity and individuality?
4. How might you check in with clients to learn about their relationship to their own individuality?
5. What two or three tactics might you employ to help a client regain and maintain their individuality?

Chapter 6

The story of life purposes

In my vision and version of existential wellness coaching, I take it to be true that there is no single or singular purpose to life and that the hunt for that unavailable singular life purpose brings pain, confusion, and unnecessary suffering.

What seems truer to me is that, instead of seeking something that does not exist, clients can be helped to understand that the path to wellness involves naming and living their multiple life purposes—that is, naming and living the many things that they themselves deem important. That is, there is nothing for them "to find." There are only and exactly choices for them to make.

Let me recapitulate some key points.

The more science taught us about ourselves and the universe, the more we shrank in size—and shrank back in horror. You could build the largest particle accelerator the world has ever seen and recreate the Big Bang—and, psychologically speaking, end up with only more of nothing. This is where we are today. We had somehow wagered that well-stocked supermarkets and guaranteed elections would do the trick and protect us from the void. They haven't. This we must now face.

This now shared certainty that we are throwaways has made life look completely unfunny. We can laugh and make small talk, but in our private moments, there is not that much laughter. There is only a deep, wide, abiding "Why bother?" Here, I think, is the answer. While we are here, we have the self-obligation to bother and the self-obligation to act as if we matter, a mattering that includes acting ethically and putting the whole world on our shoulders.

This is what existentialists call an "absurd conclusion." It is "absurd" to care about life when life doesn't care about us. But that is the right answer.

To accomplish this, you take as much control as possible of your thoughts, your attitudes, your moods, your behaviors, and your very orientation toward life, and you make use of the freedom you possess in the service of what's important to you.

DOI: 10.4324/9781003724971-6

You attend to what existentialists call "the project of your life." You identify your life purposes, and you take responsibility for your life purpose choices. You deal with meaninglessness by making daily meaning investments and by seizing daily meaning opportunities. And you dismiss absurdity as true but irrelevant.

Like it or not, we have been forced into the role of steward and arbiter of our lives. Surely no one asked for that. Who wouldn't prefer an orgasm, a tidy income, a little selfishness, and another round of golf? Wouldn't you? But is that what you really want? Is there even an ounce of goodness in that picture? No, and so, we try.

We can't escape our psychological subjectivity, as we are embedded inside of it. But we can wonder about our motives, we can make guesses about our intentions, and we can speculate about where we may be fooling ourselves. We can reflect. Inside our cocoon of psychological subjectivity, a cocoon that makes it hard to see clearly, we can aspire to self-awareness.

We choose our life purposes, and then, we live our life purposes. This sounds obvious enough. If you knew what your life purposes were, surely you would want to then live them, yes? But even people who have a good sense of what their life purposes are have difficulty actually living them.

This is because tasks, chores, errands, and everything else are allowed to come first, because juggling multiple life purposes is difficult, and because living our life purposes requires rather more effort than, say, napping or turning on the television. But let us set the bar that high: that we will live our life purposes!

6.1 As if it were step by step

Let's presume for the moment that the effort to choose and live your life purposes allowed for a step-by-step process (which, of course, it doesn't really).

Maybe you would start by considering what's really important to you at this moment in your life. Then, you would take the next step and the step after that. What might that path look like? Maybe something like the following nine steps?

6.1.1 Step 1. You decide

You decide that you and your efforts matter, that you want to live in accordance with your own values and principles, and that your life purposes are yours to name and frame. Step one involves making a certain decision and taking a certain stance. It is a bit like going to the gym—to the existential gym. You grasp that bar, put the heavy weight of your life on your shoulders, and prepare for an overhead lift.

6.1.2 Step 2. You honor the nature of the task

You recognize that naming and framing your life purposes may prove at once impossibly complicated and also simple, as simple as coming up with a life purposes statement that you follow. Maybe you create a huge list of the values that matter to you and wonder what on earth to do with that long, contradictory list. You try to factor in your circumstances, your personality quirks, everything. How complicated! Or you might decide that "do the next right thing" nicely captures the essence of your life project. How simple! Complicated? Simple? Both?

6.1.3 Step 3. You announce what's important to you

In whatever fashion you get there, you distill your list, and you announce what's important to you. Then you nod. "Yes, my health really is important to me." "Yes, my creativity really is important to me." "Yes, finding meaningful work really is important to me." "Yes, repairing my relationship with my children really is important to me." Etc.

6.1.4 Step 4. You restate those important things as life purpose choices

This is an easy step linguistically. You just say, "My health is one of my life purpose choices" instead of "My health is really important to me." Linguistically, it's that simple. But those restatements are psychologically crucial. To call something a life purpose choice is to anoint it, strengthen it, and commit to it.

6.1.5 Step 5. You elaborate on your life purposes choices, clarifying and refining them

You've announced, say, that your health is a life purpose choice. But what does that mean? Is that primarily your physical health? Or your emotional health as well? Is that more about diet and exercise or more about finally getting off that medication with all its debilitating side effects? What exactly do you mean?

6.1.6 Step 6. You translate your life purpose choices into actions

Moving from "health" to "diet + exercise + meditation + medical check-up" is brilliant. Next, what will you actually do (and not do)? Have blueberries and yogurt for lunch every day? Stop eating at 7 p.m.? Empty the cupboards of all processed snack foods? These are the mundane consequences of life purpose choosing!

6.1.7 Step 7. You align your thoughts with your life purpose choices

You want to make a career change and find more meaningful work. That's a clear life purpose choice of yours. But how well can you proceed if you are thinking "I have no chance," "All work is meaningless," "It's too late for me," and "I have no real skills"? Do we agree that those thoughts would not serve you all that well? Indeed, if those were your thoughts, would you even try?

6.1.8 Step 8. You institute practices that support your life purpose choices

Intending to write a novel is one thing. Instituting a daily writing practice is a different thing—and the best way to honor your life purpose choice of writing. A writing day that produces 20 words is far better than a not-writing day filled with regrets about not writing.

6.1.9 Step 9. You live your life purpose choices

We do not want to create a list that leads nowhere. This is meant to be a lived philosophy of life, not a lip service one. You live your life by organizing it around your life purpose choices. This isn't for next year, or for when the kitchen remodel gets done. This is for now—right now.

6.2 Supporting effort #1: your life purposes statement

How might you support clients who want to work on their life purposes? You might invite them to create a life purposes statement, a life purposes icon, and/or a life purposes mantra and keep a life purposes journal. Let's look at each of these in turn.

A life purposes statement is nothing like a life purpose statement. The notion of a life purpose statement implies that you can reduce your life to one singular purpose. You can't. A life purposes statement, by contrast, accompanies you as you live the project of your life and does a little handy reminding of some headlines that you'd like to remember. It is a reminder, not a final answer.

The one I like to suggest is "Do the next right thing." "Do the next right thing" reminds you that you'd prefer to live an ethical life rather than an unprincipled one. But it does more than that. It suggests how interesting the word "right" can be. "Right" can mean "ethical." But "right" can also mean "strategic," and it can mean "appropriate," and it can mean "out-of-the-box." It is one rich word!

Let's say that you've worked hard at one of your life purposes. The next right thing might be a snack, a hot shower, or a nap. These aren't "moral" choices, but they are contextually the next right things for you to do so as to keep yourself on track, prepare you to tackle the next life purpose on your list, and help you maintain a kind of balance between engagement and disengagement and between intensity and relaxation.

The next right thing might even be something impulsive because you need to break free just a little bit from your wise, regimented life. It might be something a little indulgent after a week of supreme carefulness. "Right" has a beautiful richness to it, because what it means as part of your life purposes statement is that you are keeping track of your life moment by moment: you know what you need, you know what to do, and you know how to live.

Naming your life purposes involves connecting the dots among your desires, your appetites, your dreams, your goals, your values, your principles, your intentions, and everything else pressing down on you and welling up within you. If you were to try to "really" connect all those dots—if, for example, you were to create a document as long as a manual by which to live—you would likely never dip into that manual or find a way to make good use of it. The better answer—and a really good answer—is to keep it simple.

This "simplicity" I am calling a life purposes statement. In one great gulp, you take into account the values you want to uphold, the dreams and goals you have for yourself, and the vision you have for comporting yourself in the world, and you spend whatever time it takes turning that unwieldy, contradictory material into a coherent statement that reminds you of core sentiments about your life.

"Do the next right thing" is one possibility. But the choice is yours. There are no rules or regulations. A few suggestions, though: you probably want to keep it short; it would be lovely if it were a bit memorable; and you might give it a trial period of a day or two to see if it is doing the work you want it to do, of reminding you of your life purposes and supporting your efforts. If it does not seem to be working quite, try again!

Here are seven that clients have created. Pamela: "Action and satisfaction, today and every day." Sylvia: "I bring my complete self to each moment." Lois: "Right here, right now, paying attention and making meaning." Harrison: "Years of creating a body of work, days of grace and enthusiasm." Judy: "Passion and presence, courage and conviction." Frank: "I take pride in working with my hands and doing the right thing." Sonia: "I am at ease in the universe, as long as I speak in my own voice."

Think of those rich slogans from AA: "First things first," "One day at a time," and "Easy does it." They don't say everything that might be said about the recovery process, and they don't say everything that might be said about how you want to live your life. But they do a lovely job of reminding. They are useful, powerful, and beautiful.

Try your hand at creating yours. Living your life purposes requires support—from you. One tool in your support tool kit is your life purposes statement, those few words that do a grand job of reminding you that your life is your project, that your life is in your hands, and that you mean to live your life purposes. Provide yourself with that sort of compact, portable help.

6.3 Supporting effort #2: your life purposes icon

Here is another gorgeous way to support your intention to live your life purposes every day. Think of the way that a Christian cross or a Jewish Star of David holds a wealth of meaning for Christians and Jews. For the religious, those icons carry volumes of information in a simple, portable, and brilliant way about what life means and about how to live. Don't those icons do a ton of work?

Other life purpose icons include the clenched fist of Black power, the dove of peace, the image of the Buddha, and the rainbow flag of gay rights. These images provide a wealth of information and meaning for those people who hold them as iconic. Does the image of the Buddha mean the same thing to any two Buddhists? No. But does it hold meaning for each? Yes!

Such life purpose icons abound. But rarely does an individual create and make use of a personal icon that she employs to encapsulate her life purposes. People tend never to do this because it doesn't occur to them to do so. It is not an assignment any fifth-grade teacher ever gave them. It is not something that was ever discussed over Sunday dinner. It just never came up.

Even if it did occur to them to create their own personal life purposes icon, they might still feel challenged to accept that they had the right to create something as weighty as a Christian cross or a Jewish Star of David. Some thoughts like "How dare I?" might leap to mind. Especially if they've gotten in the unfortunate habit of suppressing their individuality, that long-standing habit might stop them in their tracks.

However, you not only have that right, but you also have the obligation to hold your personal life purposes as exactly that important! And so, what might you choose? Well, literally anything under the sun. The world of images is your oyster. Close your eyes, mind your breath for a moment, and let an image rise to the occasion. How exciting for you!

For example, from Paula, a painter:

> My life purpose icon is the walking stick. I have a walking stick in real life and I treasure it. It is somewhat crooked, as is the path of life. But it is sturdy and I cannot break it. It is made of both light and dark wood, representing life's dualities—day and night, stormy and peaceful, happy and full of strife. And it was born from something rooted to this earth, just as I am.

From Sandra, a sculptor:

> My personal icon is a lighthouse. A lighthouse is steadfast. A lighthouse stands out and stands alone. And a lighthouse has its own beauty and strength. It's built to withstand the worst storms, it's a fantastic design with a tremendously useful function, and it's a genuinely positive image.

From Kimberly, an aeronautical engineer:

> I've chosen a rocket as my life purposes icon. My favorite fantasy is to see the earth from space. Just as ships are built to sail the seas rather than languish in harbors, rockets are built to blast off rather than stand on the launch pad. Yes, mistakes will be made, postponements will happen, and problems will arise—but persistence pays off when we blaze into the unknown.

Imagine that you could carry your life purposes around with you in a portable way by creating your own icon. What might you choose? A walking stick, a polished stone, a lighthouse, a rocket, a hummingbird, a throne, and an egg—what might your life purposes icon be? Stop for a moment. Maybe one will come to you just like that, like a bolt of lightning. Maybe it will be a bolt of lightning!

And how might you carry it around and keep it close? By making it into a necklace that you wear daily? Or a ring? By making it your screensaver image? By sculpting it or painting it and keeping the sculpture on your desk or the painting across from your bed? What if you could see it every morning when you awoke? Wouldn't that orient you in a brilliant direction?

6.4 Supporting effort #3: your life purposes mantra

A mantra might also support you. A mantra is simply something that you repeat, or repeatedly listen to, because you find that it serves you to hear it. It could be a sound, a word, a phrase, or a whole passage. It isn't the size or the shape of it that determines whether something is or isn't a mantra. It's whether it serves you to hear it.

Maybe a reminder of your many life purposes can be captured by sound? Maybe by the sound of wind chimes, some notes of music, a single musical note, or a bird's song? Something short, sweet, and memorable? Are you maybe hearing something right now?

The world is full of mournful sounds, evocative sounds, and memorable sounds: train whistles, a screen door closing, and a baby laughing. Record a sound that moves you and listen to it. Do you even have to record it? Can't you just hear it? And if you can whistle . . .

Or your mantra could be a word. It could be a word like om, courage, now, hope, or amazing. If shamanism holds power for you, it could be the name of your power animal—jaguar, crow, cougar, lynx, or eagle. Maybe it's a place: Paris, a fjord, or a valley. Or a principle: fairness, liberty, or justice. Is a word coming to mind?

For me, the word is "process." "Process" is my mantra. If something hasn't worked—if a paragraph is off, if a class hasn't filled, if a day got lost—I will intone, "Process." I know what I mean by that. It reminds me that progress is not linear, that showing up is the name of the game, and that magic can happen out of the blue, at any given moment.

Your most powerful mantra might be your own name. Think of that! What might do a better job of carrying your life purposes, your identity, and your intentions than your own name? Wouldn't it be wonderful to have your name do that work? Say your name a few times in this new, mantra-like way. Does that work for you?

Or it could be a name you call yourself. Maybe your given name doesn't work for you. Maybe you don't much like the people who gave it to you, or what seems like a mean-spirited choice on their part. How dare they name you after a fruit, a month, a gemstone, or a Brooklyn neighborhood? Flatbush? Really? Why not call yourself something else and make your new name your mantra!

Or it could be a phrase. The life purposes phrase that I've suggested you employ is "Do the next right thing." As a mantra, this could be shortened to "Next right thing" or "Right thing." Doesn't "right thing" have a ring to it? Might that serve you?

For me, a passage that reminds me of my life purpose choices is a line from a Paul Verlaine poem. The line is "Il pleure dans mon coeur comme il pleut sur la ville," which roughly translates as "It cries in my heart as it rains on the town," and which is beautiful in French.

I can't tell you why this mournful line works so beautifully for me. But it does. When I hear myself saying it, I am refreshed, reminded, and reoriented. "Process" works for me, as does that line of poetry. As do bits of Motown lyrics and certain line fragments from novels. Let your mind wander. What are you hearing?

6.5 Supporting effort #4: your life purposes journal

You may already journal. Or you may never have had a desire to journal. Let me present the idea of a life purposes journal, one that you keep that is devoted to your reflections about how choosing and living your life purposes is going. Like your life purposes icon, your life purposes statement, and your life purposes mantra, your life purposes journal might do a lovely job of helping support you in your effort to live purposefully.

You might check in with yourself each evening, spending, in what may have been an otherwise tumultuous or over-busy day, a quiet, thoughtful few minutes processing the day and reflecting on how living your intentions went. Did you, for instance, get to your business-building activities? If so, celebrate for a second. Maybe dance around the room. Celebrating these small daily victories might amount to one of your more important practices.

Did you get to your business-building activities but sourly and "against your will"? Then remind yourself that living your life purposes doesn't come with the guarantee that you will be put in a good mood. Nod, remind yourself of that truth, and congratulate yourself on successfully showing up. Living a given life purpose may make you grumpy; it may make you anxious, and it may activate some addictive craving. All of that can happen.

Maybe you've been thinking about peanuts all day long. But you survived, and now, you get to reflect during your evening journal writing about how intentional living makes for days of this sort. You get to say a kind word to yourself; you get to congratulate yourself for another day spent exactly as you intend to spend your days. Yes, you may be quite tired and a little out of sorts. But the day was a victory.

That's daily life purposes journaling. Maybe you'll also adopt a separate weekly life purposes journaling practice. This might be a more elaborate, more in-depth reflection than your daily life purposes journaling, where you reflect on the past week and plan for the new week. Here, you get to consider why you were able to exercise on Tuesday and Thursday but not on Wednesday and maybe discover that Wednesdays present certain built-in obstacles that you hadn't noticed before. That's valuable news!

This weekly reflection affords you the opportunity to do what is in fact quite a complicated thing to do, namely, keep track of your multiple life purposes. Maybe you automatically and intuitively track one or two of your life purposes, but what about life purposes three, four, and five? They may well need more mindful attention than life purposes one and two, and your weekly life purposes reflection is your opportunity to keep track of them.

You would want this to be a gentle reflection, one full of self-forgiveness and ease, because it is completely likely that you will not have lived your week exactly as you had hoped to live it or intended to live it. Indeed, it may have fallen far short of ideal. Maybe you missed attending to almost all your life purposes in the hurly-burly of living. That happens! Do not beat yourself up if this occurred.

You want to notice that but not dwell on that. Smile a little at how human plans get bashed about in the living, think carefully about how to make your coming week better, and recommit to this, the project of your life. Forgive yourself and recommit. Those are two steps of this dance!

You might also want to add another journaling practice, a monthly journaling check-in. It might serve you beautifully to provide yourself with a snapshot of how the month went. It might become clear that this or that life purpose needs more attention; that this or that life purpose isn't feeling very important at the moment; and that this or that life purpose monopolized your time, maybe in a good way, as a productive obsession, or maybe as a thief. Those would be good things to know!

Journaling brings with it real benefits. It helps you gain insight; it helps you get things off your chest; it helps you form new intentions; it helps you recommit; it helps you better understand what's working and what isn't working in your life. Even an intermittent life purposes journaling practice might serve you beautifully. Just keep your life purposes journal handy and have the occasional fruitful conversation with yourself.

6.6 Eight life purposes practices

There is no prescribed way to live. Nor can there be. There are no particular things that you are obliged to do at 4 a.m., at 2 p.m., or at 10 p.m. You do not need to turn east, west, north, or south. You do not need to come together or stay apart. That is between you and you.

But, while there are no prescribed things to do, there are many wise things to do. I think that all of the following are wise. See if you think so, too. None of these is obligatory. But they all make sense, I think. Try some out, if you like. If one serves you, keep it. If it doesn't, discard it. And, of course, think about how they might apply to your work with clients as an existential wellness coach.

6.6.1 Practice 1. Increase your life purposes vocabulary

Insert phrases like "absurd rebellion," "self-obligation," "meaning opportunities," "meaning investments," and "life purposes" into your internal conversations. Focus on a word like "individuality" or a phrase like "multiple life purpose choices." Learn this language.

6.6.2 Practice 2. Check in each morning

Start each day with a life purposes check-in. Sit yourself down, remind yourself of your current life purpose choices, and mindfully select the ones you intend to champion on that day. Or simply stretch and wonder: "What are my life purpose efforts for today?" Wouldn't that wonder serve you better than turning on the news?

6.6.3 Practice 3. Practice doing the next right thing

First, have a conversation with yourself about what the phrase "do the next right thing" signifies to you. Doing the next right thing is an art form, not a slogan! It is a big, wonderful, and humane intention, in conflict with our selfish genes and our rapacious appetites. Therefore, it needs a lot of practice.

6.6.4 Practice 4. Create a first-thing-each-day morning practice in the service of your life purposes

This might be a creativity practice, a health practice, a career-building practice, a mindfulness practice, a personality upgrade practice, and so on. You would wake up and go directly to your practice. Maybe you'd decide on multiple morning practices, providing you with multiple daily meaning opportunities. How lovely!

6.6.5 Practice 5. Redesign your mind

You can get a better grip on your mind than is usually supposed, and you can even shoot for the high-bar goal of banishing thoughts that don't serve you and only thinking thoughts that actually do serve you. At the same time, you might redesign your mind by adding windows that let in a welcome breeze, installing an easy chair, painting those dingy walls a bright white, and so on.

6.6.6 Practice 6. Practice energy management

What might that look like? Begin by making a two-column list of activities and habits that drain your energy and activities and habits that increase your energy. That would be a start! Energy is a particularly mysterious part of the human story, neither easy to grasp nor easy to manage. Isn't it time to learn more about it?

6.6.7 Practice 7. Practice surrendering to not knowing

This would help you calmly tolerate all that is not known and never can be known. You might begin to softly murmur, "I just don't know about that," rather than reeling back in horror. Maybe you'll create a daily ceremony of surrender to not knowing, bowing in the direction of mystery or nodding at the inexplicable.

6.6.8 Practice 8. Practice choosing love as a life purpose and a meaning opportunity

All that would be required is a softening of your heart and an object of affection. If you bestow love today, you might coax some new meaning into existence. And you could do that again tomorrow. Think of words in the family of love: affection, kindness, generosity, and intimacy. They paint a picture of what loving looks like. Aren't they worthy things to practice?

6.7 You and clients

I've framed this chapter as a conversation with you, as, first of all, you are the one who likely needs to grow wiser about the difference between life purpose and life purposes before you can impart that wisdom to clients.

I hope you will spend some time absorbing these ideas and follow that up with some solid thinking on how you might present these ideas to clients, either directly or between the lines. Clients understand this distinction the second they hear it. They quickly align with the idea that life has no singular purpose and that they are obliged to decide what matters to them and what is important to them. Help them make this vital discovery.

FOOD FOR THOUGHT

1. What are your thoughts about this core distinction between "life purpose" and "life purposes"?
2. If you agree with it, how might you make use of it in your existential wellness coaching?
3. If you disagree with it, what is your view? If you've never quite articulated it, might this be the right time to try?
4. If your view is different from mine, how might you incorporate your belief system around purpose into your coaching?
5. Generally speaking, how central to the idea of existential wellness coaching and the practice of existential wellness coaching do you see the concept of purpose?

Chapter 7

Coaching meaning

Say that you believe, as I do, that a lot of human distress has to do with the feeling that life isn't meaningful or purposeful. How could a person suffering from that sort of feeling get some on-point help?

The main help that existential wellness coaches could offer their clients, from my point of view, would be a clear focus on how much is gained by actively and passionately "making meaning."

Most people get stuck in a waiting mode, waiting for something to happen—a change in circumstances, fewer life difficulties, some new revelation or insight, some bolt of lightning from a workshop, or something—that, once it happens, will open a currently closed door to meaning. And, while they wait, they experience life as painful and meaningless.

An existential wellness coach can say, "It is time to open that door." They can say, "You must make meaning in the middle of things—now is the time." They can say, "Identify your life purposes, live them, and, if you are lucky, life will feel meaningful." They can paint a picture for their client of meaning as a psychological experience or, even more simply, as a certain sort of feeling, one that can be coaxed into existence, most often as the fruit of living one's life purposes.

When our younger daughter came home from college one year, she presented me with a coffee mug. The motto on the coffee mug read, "Life isn't about finding yourself. Life is about creating yourself." "Isn't that your philosophy in a nutshell?" she laughed. She was exactly right. E.W. Wilcox, to whom the quote was attributed, had captured the essence of thousands of years of existential thought: that life is as much a responsibility as a gift and that each of us is honor-bound to create ourselves in our own best image.

I make my meaning—or else I don't. All that exists until I actively and mindfully make personal meaning is the possibility of meaning and, while I wait to get started, the experience of emptiness. There is the possibility that I will experience the next hour as meaningful, a possibility that turns into a reality only

DOI: 10.4324/9781003724971-7

if I make a certain kind of decision and a certain kind of investment. If I don't make that decision and that investment, I experience myself as going through the motions and wasting my precious time. We've all had that experience—for many of us, for far too much of the time.

We are on the threshold of really understanding a shining idea: that each individual life can have meaning, even if the universe has none. Each of us comes with appetites, genetic predispositions, and everything else that "human being" connotes, and still, we are free to choose what meaning we intend to make. This is what nature has granted us. I get to decide what will make me feel righteous and happy, and you get to decide what will make you feel righteous and happy. You can turn the meaning that was waiting to be made into the meaning of your life.

You and you alone are the sole arbiter of the meaning in your life. The second you turn to someone else and say, "What does life mean?" or "What should my life mean?", you have slipped into a way of thinking that courts inauthenticity and depression. The second you agree with someone simply because of his position or reputation, whether that someone is a guru, author, cleric, parent, politician, general, or elder, you fall from the path of personal meaning-maker. All of this an existential wellness coach could communicate.

You and you alone get to decide. That is the awesome proposition facing every modern person. The revolutionary idea that an existential wellness coach floats is that, as limited as we are in a biological, psychological, and practical sense, we are exactly that free in an existential sense. If we do not live that way, honoring that existential freedom, we get sad and depressed. If we do not live that way, we find ourselves wishing that we had opted for authenticity and had decided to matter.

An existential wellness coach understands completely the extent to which people are burdened by the feeling that they and their efforts do not matter. It isn't that people don't work hard or try hard. They do. But two thoughts, that they are disposable throwaways in a meaningless universe and that nothing they do can possibly alter that painful truth, play havoc beneath the surface, draining them of motivational energy and fitting them for a depression.

These doubts must be met in the following way. You announce that meaning does not exist until you make it, and then, you don the mantle of meaning-maker. The split second you do this, all previous belief systems, both those that told you what to believe and those that told you that there was nothing to believe, vanish.

You let go of wondering what the universe wants of you, you let go of the fear that nothing matters, and you announce that you will make life mean exactly what you intend it to mean. This is an amazing, glorious, and triumphant announcement.

The instant that you realize that meaning is not provided (as traditional belief systems teach) and that it is not absent (as nihilists feel), a new world of potential opens up for you. You suddenly have the opportunity to pursue personally resonant activities and the philosophical and psychological pillars to support those pursuits. You break free of tradition, with its restrictions, demands, and narcissistic bent, and set out to make your life a thing of value. You haven't made it that thing yet, simply by announcing your intention. But you have aimed yourself in a brilliant direction: in the direction of your own creation.

All of this an existential wellness coach could communicate.

How might you discuss the difference between seeking meaning and making meaning with a client? One useful way is to provide as a journal prompt the following: "What do you see as the difference between seeking meaning and making meaning?" Let clients ponder that rich, quality question. What other ways might you try?

7.1 How meaninglessness is customarily handled

People customarily address their "meaning issues" in one or another of several unfortunate ways.

One way is to shrug their shoulders and try to ignore the problem. This sounds like, "I don't know what 'meaning' means and I'm not interested."

A second way is to hunt for meaning as if it were a lost treasure. This sounds like "I will know what life means once I get to the top of that mountain."

A third way is to bow to the authority of others, abdicating personal responsibility. This sounds like "I do what God says."

A fourth way is to take a truth, that there is only subjective meaning, and run with it in the direction of unbridled self-interest. This sounds like "Everything is permitted and I can do whatever I damn well please."

A fifth way is to stare too long at the reality that we are merely excited matter, here for a little while and at the mercy of the fates, and collapse in existential pain. This sounds like, "Nothing I do really matters, given my puny status in an indifferent universe."

These are the usual ways that people deal with their "meaning issues." An existential wellness coach could identify these five ways—shrugging meaning away, hunting for meaning, taking meaning orders, using "the problem of meaning" as a cover for selfishness, and feeling defeated in the face of human reality—as poor choices and point to a better choice: passionate meaning-making.

7.2 On meaning investments

To help a client better conceptualize this option, an existential wellness coach might introduce the phrase "meaning investments." Clients tend to understand the idea of "making meaning investments" without needing the concept explained. They typically get it instantly.

I once asked subjects in a study group the following question: "Thinking back on it, where in life would you say that you made a significant meaning investment?" Here are two characteristic responses.

Max responded:

> About eight years ago, when I had been without work for a few years and was tired of looking for employment in the financial services industry, I started playing around with the idea of doing other things. I had always been curious about acting. Breathing deeply, and telling myself that I could do this, that I could honor a promise to myself to participate wholeheartedly in a personal experiment, I was able to open the front door of an acting studio and enter the first day of acting class.
>
> I went through all the exercises that day and on subsequent days. Many of them felt absolutely stupid. But eventually I began to have fun. For our final project, we each had to deliver a monologue in front of the class—horror of horrors. So, I memorized mine until I was mumbling it in my sleep. My presentation was terrible. I was completely defensive. My character was angry, so I strutted about and ranted and shouted my lines. The audience of my classmates was quiet. I think maybe they were just politely suppressing their laughter—or maybe they were horrified that they would appear equally foolish when their turn came.
>
> But the instructor calmed me down. I had seriously embarrassed myself but I promised myself that I would stay no matter what, so I complied with his instructions. I started again, began my monologue quietly, and allowed the emotion to build slowly and naturally. He continued directing me and I could feel the shift. Something strange started to happen. I noticed that the director was no longer speaking. I noticed that people in the audience were getting emotional in various ways and that these emotions were growing. I got this strange sense of strength that I had never known before. Somehow, I don't know how, I knew to say the last few words of the monologue in almost a whisper. As I finished, I looked squarely at the group, quietly got up out of my chair, and gave one of those "Ah, forget it!" gestures and walked off stage.
>
> The instructor congratulated me and told me that my performance was the best that he had ever heard with that monologue. To this day, that is one of my proudest achievements. And also to this day, if I get a bit nervous before I act, I just take a deep breath and remember that moment, start quietly, and allow the strength to build. I know that I had "invested meaning" in that class and refused to just walk away from it; and, although I was scared and embarrassed, I also made a meaning investment in that moment on stage, an investment that allowed me to take direction, feel and use my own power, and become something that I never dreamed I could become—a real actor.

Pamela responded:

> A few weeks ago, I visited some Chelsea art galleries in wonderful autumn weather. After a while, my good mood left me. The artwork that I saw that day was not at all inspiring to me. I thought to myself, this is my goal? To exhibit in these galleries suddenly seemed meaningless. Therefore, making art seemed meaningless also. I had made a big effort to arrange my life so that I had time to focus on art and now it didn't seem important at all.
>
> When I got back to my studio it was really hard to paint. Then I realized that I had a choice, to continue feeling bad or to think of a way for my art to have meaning to me so that I'd feel motivated to do it. I decided that my art would be a positive force and uplifting to people—I "invested meaning" in that idea—and just like that there seemed like plenty of reason to paint. I decided that making my art was meaningful in part because it had the potential to be meaningful to others.
>
> From that moment on, I've painted steadily. I've also been back to those Chelsea galleries—and I've enjoyed being there, not so much because of the art on the walls but because other people are there on any given sunny Saturday afternoon enjoying themselves and benefiting from the experience. Yes, many art pieces are not to my liking and, in my estimation, are revered for the wrong reasons. But that isn't to say that art doesn't serve. I am "invested" in the idea that art can serve and I again find it meaningful to paint. I appreciate that I might change my mind once again—that meaning is that kind of fickle thing—but at least for several weeks now, meaning has felt rock-steady.
>
> Can you imagine inviting clients to consider the phrase "meaning investments" and maybe have them reflect on where in their life they consciously made a meaning investment; and maybe also reflect on where in their life they know that they didn't?

Existential wellness coaches have a straightforward goal in mind: they hope that their clients will begin to passionately make meaning and, by doing so, feel better about life. If they have a teaching bent, they can proceed to teach "passionately making meaning" as a kind of skill to acquire.

This skill can be conceptualized as having five component parts. First, you have to make a decision about how your life will be led. The decision you need to make is the following one: you need to decide to matter. Few people will support you in this decision, so you will have to fly in the face of the opinions of others. The world requires more cogs-in-wheels than independent souls and supports more those who go along than those who speak out. You, however, will be loud and independent. This is a decision you get to make.

You decide to matter—that is, you decide that you will live a principled, creative, and active life in support of your cherished ideals, that you will manifest your potential, that you will do good work, and that, in short, you will make your life matter, on your own terms and at least to you. You decide that you will make your life count for something. You do not presume that your life matters on a cosmic scale or that your efforts will move mountains. Rather, you embrace the idea of authenticity and proclaim that you intend to live an authentic life.

Second, once you decide that you intend to matter, you announce the following: "Irrespective of whether the universe is meaningful or meaningless, irrespective of whether my odds of succeeding are long or short, irrespective of everything at the existential level and at the practical level, I am going to intentionally make meaning." You decide to matter, and then, you announce that you intend to make meaning. What you are saying is "there is no meaning until I make it." What you mean is the following:

> I am not going to sit around waiting for the universe, some guru, some book, some god, some workshop, or anything else to let me in on the secrets of the universe or the shape of my personal path. I am going to decide, based on my best understanding of reality and based on my life purpose choices, how I intend to make my meaning.

Third, you ask yourself the question,

> Well, but what exactly are my life purposes? If I'm going to actively make meaning in accordance with my life purposes, I had better know them, articulate them, memorize them, and make sure that I really believe in them. So, what are they?

That is, you need to identify what you deem important in life and decide on the role or roles you intend to play in life. Your life purposes might be to fight against injustice, to live a life better than your baser instincts, to make beautiful things, to do good deeds, to live a healthy life, and/or three or four others. These are the sorts of life purposes that are rich enough and big enough to count.

Fourth, you need to hold the intention to fulfill your life purposes. That is, you need to keep your meaning-making efforts firmly in mind. How will you "hold the intention" to live life exactly the way you intend to live it? When life resumes its habitual busyness, how will you remember your intentions? Well, you might dream up something ceremonial. Maybe you'll create a rich but simple-to-remember life purpose statement, for instance, "Do the next right thing," find a smooth pebble to hold in the palm of your hand, and, while clenching it, repeat your life purpose statement. Existential wellness coaches can help their clients create ceremonies and rituals of this sort, rituals in the service of meaning creation and meaning maintenance.

Fifth, you need to tackle all of this with passion and energy. It might seem to go without saying that a person would naturally be passionate about something as central and vital to her life as her own life purposes. However, we know this isn't true. Few people live their lives passionately. Most people go through the motions in life because they are burdened by tasks, everyday work, responsibilities, and their own personality. They live closer to depression than ecstasy, often in a perpetual meaning crisis. Indeed, most people need convincing that it makes sense to be passionate about anything.

Why take the risks that opting for passion requires? People are trained to avoid displays of passion and even the feeling of passion. They settle for a life that fails to nourish them, one that feels safe rather than wild and outsized. Although they've probably never thought it through, they suspect that passion demands heroism—and they don't feel heroic. They fear that passion and madness are close friends. Yes, Beethoven was passionate—and look at him. Yes, Van Gogh was passionate—and look at him. The average person looks at the headstrong, egocentric, and heroic passion of a Beethoven or a Van Gogh and thinks, "Yikes! That's not for me!"

Existential wellness coaches can help their clients understand why passion is vital and can help them rekindle their passion. Passion is the driving force that motivates us and fuels our meaning-making journey. Without it, we are exactly like a car without gas or a love affair without love. The first step in becoming more passionate is announcing that you accept the basic idea that passion is a necessity.

To summarize the elements of the "skill" of passionately making meaning: (1) you decide to matter; (2) you accept that you must make meaning; (3) you identify your life purposes and, if it strikes you as valuable to do so, articulate a life purpose statement; (4) you hold the intention to fulfill your life purposes; and (5) you passionately act to fulfill your life purposes and, as a lucky consequence, maybe garner the experience of meaning.

7.2.1 *Can you imagine teaching your clients these five steps? Does this way of thinking about meaning-making resonate for you?*

If we were to ask what essential message existential wellness coaches are trying to communicate to their clients, the answer would be, "You matter." Why is this message necessary, given that it might be presumed that people already feel that way about themselves? Because, unfortunately, they don't. A client's upbringing might be one impediment. She might have grown up being lectured about the extent to which she didn't matter and punished for attempting to matter. Her culture, too, might have drilled into her the idea that she was merely one of many and that group norms always come first: that religion comes first, that fitting in comes first, and that not making waves comes first. Many life lessons might have taught her that it was wrong or pointless to opt to matter.

Still, the magnitude of her difficulty in opting to matter is not really explained even by a great many negative life lessons. It turns out that the main obstacle she faces is her belief, shared by every modern person, that human life is "ultimately" meaningless. Any reasons that she tries to adduce for mattering are overwhelmed by the possibility, bordering on a certainty, that she and her fellow human beings are only excited matter put on earth for no reason except that the universe could do it. All life, hers included, is mere pointless happenstance, not worth crying about or taking seriously.

This bitter pill is a new view, barely 200 years old. Before that, life seemed special. For thousands of years, the idea of life as categorically different from nonlife, unique, and important in the cosmos was a core tenet of natural philosophy. That point of view, a hallmark of the philosophy known as vitalism, seemed compelling until biologists found, beginning with Wohler and the synthesis of urea in 1828, that organic compounds could be created from inorganic materials. We can date our present difficulties in making and maintaining meaning from that single event, the synthesis of urea. From that day forward, a new philosophy was needed, since life lost much of its mystery, sanctity, importance, and glamour.

Once you join the scientific materialists, as all of us have done to a lesser or greater degree, and believe that you can make human beings simply by striking dead atoms with powerful but meaningless forces, life turns meaningless. That is the basic problem with which we've been wrestling for 200 years. We manage to bear up despite the suspicion that we are merely excited matter. We find ways to bear up every day. But, on many days, we discover that we can't bear up; on those days, we despair about our cosmic unimportance and grow furious with the facts of existence. The very word "meaning" strikes our ears as a cosmic joke. Because of our fear that we are merely excited matter and the consequent grudge that we hold against the universe, we feel lost and alienated.

Battered by such thoughts, a modern person is driven to throw up her hands and cry, "Why bother! Why wrestle this stupid novel into existence? I might as well find some simple pleasures, eat chocolate, take a bubble bath, and to hell with the idea of making meaning!" So she eats chocolate and takes a bubble bath. But, within minutes, she is forcibly struck by the counter-thought that meaning must have meaning, so devoid of meaning does it feel to have thrown up her hands. A countervailing energy arises in her, something like hope and something like pride, an energy that readies her to do combat with her sincere belief that she is utterly unimportant.

When people try to throw up their hands and resign themselves to accepting postmodern meaninglessness and the illusory nature of meaning, they find that they can't. "Meaning" continues to vibrate in a way that convinces them that, while it may be a difficult and even a suspect word, it is not an empty word. Meaning means something, and, as a consequence, an authentic life is possible. At the last instant, they return with a vengeance to the belief that a meaningful life can be led and that they are obliged to choose that way.

In our hearts, we opt for life. We opt to live the 20 years or the 60 years ahead of us. This may be all that we have, but it is exactly what we have. As the vitalist Schubert-Soldern aphoristically put it, "To understand life, we must contrast it with death." We force life to matter because we are alive and not dead. We say, "While I am alive, I can love." We say, "While I am alive, I can learn a few things." We say, "While I am alive, I can help in some ways." We say, "While I am alive, I can create." We live because we can and because, unromantically but utterly sincerely, we must.

The most important shift for the contemporary person to make is the one demanded by the existentialists, the shift from the despairing "Why do I exist?" to the steely "I exist." People must stop pestering themselves with the unanswerable questions that plague them—the need to know why they are alive, what made the universe, who can teach them about the meaning of life, and what are the first or final causes—and accept as their mantra, "I am alive."

In their aliveness, they find everything they need to know about how to live. All they need to do is accept their purest understanding of their own meaning-making responsibilities. They don't have to adapt to existence any more than a bird has to adapt to the sky. They and existence are already adapted together. They simply have to accept that they are the only possible maker of personal meaning. Part of them wants to cry out, "I don't belong here, there's no place for me here, the hell with it!" But they do belong here, and they must pull their chair up to the table.

We opt to matter irrespective of the fact that life stands squarely in the way of our ability to matter. If we refuse to opt to matter, our meaning-making efforts peter out, and we end up settling for second-rate meaning substitutes or meaninglessness, each with its attendant depression. But, if we hold ourselves up to a lofty, entirely self-imposed standard—that we are determined to matter, in accordance with our highest principles—then we imbue our meaning-making efforts with the seriousness that we know they require.

Opting to matter does not answer every meaning question, nor is it a complete program in and of itself. It alone will not make a boring meeting meaningful or a mistake that ruins a novel a pleasant experience. It alone will not keep meaning afloat on gloomy days when nothing feels worth attempting. Still, it is a vital step on the path to meaningful and purposeful living. Once meaning becomes an issue, as it does for millions, then a state of crisis exists. Crisis management begins with the decision to matter. Then, on the tactical level, you engage in passionate meaning-making, which I've described above as a certain five-step process.

This is one way to think about meaning and one way to think about how a person, an existential wellness coach, can help another person with their meaning and life purpose issues. This is not the only approach, of course. But I hope that it makes a good case for the possibility that help could be available if helpers were trained in these ideas. We currently do not have many helpers who are trained in this or good at this. That is a shame, as so many human problems with names like anxiety, depression, and addiction might be resolved if more help were available in the realm of meaning.

FOOD FOR THOUGHT

1. What are your thoughts about existential wellness coaches focusing on "meaning issues" with their clients?
2. Do you have a personal, clearly articulated view as to "what meaning is?" If you don't, might it pay dividends to try to arrive at your own understanding?
3. What are your thoughts about inviting clients to begin to use phrases like "meaning investments," "meaning opportunities," and "making meaning"?
4. What have you experienced as meaningful in life? Why do you think those experiences felt that way?
5. What do you know to do when "meaning leaves the building"? How might you help clients when they experience meaning as lost or vanished?

Chapter 8

The pain of meaning crises

Meaninglessness may be—is—only a feeling. But, when we feel that way, we can feel that we are wasting our lives, and that is a true crisis.

If our job doesn't feel meaningful, if our spiritual path doesn't feel meaningful, and if our marriage doesn't feel meaningful, yes, those are just feelings. But they are feelings that can break a person.

So, existential wellness coaches, even as they understand the subjective psychological nature of meaning, also understand that if and when a person experiences a pursuit or a situation as meaningless, a genuine crisis has struck.

Meaning crises cause profound unhappiness. When your subjective sense of the meaningfulness of a situation, activity, or experience moves from positive to negative, you've hit a meaning crisis. Even if you just move from positive to neutral, from a feeling of "wow!" to "who cares?", a crisis has struck. Any time meaning leaks out of life and your subjective psychological experience no longer has a positive valence, you are obliged to deal with that crisis or else find yourself bored, unhappy, or worse.

Maybe you loved reading mysteries, and suddenly one day, for no reason that you can name, mysteries just don't seem meaningful to you any longer. Maybe environmental issues always held meaning for you, but one day you notice that another species is about to go extinct—and you find that you don't care. Somehow, the meaning has drained out of saving species. These shifts and changes, some of them on the small side and some of them enormous, bring existential pain and confusion in their wake.

Consider the following three scenarios. In each scenario, someone has been doing something for a long time, something that once felt meaningful but that no longer holds enough meaning. A meaning crisis has occurred: meaning has leaked out, and unhappiness has leaked in.

1. You've been teaching the same subjects for the past 20 years. You like teaching, you like your students, and you like the subjects you teach, but mostly,

DOI: 10.4324/9781003724971-8

you have to teach to the tests, and every year, you are given more duties that have nothing to do with teaching. You are now about to start your 21st year of teaching, and you are not really looking forward to the coming year. Your predominant feeling is sadness mixed with fatigue.

2. You have a strong interest in bees and have been an avid beekeeper for the past 15 years. Lately, your hives have been hit hard by an inexplicable epidemic, and most of your bees have died. Now, as you are about to start your 16th year of beekeeping, you could start fresh with new bees—but you would do so without any guarantee that your hives won't be hit again. Your predominant feeling is sadness mixed with anxiety.
3. You are a lawyer specializing in death row appeals. It is a branch of the law that pays very little money and that you choose on principle. However, during your decade of doing this work, virtually none of your appeals have ever saved an inmate from execution. You are about to start your 11th year of this work. Your predominant feeling is sadness mixed with anger.

What do human beings do in these situations? They tend to try one or another of the following seven options.

1. *They deny what is going on*

   The teacher goes on antidepressants for her "depression," focuses her attention on hating her principal, gives her students lower grades than she has in the past, and finds herself uncontrollably sobbing at unexpected moments.

   The beekeeper goes on antianxiety medication and further tries to quell his anxious feelings by going on a hunt for bees "guaranteed to survive," even though the bees he locates cost more than he can afford and even though he has the suspicion that he is being duped about their hardiness.

   The lawyer goes on angry tirades with clerks and waiters, seeks out therapy to help with her "anger management issues," gets sicker than she has in many years, and finds herself verbally attacking her clients, which she attributes to "dealing with a crop of losers."
2. *They consciously try to make the best of it*

   The teacher reminds herself that she is helping her students, even if not as much as she would like because of the narrowness of the curriculum; she gets out of bed, puts one foot in front of the other, and gets through the new school year by trying to "turn her frown upside-down."

   The beekeeper acknowledges his anxiety, crosses his fingers, begins with new bees, does what he has always done (because he doesn't know what to change or where the problem is), and wakes up each morning wondering how many bees he will find still alive.

   The lawyer immerses herself in her next appeal, taking some comfort in the fact that her presence and her efforts reduce the pain and anxiety of her client, who is awaiting death. She works hard to produce a brief that may do the trick, although she knows that it almost certainly won't—that "almost" being just about everything that she hangs her hat on.

3. *They try to reframe the situation*
The teacher reminds herself that she has her vacations and summers free, congratulates herself for choosing a profession that allows her that much free time, and pledges to enjoy herself more, both at school and away from school.
The beekeeper reminds himself that the natural world is exactly what it is, so little in his control that he might as well smile at the idea of controlling it, and pledges to enjoy each bee while it lasts and experience pleasure at every drop of honey he gathers.
The lawyer reminds herself that she can live, albeit modestly, on only four or five death penalty cases a year, providing her with four or five righteous challenges annually, coupled with more free time than a corporate lawyer could ever dream of having.
4. *They make changes that they hope will improve the situation*
The teacher creates new lesson assignments that she hopes will spark some interesting class discussions and that will make the material feel fresh and new to her.
The beekeeper purchases, at a modest cost and from a reputable source, a strain of bees with a track record of being less susceptible to the recent epidemic.
The lawyer decides to reduce her client load from five annual cases to three annual cases so as to reduce the time she spends worried and frustrated.
5. *They try something new "over there" while "making do" over here*
The teacher takes some online classes in knitting so as to pursue an old love and cheer herself up when she is not in the classroom.
The beekeeper decides to raise alpacas so as to gather fleece as well as honey.
The lawyer takes on a couple of clients whose issues do not bring her into contact with the criminal justice system.
6. *They get out of the current situation without a plan in place*
The teacher walks into the principal's office one cloudy morning and tells him that she is quitting.
The beekeeper suddenly takes his entire beekeeping operation to the equivalent of the dump.
The lawyer wakes up one morning and begins calling all the death row appeals lawyers she can locate to see if any of them are willing to take over her current cases.
7. *They get out of the current situation with a plan in place*
The teacher investigates the profession of coaching, calculates that it might take her about five years to build a practice large enough to allow her to quit teaching, and signs up for her first coaching class.

The beekeeper makes the decision to become a lay expert on the stressors facing bees with an eye to moving from keeping bees to writing popular articles about the dangers that bees face.

The lawyer decides that she will pursue the only other area of the law that interests her, intellectual property law, and creates a plan that will allow her to make the transition over the course of a few years from death row appeals law to intellectual property law.

This, then, is our beginning picture of what meaning crises look like—and how people react to them.

8.1 What actual people try

When a meaning crisis hits, people try all sorts of things to deal with that crisis. What follows are some real-life examples of those efforts. Here's how one teacher, Samantha, tried to make teaching feel meaningful to her again. Samantha explained:

> For the past six years, I've tried to reinvest meaning in my teaching. I've taken on new challenges and roles. I've worked harder—and I've also tried not to work as hard. I've tried to change my attitude and my expectations—this has proven the least successful. I haven't managed to change my attitude or expectations at all, no matter how many times I try! I've sought support by talking to my boss, trying to use my regular appraisal more productively, and problem-solving with peers. I've reduced my teaching load from five days to four days to two days.
>
> I've tried to balance my two teaching days with meaningful activities on the other days. This worked for a while, but then I realized that on the two days I did teach I still felt no better and that those two days every week amounted to days of frustration and meaninglessness. I tried to find enough meaning in my teaching job by talking to myself about job security and guaranteed income. I tried changing my mind, altering the situation, making meaning elsewhere: I've tried everything. But there's no question about it: the meaning is gone.

Mirella, also a teacher, tried a combination of "reframing" and "innovation":

> For me, being innovative means taking a step back from the expectations and associated guilt that comes with being seen as "not a good teacher." Since schools are often such closed communities and run on a system of "good will," teachers are often made to feel guilty if they are not extending enough good will to their school and students (i.e. not doing enough work for free). Creating my own meaning at my school meant stepping away from that mindset and focusing just on the classroom and my own smaller microcosm.

> I also tried finding and defining a new role for myself within the school by offering to teach a "making meaning class" before or after school. That went nowhere. When I realized that there wasn't really any way to innovate, I went into a tailspin, but focusing on the classroom is working decently enough these days. As long as I enjoy classroom teaching and as long as I don't fret about whether I am "doing enough" for the school, I may be able to keep meaning afloat here.

Leslie, a college professor, tried a variation of the seventh option by planning for new meaning as she withdrew meaning from her current teaching. She explained:

> As I struggled with whether or not to leave my tenured academic job, one of my issues was that though I was working in the field of my choice, which was music, I wasn't doing enough of precisely what I wanted to be doing in that field, which was performing chamber music.
>
> After a day of teaching, furthering other peoples' causes, and dodging political bullets, I didn't feel I had the energy to do anything personally meaningful. I was beginning to lose my love for music and that wasn't okay with me.
>
> I chose to give up one meaning container, academia, in order to recommit to an older but much more personally compelling meaning container, music. I created a plan and set it in motion. I quit my day job, moved to a town where I had performing connections and a better support system, started my own chamber ensemble. And I started to think bigger thoughts about who I was. I started consciously thinking, "I am a pianist, I am a musician, I am an artist, I am an entrepreneur, I am a creative force, I am a work in progress, my life is just beginning" instead of thinking, "I am an Associate Professor, I am tenured, I am a teacher, I have financial stability and security, I have a retirement account, I have a finished life—game over."

Consider a teacher we'll call Brad. Say that Brad no longer finds his 15-year teaching job of high school chemistry meaningful, but he is still passionate about his first love, musical theater. He might try some combination of options four and five by helping students write and produce a musical—say, about two characters, hydrogen and oxygen, and how they get together to create water. This is a project that might bring something that he loves into the mix, changing the focus of his day and his job. If he could pull this project off, it might constitute a sufficient answer to his meaning crisis.

But, for this solution to work, all of the following must fall into place.

- Brad's school must be the kind of school where the chemistry teacher can double as the drama teacher (and how many schools are like that?).

- Brad must convince his principal that his students will not do poorly on their chemistry APs despite the fact that he is now putting on a play (and if their scores drop for any reason, that is probably the end of Brad's theater career at that school).
- Brad must fundraise for props and scenery, which is a separate job from running rehearsals and putting on the play.
- Brad must not hate his chemistry classes even more than before, now that he has this exciting other thing to turn to; that is, he must still find a way to tolerate teaching chemistry.

Even if all this falls into place, will this picture work for Brad? Will a regimen of boring chemistry classes punctuated by three nights of performance a year work to solve his meaning problems? Who can say? When what we are doing doesn't feel meaningful—when the life we are living doesn't provide us with sufficient experiences of meaning or the sense that "this life is worth living"—a crisis has occurred. Then, we must make some valiant effort of the sort we've been discussing. We can't know if our effort will prove sufficient—but we are obliged to try.

8.2 When meaning vanishes in an instant

Think of a feeling like happiness. Can't happiness be wiped out in a moment? Of course, it can. Something bad happens—a medical diagnosis and an accident befalling your child—and your happiness vanishes.

The same is true for meaning. If you aren't alert to this reality, you may feel supremely disconcerted that "the meaning of life" disappeared just like that. Where did meaning go? Well, it went away, just as happiness can and does go away.

Consider the following. You listen to a talk given by a well-known rabbi, Indian mystic, or New Age spiritual leader. His voice is comforting, his delivery is seamless, his demeanor seems grounded and centered, and you experience your time there as meaningful. The event provokes a certain feeling.

Then, as you are leaving, you overhear two women talking about the speaker's predatory nature: that he is a well-known pedophile and rapist. There goes your feeling of meaning, just like that, in an instant.

How will you interpret this loss of meaning, and how will this unfortunate event make you feel? You're likely to feel duped, conned, and seduced by a practiced conman who has honed his persona. You will blame him—but you're likely to blame yourself, too, for falling for it.

Certain other unfortunate thoughts and feelings are likely to pounce on you in the aftermath of that betrayal as well. You're likely to feel *once again* that life really has no meaning and that life is just fluff, nonsense, lies, and death. And you're likely to feel *once again* that if "life does have meaning," you have *once again* looked in the wrong place for it.

If, by contrast, you are living your life purposes, then if by chance listening to that celebrity huckster did provoke a certain feeling in you, that feeling of meaning, which then vanished when you learned the truth about him, you would know that all that had happened was that you had felt something, that certain feeling of meaning, which you would have by now come to understand is no big deal.

Hearing about his depravity would produce no pain and no sense of betrayal. You would nod, maybe even smile, and say to yourself,

> Yup, we are built to feel meaning at the hands of folks like that—glad I know better! Glad I know that nature has provided us with lots of seductive feelings that I'm now able to hold as lightly as soap bubbles!

If you hold meaning to be something out there, something that other people know about, something that resides outside of yourself, and something that must be searched for and, if you are lucky, maybe found, then every event of this sort will disturb you, demoralize you, and maybe even seriously harm you. *This person had the answer*—oh, foolish you, no, he didn't. Betrayed again! And lost again, back in the tangled wilderness of pining for meaning.

Understanding this truth about meaning that meaning is merely a feeling that comes and goes, one that nature often provides us with for less than stellar reasons, inoculates you against blows of this sort. Betrayals may still hurt—but they won't rock you to the core. One answer to a meaning crisis of this sort is to be smart enough about meaning to know not to consider it a crisis!

Consider a second scenario. Maybe you picture the universe as having purpose—for you, for the species, and for everything. Maybe you believe that these purposes have a positive valence—that the universe is for love and not hate, for justice and not injustice, and so on—and that this worldview helps keep you essentially optimistic.

At the same time, you know that "life is not fair." You have a way "beyond words" of melding these two contradictory views, such that the bad things that happen—the earthquakes that kill 20,000 people and the way that your promotion was given to your boss's nephew—do not invalidate, destroy, or even wobble your view of a "good universe." You "possess meaning" that works for you, and you would likely score well on any "meaning in life" questionnaire.

This sounds like a success story. But what regularly happens, if you are holding views like these, is that your system can't withstand significant personal loss. As functional and resilient as your worldview scheme appears, it can suddenly break down almost completely into the deepest sort of despair. You fall in love, the love of your life walks out on you, and something essential crumbles.

Your way of avoiding admitting that life has no meaning or purpose of the sort you ascribed to it worked well in an everyday way, but it made you susceptible to the whole edifice collapsing. Serious collapses and crashes can occur if you don't understand and admit that this thing you are pinning your hopes on—a loving universe run with a beneficent purpose—is a shaky bit of wishful thinking.

When a person understands that the feeling of meaning comes and goes, that its presence does not, by its mere presence, signify anything spectacular, and that its absence is nothing tragic, then they have put life on a solid footing. They will not stand mortified when a hero turns out to have feet of clay, they will not feel their world crumble when a lover leaves town, and they can say in those and all similar instances, "Back to the project of my life, back to doing the next right thing, back to deciding what's important and plucking motivation from that well of motivations that nature has provided for me."

Painful events will still prove painful. This updated and upgraded understanding of life, with its focus away from meaning and toward instrumentality, will not provide a complete cure or full immunity. But it is bound to make a real difference. Imagine investing in that guru to the extent of following him to Nepal and joining his dogmatic community versus smiling to yourself as you listen to him and whispering to yourself, "He sounds good, he's even given me a tingling feeling, but as soon as this lecture is over, back to my life purposes!"

That first way might cost you a decade or a lifetime. That second way costs you nothing more than an hour or two of your time, or at most an evening.

8.3 The double whammy

It is one thing if meaning vanishes. That is just a feeling disappearing. It is another thing if what vanishes with it is our sense of purpose. That's a powerful double whammy that produces the deepest crises.

Consider the following. You enter a graduate program with high hopes, excitement, and enthusiasm. You feel on what you are internally calling a meaningful path. Looking at the description of the classes feels exciting—those descriptions generate the feeling of meaning. The program "feels meaningful." You can't wait to get started, you find yourself in a good mood (because experiences of meaning elevate mood), you splurge on a new computer, you sharpen your pencils, and you practically sing your way to your first classes.

You begin your program—and none of the classes meet your expectations. One is taught by a bully; one is dull and detail-oriented; one makes no sense to you; one is flat-out boring. In none of those classes do you experience the feeling of meaning. Not used to using the language I'm proposing, you may not say to yourself,

> It looks like these classes aren't going to provide me with the experience of meaning. Maybe getting my degree is still a valuable idea, for certain reasons, but I see that the program is not going to meet my meaning needs or feel very meaningful.

Instead, rather than speaking to yourself that way, you're likely to say, "This is so depressing," and "I think I ought to quit."

The worst part is that suddenly you no longer believe in either the subject or the profession. You thought that the subject would feel more special—that cognitive science would have more interesting things to say about consciousness than it appears to have, that art history would feel like an adventure, more like going to Florence than learning names and dates, and that clinical psychology would be more about human nature than it appears to be. You suddenly "see through" your chosen profession and have no idea what to do next. You've taken out loans; you have no alternative plan; you're apparently committed to this path; and yet you hate where you are.

What naturally follows? You begin to skip classes and procrastinate on assignments. You find yourself unable to sleep as your mind pesters you with thoughts like "How can I make this better?", "These classes are so awful!", "Should I drop out?", and "If I drop out, what would I do with my life?" For the first time in your life, you experience serious insomnia. You also find that you have no appetite, which mirrors your loss of appetite for life, and you find yourself losing significant weight. On many days, you find it hard to get out of bed.

This is one typical meaning crisis and its predictable rhythms. Nothing "clinical" happened: your brain did not suddenly become disordered. Exactly the following thing happened: a person invested meaning in the idea of something, and its reality badly disappointed her, thus failing to provide her with the experiences of meaning that she had hoped to receive and precipitating a crisis.

What our graduate student needs to do is one of the following two things. She might try to reinvest in her life purpose of becoming a professional of a certain sort (a cognitive scientist, an art historian, or a psychologist), to hold her nose, to make it through her classes, and to find other ways to coax some meaning into existence even while her program is devoid of meaning. That is, she might still be able to keep her profession as a life purpose, even if her graduate studies feel meaningless.

Or she might catch her breath, announce that her professional choice no longer makes sense to her, not bad-mouth herself about "abandoning her program" or "quitting" or "making a tragic mistake," and either plot a new course or, if it is too soon for that, take a break, consciously announce that for a period of time she will not be hunting for meaning or even needing meaning, and deeply relax. And she will also need to do some forgiving—herself, for having been seduced by this shiny path, and the universe, for cheating her out of that path.

If she drops both her graduate studies and her chosen profession, two crises will have occurred, a crisis of meaning and a crisis of purpose. Consider a second example. Say that you are teaching at a certain school and things change—the curriculum changes, a new principal arrives, your workload increases, or maybe many negative things descend all at once—and teaching *at that school* no longer feels meaningful.

That will likely be experienced as a meaning crisis. But your purpose hasn't crashed. In this scenario, you still love teaching children—you just don't want to be at this school. So you look for a new job at another school, and, with luck, you find one. Because the challenges at your last school soured you on *that school but not on teaching*, you didn't find yourself falling off the precipice into that deeper double crisis of both a meaning collapse and a purpose collapse.

This calamity happens much more often than we realize. Even a small event can precipitate it. You've organized your life and identity around acting. You have a terrible audition; meaning and purpose both crash, precipitating a dramatic reaction: you pack up your car, leave L.A., and never act again. Or it might be a medium-sized event: you've organized your life and identity around being a well-known physicist, a rival wins an award you coveted, and you plummet into a very dark place. Or it might be a large event: you've organized your life and identity around being in a relationship, your lover of many years has an affair, and both meaning and purpose leave the building.

Whether the precipitating event is small, medium, or large—or even just a passing thought, the idle thought that everything that a moment ago felt important to you no longer does—if this crisis happens, it is about as severe a crisis as a human being can experience. Some absence of meaning can be dealt with—but an absence of both meaning and purpose? That produces despair.

How can you reinvest life with the feeling of purpose when that feeling has evaporated? Is the answer the same as it is with meaning? With meaning, we can do several things: we can remind ourselves that meaning comes and goes and that its absence is no tragedy; we can repeat things that we've experienced as meaningful in the past, with the hope that they will feel meaningful still; we can try new things that we think might coax the feeling of meaning out of hiding; and so on. But will those same tactics work with purpose?

Can we operate "without purpose," telling ourselves that "purpose is bound to return"? You can see the dilemma here. Losing purpose is a bigger deal than losing meaning. Meaning is merely a feeling, but purpose amounts to our operating instructions. If we "lose the plot," how can we live? Why brush our teeth? Why not have another candy bar? Why not be irritable, lethargic, indifferent, or cruel? Won't anything we choose to do feel completely arbitrary, and won't doing nothing make the most sense?

At such an extremity, we must return to our most basic understanding of the human situation: that unless we announce our life purposes, we will be bereft of them. We return to where we started, making a new list of life purposes, which may no longer include those purposes from before, like that particular graduate program and that particular profession, but which represents our best understanding of what is newly and currently important to us. We go there—if we don't, isn't despair a certainty?

These are the issues that occupy existential wellness coaches. Our clients are bound to experience the pain of meaning crises—those crises will hit every smart, sensitive, and creative person at some point in their life. We understand that, and we stand ready to help.

FOOD FOR THOUGHT

1. Describe "meaning crisis" in your own words.
2. How might you help a client suffering from a meaning crisis? What might your top two or three tactics be?
3. Is the difference between a crisis of meaning and a crisis of purpose clear to you?
4. How might you help a client distinguish between a crisis of meaning and a crisis of purpose?
5. Have you personally experienced meaning crises? What did they teach you?

Chapter 9

On existential sadness

The thing called "depression" is epidemic, for many obvious reasons having to do in part with the challenges associated with living in this contemporary world. Every existential wellness coach will encounter clients challenged by "depression." And so, how can existential wellness coaches be of some real help?

There are many ways to conceptualize "depression" and other "disorders of mood." For many people, and for smart, sensitive, and creative folks especially, much of their sadness, despair, and "depression" arises because keeping meaning and purpose afloat is a real, even a relentless, problem. That is, much of their sadness is existential in nature.

We get sad because we have consciousness of many things, including our own sadness. We have consciousness of pain, consciousness of the fragility of life, consciousness of evil, consciousness of the unfair distribution of wealth, and consciousness of the misery that people make for each other. The amount of consciousness we possess is a defining feature of our species.

Other species are no doubt aware of many things, including the loss of loved ones and imminent death. But we are aware of a million things, from the extra weight we're carrying to the piles of unsold paintings in the studio to the inexorable crawl of time.

These are existential matters, about who we are as a species, about what we want, about how we operate, and about how we live and die.

In this sense, all of our sadness is existential in nature, having to do with our built-in awareness, our attempts to be less aware, and the complicated nature of our wants. Every day, we are making subtle existential calculations regarding how our life is going—and, very often, about how our life is falling short.

We start with an original personality—we are already very much ourselves at birth, already a unique exemplar of the species—and then, we accrete a lifetime of calculations about how we are faring and how life is treating us. Very often, the results of those calculations are a negative number, a number that brings with it despair.

Therefore, the first step in reducing your experience of sadness is making explicit the relationship you intend to have with life. This is true for you, and

DOI: 10.4324/9781003724971-9

this is true for your clients. Do you want to think thoughts that don't serve you in order to preserve your illusions, or do you want to think thoughts that support your intentions? Do you want to experience life as if you were a puppet on a cosmic string, being driven by unseen forces that demand that you hold meaningless jobs and renounce what you love in favor of rat race dynamics, or do you want to manifest your values and principles in the service of the most self-directing, instrumental life you can construct? How do you want to deal with life?

The instant you decide to deal with life a certain way, as the hero of your own story, and reframe the facts of existence as a supreme challenge but not as a life sentence, you release a significant portion of your sadness and "depression."

How you face life determines how sad you will feel, which makes existential self-help a top priority. Here are three tips for exercising existential self-help, tips that you can share with your existential wellness clients directly or subtly "between the lines" and/or use yourself.

9.1 There is no choice but to live with complexity—simplicity is a denial of reality

We would love life to come with slogan-sized affirmations and admonitions. It can't—not if we are real. Is it really so easy to know how to create images that move people? Is it really so easy to know how to maneuver when a photographic technique that we know well is replaced with a new technique and requires our complete retraining? Is it really so easy to know what to do if our son is drinking alcoholically or if our parents are growing more confused daily? Do slogans like "Just do it!" or "Everything is for the best!" really meet such challenges? They don't. Life is exactly as complex and difficult as it is. To hunger for a simplicity that doesn't exist is a desire that *creates* sadness.

9.2 Life is a mistake-riddled and challenge-riddled process

We have a longing and a craving for life to "finally settle down" and "finally become comprehensible." Surely, we don't have to repeat our mistakes, make new whopping mistakes, stand before life not knowing what to do next, or experience serious doubts and anxieties, do we? Unfortunately, we do. Life can't settle down and become comprehensible in the ways that we crave.

Tomorrow I may lose a parent or a child—that may change everything. Tomorrow I may start on a series of paintings more ambitious than anything I've ever tackled before, something with a steep learning curve—of course, I may doubt, grow anxious, and make mistakes. We want something like a guarantee out of life: if I reach a certain age or take enough workshops, I can finally stand in a place of certitude. But life only allows for process, not certitude. When you accept that you still have more mistakes to make, your next mistake need not come accompanied by sadness.

9.3 You choose your life purposes and then live them

Existential self-help consists of grounding yourself in a pair of realities: that life is exactly as it is and that you are obliged to keep your head up and make yourself proud. Most people make the mistake of supposing that if they don't look life squarely in the eye, they can avoid noticing what's making them unhappy. Instead of their dodge proving successful, they simply increase their unhappiness. By accepting the realities of life, by announcing that you intend to direct life as best you can, and by asserting that what matters to you is what you decide matters to you, you stand up straighter—and that gesture of getting to your feet opens the door for some significant portion of your sadness to leave.

Many, if not most, of your clients will arrive announcing that they are depressed, and many of these clients will bear a "clinical depression" diagnosis or a "bipolar" diagnosis and will be on psychiatric medication. Your job as an existential wellness coach is not to try to determine whether their sadness is a biological matter, a social matter, a psychological matter, an existential matter, or something else. Your job does include, however, manifesting a deep appreciation for the prevalence, reality, and painfulness of existential sadness, sorrow, and despair—and, over time, acquiring your ways of helping to reduce that.

9.3.1 Sorrow versus depression

It would be a very long detour to try to make the full case as to what "depression" is or isn't, whether it should really be construed as a "mental disorder," or whether it is more a construct and a label, etc. For our purposes, what we want to get clear on is the truth that sorrow exists and that sorrow isn't "clinical depression." As an existential wellness coach, you want to get very clear on this distinction.

We know that the world is the world. We try to prepare ourselves for the perplexing, disturbing reality of now—we ready ourselves, smiling a small smile and exclaiming, "Okay! Disturb me, world! Confound me, life! Confuse me, mind! I get you!" As a result of our clear thinking, we come to understand the nature of sorrow. We know that sorrow is not "depression." We know that sorrow is the song of a world in mourning, a world mourning its injustices, its tragedies, and its very nature.

There is also something about love wrapped up with sorrow and something about compassion. Sorrow is part sadness, but "sadness" does not capture the special quality of sorrow. Sorrow is something like the embrace of a long-lost comrade. We celebrate our comrade's return while mourning all those lost years. Love and sadness, and happiness and grief are all mixed together. Maybe sorrow is a teaching feeling. Why would nature do that? Maybe so that we are forced to live with our eyes wide open.

The pain of sorrow, which we do not crave and which we do not want, is maybe like the pain that tells us that our hand is too near the fire. Maybe it is crucial for our well-being. We do not love such reminders, but maybe we need that reminding. Holding our child's hand, feeling the pain of it as well as the joy of it, we are reminded of what we have and what we will lose. That experience of sorrow resets our compass, and, as a result, we decide to bake cookies with our child or go out for ice cream with him, rather than go back to our daily grind.

Had we not felt that sorrow, we might have been inclined to do the laundry or clean up the living room. But, because we got that whiff of mortality, we decided that baking cookies was our way to love and to live wisely. It was the next right thing to do. Sorrow invited in love, and we decided to love.

Sorrow is such a complicated feeling because a large part of what we're experiencing when we feel sorrow is our love of life. We feel sorrow because we can love, because we have loved, and because we still can love. Maybe sorrow only comes to someone who still loves life? Existential wellness coaches get to think about such matters.

But, of course, that doesn't mean that we invite it. Sorrow may be a great reminder that we love life, but it is also an anchor capable of dragging us into the depths of despair. It does not feel good, and we do not want it. To our not wanting it, nature says, "Ha!" and readies its piercing arrows anyway.

Maybe you are getting ready to travel. You read your guidebooks in anticipation of your six-month sojourn in Paris, where you'll be strolling the streets and writing in cafés. You grow giddy with anticipation. You arrive. You walk down some charming street. And suddenly you feel sorrowful. You couldn't be happier, and you also couldn't feel lonelier. Something is tugging at your heart and angling you toward despair. You anticipated a beautiful experience, and it is indeed a beautiful experience. But, inexplicably, it's also a mournful one.

What are you feeling as you walk down that Parisian street? Is it something about the nature of beauty, about how beauty can mesmerize us and seduce us? The street is everything that it ought to be, but are we somehow being fooled by its beauty?

Might it be something about the Jews rounded up from this very street and deported to their deaths? Is it something about humanity's horrors, about collaborators, about neighbors betraying neighbors, and about unbearable malice and enmity?

Is it something about the philosophers who lived hereabouts, who were sometimes such eloquent thinkers and often so weak as people? Is it something about the vast distance between people as they are and people as we wish they would be?

Is it that you've been reminded that you can't bottle this, that you can't keep this, that this is just a passing moment, that you must find a job when you return home, and that probably it will be an awful one? Has "now" already become "tomorrow"?

Or maybe it is partly regret. Nature provides regrets. We walk down that Parisian street, feeling the psychological experience of meaning, and at the same time, we hear ourselves say, "You idiot, you could have had this twenty years ago!"

"Now" is always ripe for regrets. We feel proud that we are loving our child so well. An instant later, we hear ourselves say, "Why didn't I stand up for my little sister against that bullying father of ours?" Regrets are right there, all around us, waiting.

The world creates sorrow. Circumstances create sorrow. The human experience creates sorrow. And human societies and cultures create sorrow. A real, true-to-life philosophy of life must concern itself with human society, since everyone lives in its confines.

There is the world of plagues, typhoons, and earthquakes: the natural world. Then, there are the man-made worlds of society and culture. Those man-made worlds can be as venomous as a snake, as restrictive as a prison cell, and as relentless as a tsunami.

Societies are authoritarian by nature and by habit. We and our clients are likely antiauthoritarian by nature and by habit. Even if they have made the decision to fit in and get along, they are likely to find themselves in a tense, adversarial relationship with their own society.

This produces all sorts of difficulties and its own full measure of sorrow. It makes us sad that society is what it is and not a more welcoming place. It aggrieves us that we can't just love it and embrace it and that it can't just love us and embrace us back.

Your client has three basic choices: to blend in, to remain aloof, or to stand up. If she decides to blend in, her acquiescence makes her sad. If she decides on aloofness, her alienation makes her sad. If she decides to stand up, society's retribution makes her sad. We understand the absurd irony of this.

She would love to stand up. But she knows that, if she does, she will likely be punished. She may be fired, sued, tormented, and hunted. The history of the species tells a single tale: dispute society and pay the consequences. We understand clearly why sorrow isn't a "mental disorder." It is exactly the pain you would expect, given life's realities.

9.3.2 *A guaranteed measure of sorrow*

We could draw a picture of a beautiful world, and certainly, we strive to make this recalcitrant world that beautiful one. We aim to increase its goodness, its fairness, and its wisdom. We march in that direction, maybe with some comrades. That's our agenda. We have intimations of paradise, glimpses of heaven on earth. Paradise is a healthy baby born into a happy family. Heaven on earth is freedom, friendship, a soft cheese, and a crusty roll. We could easily draw that picture if only the world would let us.

But, instead, the world gives us genetic abnormalities, angry parents, and political tyrannies. It gives us pandemics and mindless cruelties. It gives us this group pitted against that group. Sorrow comes, and we cry dry-eyed. The world gives us despondency. Yes, we can also have joys and pleasures. We can rise up, feel proud, and sing songs. We can pass some time in a trance, consuming culture's relaxations. But there the world is, again, deflating us, demeaning us, and constraining us.

Imagine a 15-year-old struggling with his world. His world is home, high school, the Internet, mass culture, text messages, constant news, plus all the cataclysmic events that affect him: a rash of suicides, a rash of school shootings, and a rash of expectations. He is sorrowful. Call it despondent. Call it melancholic. Call it down. What he is not is "depressed," if by that we mean that he is having a problem with his hormones, his genes, or his neurotransmitters. The world has made him despondent.

What should we invite him to do? How can we help him? We can take him fishing for the weekend or enlist him in a project to get his mind off the world. But, most crucially, we can invite him to become a philosopher. We can paint him a picture of how to live in this exact world, with its precise difficulties. We can help him understand why it is his obligation to stand up, to absurdly rebel against the facts of existence, to identify, and then to live his life purpose choices.

But he is just 15, after all. He will have a lot on his mind. Much of it will feel obsessive: pimples, video games, the girl who isn't giving him the time of day, the car he wants, the band he'd love to start, and the way his grades aren't what they should be. He keeps his headphones on to drown out his parents' fights. In his peripheral vision, he sees that the polar ice caps have melted some more. Then, there is the teacher who has it in for him. And the pimples! And so much Spanish vocabulary homework!

Into this obsessive, claustrophobic, melancholy world, we nevertheless try to drop hints about his obligations, his choices, and his possible path. We may pry him from his video games a little and invite him to think. We invite him to think about the world. It is not an invitation he is usually offered. What he is usually offered are trailers for the blockbuster films coming out at Christmas. We offer him something very different: a philosophy of life to chew on—one that includes the reality of sorrow.

We invite clients to think about life and, as they plot their course, to factor in the realities of the world. Those hard realities will leave them shaking their heads. What are they supposed to do about climate catastrophes, the reappearance of plagues, shameless greed, religious warfare, the return of fascism, and even small events like fender benders and pimples appearing? And what about the sorrow that comes with all that?

What is a human being supposed to do? Well, he returns to a rock-solid first principle: that we demand of ourselves that we make life purpose choices and that we strive to live our life purposes, even as we are forced to take the world and all of its arrows into account.

That is, we try. We make an effort. We understand that the world is hard. We understand that the world is not concerned about fairness. We understand that tornadoes don't target us and that tyrants may. For tornadoes, we build storm cellars. For tyrants, we resist. We make an effort.

We make decisions based on our understanding of the world, and, often enough, the world informs us that we've gotten the picture wrong. Maybe we thought that this or that plausible pursuit would prove a golden meaning opportunity. It didn't. Yes, that amounts to a crisis. But we stand ready to make the next effort. We do not say, "I am defeated."

You will experience sorrow. You are a human being, and all human beings experience sorrow. And, being human, you'll experience sorrow at the very oddest moments, even, say, when life is quite good or when something unusually excellent happens. Life can be good. Life can even exceed our expectations. But, even at such moments, and often especially at such moments, feelings of sorrow, melancholy, and regret invade us. We wish that the moment would never end, but we know that it will. More sorrow!

That a given moment can be at once wonderful and full of sorrow speaks to the layered nature of now. Now is no simple thing. We know this. Nature did not build us to just peel a potato. It built us to sometimes think about death even as we peel that potato. How hard!

You hold your child's hand and experience a truly wonderful moment. Suddenly, you grow sorrowful. You're confronted by the inevitable passage of time and by the knowledge of all that your child will be obliged to experience, the bad with the good.

You are invaded by the knowledge of the impermanence of life. That touch of flesh provokes that knowledge, and tears start flowing. Those aren't happy tears. They are the tears of sorrow that want to well up when we are reminded of what life brings. The world is, and we are in it. Those facts don't guarantee only sorrow, but they do guarantee a measure of it.

9.3.3 *Coaching a sad client: a vignette*

When Clara first walked into Emily's office, she carried herself with a kind of quiet heaviness, not the dramatic, visible grief of recent loss but the muted, pervasive sadness of someone who had grown accustomed to feeling life as dim and colorless.

At 48, Clara described her life as "fine on paper"—a steady job, two grown children doing well, and a supportive husband—but she confessed that none of it seemed to matter much to her anymore.

"It's like I'm living behind glass," she told Emily in their first session. "I can see the good things, but I can't feel them. Sometimes I wonder if I'm just waiting around to die."

Emily, an existential wellness coach, didn't rush to reassure her or reframe her sadness as a problem to be solved. Instead, she leaned forward slightly and said,

> What you're describing—this feeling of watching life rather than living it—many people experience it at some point. It can feel unbearable, but it's not a sign that something is broken in you. Often it's a sign that you've outgrown the meanings that used to work for you.

Clara frowned, considering. "So, you're saying my sadness isn't necessarily depression?"

Emily nodded. "What you're describing sounds like existential sadness—a loss of connection to meaning, to vitality, to a sense of mattering. It doesn't mean you're defective. It means you're human, facing the big questions that none of us can avoid."

For Clara, even just this reframing provided some relief. Instead of pathologizing her sadness, Emily had contextualized it as part of the human condition.

In their next session, Emily invited Clara to describe when she felt her sadness most sharply. Clara spoke of waking up in the mornings with a sense of futility, of scrolling through news feeds and feeling overwhelmed by suffering in the world, and of sitting at family dinners and feeling like she was going through the motions.

Emily asked, "When you're in those moments, what are the thoughts that accompany the sadness?"

Clara paused. "Mostly, I think: What's the point? Why bother with any of this if everything ends?"

Emily didn't flinch.

> That question, "What's the point?", is at the very center of existential sadness, isn't it? It touches on mortality, futility, the impermanence of things. These are painful truths. But they're also the same truths that have inspired people throughout history to create art, to love fiercely, to make meaning while they can.

Clara looked at her coach curiously. "So, how should I think about that sadness?"

"Maybe as a signal," Emily said gently. "It's telling you that something in your current way of living feels too small for the bigness of your questions."

In session three, Emily introduced Clara to the idea of "active meaning-making." She explained that many people wait for meaning to arrive passively, like a gift from outside, but meaning more often emerges from intentional engagement.

"Think of it as weaving a fabric," Emily said. "Every act of caring, creating, choosing—these are threads. They don't erase the sadness, but they give you something to wrap around yourself."

She asked Clara to list activities that once brought her even a flicker of aliveness. Clara hesitated but eventually mentioned painting, which she had abandoned years ago, and volunteering at an animal shelter, which she had loved in her twenties.

"Your sadness may be inviting you back to those places," Emily said. "Not because they'll solve the big questions, but because they'll give you a way to live alongside them."

Clara agreed, somewhat skeptically, to try setting aside one hour in the coming week to paint.

Clara arrived at her fourth session wearing a faint smile. "I painted," she reported. "It wasn't great, but for the first time in months I felt . . . engaged. The hour went by quickly. I was absorbed."

Emily highlighted this as evidence that even small acts could puncture the numbness. "Notice that the sadness didn't vanish," she said. "But you weren't only sad. You also experienced concentration, maybe even a little joy. That's what it means to live with existential sadness—not to eliminate it, but to create moments that coexist with it."

Clara nodded slowly. "It felt good to be reminded that I can still care about something."

By their sixth session, Clara had returned to painting weekly and had reached out to volunteer at the local animal shelter. She admitted that she still had mornings when she woke up with dread, but she noticed a subtle shift: "I don't feel as trapped. I have things to look forward to, even if the big questions remain unanswered."

Emily encouraged her to see this as progress rather than as a failure to "fix" herself. "Existential sadness doesn't necessarily disappear for good. But we can learn to metabolize it, to channel it into meaning-making, compassion, and creativity."

She then guided Clara through an exercise of articulating personal values—not abstract ones, but those that resonated in her bones. Clara identified care, creativity, and presence as her core values.

"Each time you live from these values," Emily explained, "you give yourself an antidote to that abiding sense of futility. You're choosing meaning, rather than waiting for it to appear."

Weeks later, Clara reflected on how her sadness had changed in quality. "It's still there," she admitted,

> but it's not crushing me. It feels more like background music than a constant weight. Sometimes it even feels like . . . fuel. When I volunteer, I think: the world is broken, yes, but here I am, helping this one scared dog feel safe. That feels like something.

After three months of coaching, Clara reported a noticeable reduction in her existential sadness. She still faced mornings of heaviness, but she no longer experienced life as flat or meaningless. She had reengaged with painting, felt revitalized by her volunteer work, and begun speaking more openly with her husband about her inner struggles. Most importantly, she had shifted from seeing sadness as a sign of something wrong with her to viewing it as a natural part of being human, one that could sit alongside creativity, love, and contribution.

9.3.4 Reducing the power of "mood"

An existential wellness coach is attempting four things with respect to his client's announced "depression": (1) she is helping her client think about his depression in new ways, especially in ways that include thinking about the possibility that the depression is not biological or psychological in nature, but existential; (2) she is providing her client with a picture of what "reducing existential despair" can look like; (3) she is helping him arrive at tactics and strategies that can actually reduce that despair; and (4) she is inviting him to come to the conclusion that "mood" is a less important thing than he currently thinks it is. Let's focus on that last.

Remember that "mood" is the thing we are talking about when we talk about "depression." "Mood" only means a state of mind or emotion. But, somehow, it has been twisted into a word that now stands for a state of mind or emotion existing along a happiness–unhappiness continuum. The word as commonly used today implies that we are always to some degree happy or unhappy and that we should be monitoring those degrees so that we know when our mood is "disturbed."

But are human beings really always happy or unhappy? Aren't we often "in no particular mood"—that is, in a kind of neutral mood? Not only do we take the temperature of our mood far too often nowadays—we have created a monster out of the word. Our current construction of the word "mood" gives unhappiness more of a central position in our lives than it ought to command. Unhappiness is a reality, but "mood" is a construct—and a tyrant.

Is there really some continuum on which we can always find ourselves, with euphoria on one end and grief on the other end? Isn't it more the case that for large portions of our day and for large portions of our life, we are "mood neutral" and feeling perfectly fine in that gear? Isn't it highly artificial and unhelpful to check in with ourselves to see how happy or unhappy we are when we may not be in any particular state of mind or experiencing any particular emotion?

This is no small point. If you think that you are supposed to be "in a good mood" and you check in with yourself and don't find yourself happy, you are likely to think that you're unhappy. But what if you were under no obligation to be "in some mood" all the time? What if it were perfectly acceptable to be "mood neutral"? When you recognize these two important truths—that you can pay less attention to your mood and more attention to your intentions, and that experiencing "no mood" or a "neutral mood" is perfectly acceptable—you rid yourself of a mindset that keeps you primed for unhappiness.

This is another area where a culture-wide shift in language would alter our experience of reality for the better. Instead of having to be in a "good mood" or a "bad mood," we could be in a "perfectly satisfactory neutral mood." We could watch a ball game, answer emails, stand in line at the supermarket, and not pester ourselves about our mood. We could "talk ourselves down" from opting for unhappiness when we find ourselves in snarled traffic by reminding ourselves that a neutral mood is probably our best bet. We could live in the now and be more present by focusing on our current meaning opportunities rather than our mood fluctuations.

If we take our pulse too often, what we come up against is our experience of the void. You can take better charge of your mind and your life by not continually checking in on your moods, by not taking thoughts like "Since I am not happy, I must be unhappy" at face value, by monitoring your self-conversations, and by keeping an eye peeled for the tricks you're inclined to play. If, during a bit of a dull time, you ask yourself, "How do I feel?", what do you think you are going to say? Get smart not only about what you ask yourself but also *when* you ask it. And when you shouldn't ask it!

Focus on your intentions, not on your mood. Do not zealously take the temperature of your mood as if it were a life requirement. Accept that a certain neutrality of mood is not negative but perfectly acceptable. Let go of the idea that "mood" is the measure of your well-being. It is far better to spend time in a neutral mood engaged in authentic work than to pester yourself about your happiness or unhappiness. Focus on purpose and not mood, and you will reduce your experience of unhappiness.

We are at least lucky that our language doesn't allow for an infinite number of compound words, as do German or Eskimo. Eskimos have so many words for snow because their language allows for compound words. The-snow-on-Bob's-roof becomes one word, and the-snow-I-hate-to-sweep-out-of-my-driveway becomes another word. If English worked like Eskimo, we would have millions upon millions of compound words for our sadness and our experience of emptiness. We would have compound words manufactured from feelings like the-sadness-I-feel-when-I-realize-it-is-Monday-again and the-emptiness-I-feel-when-I-remember-that-I-will-be-gone-in-another-decade-or-so. If we possessed a vocabulary like that, how nuanced and horrible we'd experience our "mood check-ins"!

In this extended age of reason of ours, we chat with ourselves endlessly and pay close attention to what we are saying. We are not only engaged in lifelong self-conversation, but we have also gotten into the bad habit of taking each of our thoughts as gospel. We think "Life stinks" and then believe that it does stink just because we had that thought. But could it be the thought that stinks? Could it be that such a thought only supports our alcoholism, our pessimism, our anorexia, our discontent, and our black moods and serves no good purpose? You may never directly say to a client, "Please stop thinking about your mood so much," but keeping an awareness of this idea in your back pocket will help you orient clients away from "too much mood thinking" and toward purposeful living.

This chapter amounts to only a brief introduction into how existential wellness coaches—or any helper—can begin to conceptualize their clients' depression, sadness, despair, sorrow, and mood in fresh, nonclinical ways, ways that are true to life and as rich as life itself. This is not the complete story. But maybe it has opened the door—and a few windows—to some useful, new thinking.

FOOD FOR THOUGHT

1. What are your thoughts about the differences between the word "depression" and words like "sadness," "melancholy," "sorrow," and "despair"?
2. If a client came in and said, "I'm always sad," what might you try or offer?
3. If a client came in and said, "I'm always depressed," would you offer something different from what you offered your sad client? If so, why?
4. How might you factor in "the reality of sorrow" into the work you do with clients?
5. Do you check in on your mood "too often," "not enough," or "just about the right amount"?

Chapter 10

On existential anxiety

Anxiety as a concept has always been a bit of an odd duck. On the one hand, we understand it to be a natural feature of our evolutionarily sensible warning system against danger. Venturing into the jungle at night should make us anxious, wouldn't you say? We wouldn't want fearless or anxiety-free four-year-olds wandering off and getting eaten by tigers—or us getting eaten, either.

At the same time, we see anxiety as the enemy, as something that prevents us from performing, from getting on a plane, from cohabiting a space with a harmless spider, from sleeping, from dating, and from every manner of thing we would like to get done and need to get done. Which is it, then, friend or enemy? Well, of course, the answer must be "both."

If we think about it, would we even trust someone who has never experienced anxiety? They might be a very evolved creature . . . or, maybe just as likely, a sociopath. Imagine a soldier who experiences no anxiety. Is he brave . . . or a killer? A complete absence of anxiety doesn't sound very human or even very moral. Don't we suspect that the meanest among us also experience the least anxiety?

So, anxiety has always been a difficult concept, despite the millions and billions of words written about it. The common-sense approach to it seems to be to see it as something that we shouldn't think of trying to eliminate but rather as something that we want to be able to "reduce" and "manage" when we're experiencing too much of it.

We don't want to feel severely anxious before each small event in life: before visiting our parents, before dropping in at a party, and before doing some necessary research on our dissertation. We don't want those small events to feel like lions and tigers approaching. That seems to be the right approach: to not see anxiety as the enemy but rather as a human ingredient that can increase beyond proper and comfortable limits and negatively affect our whole life.

DOI: 10.4324/9781003724971-10

That is everyday anxiety. And what about that special anxiety that existentialists consider a ground of being: existential anxiety? Let's take a look at the history of that idea.

10.1 The history of the concept of existential anxiety

The concept of *existential anxiety* occupies a central place in existential philosophy and psychology. Unlike ordinary anxiety—linked to identifiable dangers or stressful life events—existential anxiety arises from the recognition of human finitude, freedom, and responsibility. It is anxiety about existence itself, not about circumstantial threats.

The history of existential anxiety stretches across centuries, from early philosophical inquiries into dread and fear, through the systematic accounts of Søren Kierkegaard, Martin Heidegger, and Jean-Paul Sartre, to its clinical applications in existential psychotherapy. As a concept, it is situated in philosophy, theology, psychology, psychiatry, and coaching and has evolved into a vital category for understanding human life.

Although the explicit concept of "existential anxiety" belongs to modern thought, its roots can be traced to antiquity. Greek philosophy recognized the inevitability of death and the anxiety that follows from human awareness of mortality. Epicurus, for example, attempted to dissolve the fear of death by arguing that "when we exist, death is not present, and when death is present, we do not exist." Still, the very fact that he felt compelled to address death anxiety indicates that it haunted the ancient imagination.

The Stoics likewise confronted anxiety about fate and death. Their emphasis on cultivating *apatheia*—freedom from destructive passions—was, in part, a response to the existential insecurity of being subject to forces beyond their control. For them, anxiety was less about neurotic fear and more about misplaced judgment about what truly matters.

In the medieval Christian tradition, Augustine and later theologians reflected on the restlessness of the soul before God. Augustine's famous declaration in the *Confessions*—"Our heart is restless until it rests in You"—foreshadows later existential accounts of anxiety. Human beings, in this view, experience anxiety not only from temporal threats but also from alienation from the divine ground of existence. Anxiety here appears as a symptom of metaphysical estrangement.

The modern history of existential anxiety begins with Søren Kierkegaard (1813–1855). In his 1844/1944 work, *The Concept of Anxiety* (*Begrebet Angest*), Kierkegaard introduced a decisive distinction between ordinary fear and existential anxiety (angst). Fear has an object—one fears a wild animal, a storm, or social rejection. Anxiety, by contrast, has no definite object. It arises from the possibility of freedom itself.

Kierkegaard defined anxiety as "the dizziness of freedom," the vertigo experienced when confronted with the openness of possibility and the responsibility that comes with it. For him, anxiety was intimately tied to the Christian doctrine of original sin. Adam, standing before the possibility of disobeying God, experienced anxiety—not fear of something external but anxiety about the possibility of choosing wrongly. In Kierkegaard's account, anxiety precedes guilt and is a necessary precondition of selfhood.

This conception marks a turning point. Earlier thought tended to pathologize anxiety or treat it as a weakness of faith, whereas Kierkegaard elevated it to a universal, structural condition of human life. Everyone who is free must experience anxiety, for freedom is inseparable from risk, choice, and the potential for despair.

In the twentieth century, Martin Heidegger (1889–1976) secularized and radicalized Kierkegaard's insights. In *Being and Time* (1927/1962), Heidegger distinguished between *fear* (*Furcht*) and *anxiety* (*angst*). Fear always has an object—something threatening within the world. Anxiety, however, is objectless. What anxiety reveals is not a particular danger but the fundamental condition of *Dasein* (human existence).

For Heidegger, anxiety strips away our everyday absorption in tasks, roles, and distractions, revealing the naked fact that we are "thrown" into existence without ultimate grounding. In anxiety, "the world as such slips away." One is left face-to-face with one's own being-toward-death, the awareness that existence is finite and cannot be outsourced to anyone else.

This disclosure has a paradoxical structure. While terrifying, anxiety also reveals authentic possibilities. By confronting anxiety, Dasein can break free from inauthentic conformity to the "they" (*das Man*)—the anonymous social order—and take ownership of its existence. Anxiety, thus, serves both as a profound disturbance and as a potential gateway to authenticity.

Jean-Paul Sartre (1905–1980) further developed the theme of anxiety in his phenomenological existentialism. In *Being and Nothingness* (1943/1992), Sartre described anxiety as the recognition of one's radical freedom. Unlike Heidegger, who emphasized finitude and death, Sartre stressed the unbearable burden of absolute responsibility.

His famous example is that of a man standing on a cliff. Fear concerns the possibility of slipping and falling; anxiety concerns the possibility that he might *choose* to jump. Anxiety, then, reveals the fact that nothing compels human beings to act in one way or another. Even in oppressive situations, one is free to choose—though choices are necessarily constrained by facticity, by the given conditions of life.

Sartre's account underscores the anguish (another translation of *angoisse*) of recognizing that one cannot escape freedom. Even refusing to choose is itself a choice. Sartre argued that many people flee from this anxiety into "bad faith," pretending that they are determined by roles, institutions, or external authorities. But the confrontation with existential anxiety is unavoidable: to exist as a conscious being (*pour-soi*) is to be free, and to be free is to be anxious.

In the domains of psychology and psychotherapy, Sigmund Freud, for one, distinguished among realistic anxiety, neurotic anxiety, and moral anxiety. Although not explicitly existential, Freud's theories paved the way for understanding anxiety as a fundamental human affect; however, Freud tended to interpret anxiety as a symptom of repression rather than as anything that could be construed as inevitable or positive.

In contrast, existentially oriented psychologists and psychotherapists reinterpreted anxiety in line with Kierkegaard and Heidegger. Rollo May, in *The Meaning of Anxiety* (1950), argued that anxiety is not only pathological but also constructive, signaling the possibility of growth and change. For May, existential anxiety arises when individuals confront challenges to their values, commitments, or selfhood. Avoiding this anxiety leads to stagnation, while engaging with it promotes creativity and authenticity.

Similarly, Viktor Frankl, the founder of logotherapy, emphasized anxiety as a symptom of the search for meaning. His experiences in Nazi concentration camps convinced him that existential anxiety—particularly anxiety about meaninglessness—is intrinsic to human life. Frankl reframed this anxiety as a "will to meaning," a striving that can be guided toward constructive ends.

Irvin Yalom later codified existential anxiety into four ultimate concerns: death, freedom, isolation, and meaninglessness. Each generates anxiety because each confronts human beings with limits and possibilities that cannot be evaded. Existential therapy, in Yalom's view, does not eliminate anxiety but helps clients face it openly, thereby deepening their engagement with life.

In contemporary psychology and philosophy, existential anxiety continues to generate debate. Some argue that modern culture, with its emphasis on distraction and consumerism, fosters widespread avoidance of existential anxiety. Others see new forms of existential anxiety emerging in response to ecological crisis, technological change, and political instability.

For instance, eco-anxiety—worry about climate change and environmental collapse—bears strong existential features. It is not just fear of specific disasters but anxiety about the viability of human existence itself. Likewise, anxieties surrounding artificial intelligence (AI) and biotechnology often involve existential stakes, questioning what it means to be human in an age of radical transformation.

In clinical contexts, existential anxiety is increasingly recognized as distinct from pathological anxiety disorders. Generalized anxiety disorder or phobias may respond to behavioral interventions, whereas existential anxiety calls for philosophical and meaning-centered dialogue. Therapies drawing on mindfulness, acceptance, and existential philosophy all converge on the idea that existential anxiety cannot, and maybe should not, be eradicated. It is a structural dimension of life, demanding acknowledgment and integration rather than suppression.

The concept of existential anxiety has also permeated literature, art, and popular culture. Dostoevsky's novels dramatize the torments of characters who face the vertigo of freedom and the fear of meaninglessness. Kafka's surreal worlds depict protagonists paralyzed by anxiety in the face of incomprehensible systems and inscrutable guilt.

In modernist and postmodernist art, themes of alienation, absurdity, and anxiety abound. The theater of the absurd, exemplified by Samuel Beckett's *Waiting for Godot*, stages the anxiety of existence without ultimate purpose. Film, too, has taken up existential anxiety, from Ingmar Bergman's *The Seventh Seal* to more contemporary works exploring identity, mortality, and freedom.

These cultural expressions demonstrate that existential anxiety is not confined to philosophy or psychology. It is a lived reality that artists and audiences continually wrestle with, seeking forms of expression that give shape to what is otherwise ungraspable.

However, not all thinkers embrace existential anxiety as a helpful or coherent category. Some critics argue that existential philosophers overgeneralize from personal feelings of unease, projecting them as universal. Others worry that valorizing anxiety risks romanticizing suffering.

From a clinical perspective, some psychologists maintain that distinguishing existential anxiety from pathological anxiety is difficult in practice. They question whether confronting existential anxiety always leads to growth or whether it can exacerbate despair. Critics from religious traditions sometimes contend that existentialist accounts omit the possibility of transcendence or divine consolation, reducing anxiety to a secular condition without resolution.

Nevertheless, even critics acknowledge that existential anxiety names a dimension of experience inadequately captured by other categories. It points to the depth of human self-awareness, finitude, and freedom—realities that cannot be dismissed.

The history of existential anxiety reveals a trajectory from ancient reflections on fear and mortality, through Kierkegaard's theological framing of anxiety as the dizziness of freedom, to Heidegger's ontological interpretation and Sartre's emphasis on radical responsibility. In psychology, existential anxiety has been reinterpreted as a vital clue to meaning-making, growth, and authenticity, with therapists like Rollo May, Viktor Frankl, and Irvin Yalom applying it clinically.

Today, existential anxiety remains a core concept for understanding the human condition. It is not reducible to pathology nor eliminable through technique. Rather, it reflects the unavoidable fact that human beings exist in freedom, finitude, and uncertainty. To acknowledge existential anxiety is to acknowledge what it means to be human. Its history is therefore not only a history of philosophy and psychology but also a history of humanity's confrontation with itself.

An existential wellness coach approaches existential anxiety not as a pathology to be eradicated but as a natural and often valuable dimension of human existence. Rather than aiming to eliminate this anxiety, an existential wellness coach helps clients reframe it as a signal, a teacher, and even a source of vitality that can guide them toward greater authenticity and purposeful living.

From this perspective, existential anxiety differs from clinical anxiety. It is not simply about excessive worry, rumination, or physiological arousal. Instead, it reflects a deeper confrontation with life's givens: "What should I do with my freedom?" "Does my life matter?" "How do I live knowing that I will die?" Clients may feel restless, dissatisfied, or unmoored when these questions surface, especially at life transitions—changing careers, ending relationships, or facing aging. An existential wellness coach normalizes these experiences and frames them as invitations to growth rather than as symptoms of dysfunction.

In practice, an existential wellness coach begins by creating a safe, nonjudgmental space where the client can name and articulate their anxiety. Many people carry existential concerns privately, fearing they are unusual or inappropriate. Simply hearing that such anxieties are universal can bring relief.

The coach affirms the courage required to voice these concerns and gently guides the client toward clarifying the nature of the anxiety—whether it stems from uncertainty about choices, confrontation with mortality, or a perceived lack of meaning.

Once the anxiety is clarified, the coach works with the client to identify constructive responses. If the anxiety arises from freedom and choice, the coach might explore decision-making frameworks that balance responsibility and self-expression. If it stems from issues around mortality, the coach might guide the client in legacy work, mindfulness practices, or values clarification to help them live more fully in the present. If meaninglessness is at the core, the coach can encourage meaning-making strategies such as creative engagement, service, or alignment with deeply held values.

Importantly, the coach does not rush to soothe or distract from the discomfort. Existential anxiety is respected as a necessary part of the human condition. Rather than suppressing it, the coaching stance is to integrate it—to allow the client to carry it alongside joy, love, and purpose. The coach might introduce practices like journaling, reflective dialogue, or symbolic rituals to help the client metabolize their anxiety into insight.

10.2 Existential anxiety and the twelve pillars of wellness

You will remember that I floated the idea that existential wellness rests on certain 12 pillars. Let's take a look at how existential anxiety might interfere with a client's successful negotiation of these categories and what an existential wellness coach might do to help.

10.2.1 Life philosophy

10.2.1.1 How existential anxiety interferes

A coherent life philosophy provides a framework for navigating choices, sustaining values, and orienting oneself toward meaning. Existential anxiety, however, often manifests as doubt and fragmentation: "What if no philosophy can be true?" or "What if my chosen philosophy is meaningless?" Such anxieties can prevent clients from committing to a worldview, leaving them adrift in uncertainty or cynicism.

An existential wellness coach might:

- Encourage clients to view a life philosophy as a *chosen orientation* rather than an absolute truth.
- Normalize uncertainty by introducing the idea that philosophies need not be perfect or permanent to be useful.
- Use reflective writing exercises where clients articulate and refine their guiding principles, highlighting how these principles already help them cope with anxiety and make decisions.

10.2.2 Peaceful mind

10.2.2.1 How existential anxiety interferes

Peace of mind requires a measure of calm and freedom from persistent worry. Existential anxiety disrupts this by fueling obsessive ruminations about mortality, identity, or purpose. Even moments of rest may be pierced by intrusive thoughts such as "What's the point of all this?" or "Am I living wrongly?"

10.2.2.2 An existential wellness coach might

- Introduce existential grounding practices, such as the mindful acknowledgment of mortality without catastrophizing.
- Help clients create "containment rituals" where existential concerns are given space in journaling or dialogue, preventing them from dominating the entire mental landscape.
- Employ relaxation techniques, not to escape anxiety but to coexist with it, reframing it as evidence of caring deeply about life.

10.2.3 Healthy body

10.2.3.1 How existential anxiety interferes

Anxiety about existence can undermine care for the body. For some, it manifests as health anxieties and obsessive monitoring of symptoms. For others, the sense that "the body will fail anyway" leads to neglect, poor diet, or sedentary habits. Existential dread about aging or mortality can either paralyze action or foster compulsive overcontrol.

10.2.3.2 *An existential wellness coach might*

- Reframe physical care as an act of meaning-making rather than as an attempt to escape mortality.
- Use motivational interviewing to help clients articulate body-care practices as values-driven choices (e.g., exercising not to avoid death but to experience vitality today).
- Encourage rituals of gratitude toward the body, shifting focus from fear of decline to appreciation of present capacities.

10.2.4 Positive outlook

10.2.4.1 *How existential anxiety interferes*

Existential anxiety tends to skew perception toward futility and negativity: "Why try if everything ends?" This undercuts optimism and resilience. A client may feel perpetually disheartened, unable to sustain hope in personal or collective futures.

10.2.4.2 *An existential wellness coach might*

- Distinguish between *false optimism* and *authentic hope*. Coaches can help clients embrace realistic positivity grounded in daily meaning rather than denial of reality.
- Introduce practices of *existential gratitude*, where clients list not only material blessings but also moments of beauty, connection, and creativity.
- Use narrative re-authoring: clients retell personal stories highlighting strength and choice even under existential duress.

10.2.5 Helpful thoughts

10.2.5.1 *How existential anxiety interferes*

Thoughts shaped by existential dread often spiral into unhelpful patterns: catastrophic thinking, nihilistic loops, or perfectionist demands. These distortions corrode self-trust and decision-making.

10.2.5.2 *An existential wellness coach might*

- Teach clients to identify *existential cognitive distortions,* such as absolutist thinking about meaning or exaggerated fears of insignificance.

- Guide clients toward *both/and thinking:* life can be finite and still worthwhile; meaning can be constructed even without cosmic guarantees.
- Use thought experiments: "What if meaning doesn't have to be singular?" or "What if ordinary acts carry as much value as extraordinary ones?"

10.2.6 Safe environment

10.2.6.1 How existential anxiety interferes

While a safe environment generally refers to physical and emotional security, existential anxiety can make the world feel unsafe even in the absence of concrete threats. The awareness of mortality or unpredictability can heighten fears of accidents, violence, or loss, creating chronic vigilance and mistrust.

10.2.6.2 An existential wellness coach might

- Help clients distinguish between *existential vulnerability* (inescapable) and *situational danger* (addressable).
- Encourage environmental modifications—decluttering, calming spaces, and safety routines—that foster a sense of groundedness.
- Explore existential acceptance: recognizing that total safety is impossible, yet meaningful living remains possible.

10.2.7 Integrated personality

10.2.7.1 How existential anxiety interferes

Integration involves harmonizing one's roles, values, and desires into a coherent self. Existential anxiety often fragments the personality: one part seeks authenticity, while another part fears rejection; one part yearns for adventure, while another part clings to safety. Clients may feel split, inauthentic, or unstable.

10.2.7.2 An existential wellness coach might

- Facilitate *dialogues between inner voices* (through journaling, role-play, or chair work), helping clients integrate competing aspects of self.
- Normalize ambivalence as a human condition rather than a personal failure.
- Encourage identity construction as a *dynamic project* rather than a quest for a final, perfect self.

10.2.8 Purposeful occupation

10.2.8.1 How existential anxiety interferes

Work is a central arena where meaning and contribution are tested. Existential anxiety can make clients doubt their career choices ("Am I wasting my life?"), paralyze them in indecision, or push them into burnout from trying to justify existence through overwork.

10.2.8.2 An existential wellness coach might

- Help clients differentiate between *livelihood* and *life purposes*—a job can be dignified and reasonably tolerable without needing to serve every life purpose.
- Use values clarification to identify what dimensions of work (creativity, service, and autonomy) matter most.
- Encourage clients to design small, meaningful projects alongside or within their occupation, reducing pressure on a single career to bear all existential weight.

10.2.9 Sustainable meaning

10.2.9.1 How existential anxiety interferes

Meaning is easily destabilized by existential doubts. A sudden confrontation with mortality or absurdity can erode once-sustaining beliefs. Clients may cycle through pursuits, abandoning them as "ultimately meaningless," or despair when meaning feels fragile.

10.2.9.2 An existential wellness coach might

- Normalize the ebb and flow of meaning as part of human life.
- Encourage the cultivation of *multiple sources of meaning* (relationships, creativity, learning, and service) so that meaning is diversified and sustainable.
- Use existential reframing: meaning is not discovered like a buried treasure but *created through committed engagement.*

10.2.10 Valuable relationships

10.2.10.1 How existential anxiety interferes

Relationships both soothe and provoke existential anxiety. Fear of loss, betrayal, or mortality may keep clients from investing deeply, while loneliness intensifies anxiety about isolation. Others may cling to relationships for security, stifling authenticity.

10.2.10.2 An existential wellness coach might

- Explore the paradox that intimacy heightens vulnerability yet enriches life.
- Teach clients to express existential concerns in relationships, deepening authenticity.

- Encourage practices of presence—truly noticing loved ones—as a way of countering anxiety about eventual separation.

10.2.11 Daily steadiness

10.2.11.1 How existential anxiety interferes

Steadiness depends on routine, reliability, and grounded practices. Existential anxiety often disrupts this rhythm by fostering sleeplessness, intrusive thoughts, or compulsive searching for answers. Days may feel chaotic, with erratic motivation and mood swings.

10.2.11.2 An existential wellness coach might

- Encourage the creation of *anchor routines* (morning rituals and evening reflections) that provide stability amid existential uncertainty.
- Introduce *time-blocking for existential reflection*—scheduling periods for deeper questioning so that they do not consume the whole day.
- Reframe steadiness as a strength, rather than as a denial of depth or spontaneity: routines allow space for meaning-making.

10.2.12 Purposeful living

10.2.12.1 How existential anxiety interferes

Purposeful living synthesizes all other pillars into a coherent trajectory. Existential anxiety can derail this by magnifying doubt: "Are my purposes real?" "Am I living fully enough?" This can lead to paralysis, constant self-comparison, or frantic overcompensation.

10.2.12.2 An existential wellness coach might

- Guide clients to embrace *plural purposes* instead of chasing a single, ultimate one.
- Encourage experimentation with purpose projects, emphasizing process over perfection.
- Help clients craft a *life purpose statement*, subject to ongoing revision, which honors both commitment and openness.

Existential anxiety, rooted in the core dilemmas of being human, is both unavoidable and profoundly disruptive. It can obstruct wellness by sowing doubt, undermining peace of mind, fragmenting identity, destabilizing meaning, and corroding relationships. An existential wellness coach's efforts are aimed not at eradicating existential anxiety but at guiding clients toward strategies of reframing, grounding, integration, and meaning-making.

Hardly ever will a client present the complaint, "I'm suffering from existential anxiety." Rather, they'll present with more "ordinary" complaints: difficulties at work, challenges at home, despair about their situation or their circumstances, regrets about the past, fear that they are out of control or untethered, and so on. But the clues that they are suffering from existential anxiety will likely be abundant and apparent. You will get very practiced at knowing what angst sounds like—and very practiced at knowing how to respond and how to help.

FOOD FOR THOUGHT

1. How would you describe the difference(s) between normal anxiety and existential anxiety?
2. Does the concept of "existential anxiety" resonate for you? If not, what feels "off" about it?
3. Given that clients are unlikely to present with existential anxiety, how will you "test" to see if it is present?
4. What are two or three top tactics might you employ in working with someone suffering from existential anxiety?
5. How does existential anxiety manifest in your own life?

Chapter 11

Dealing with ambiguity and uncertainty

Let's refresh our memory about the differences between those very similar ideas, ambiguity and uncertainty, both of which existential themes loom large in the lives of our clients.

Ambiguity typically refers to the present moment: to not knowing what something means right now. The situation itself is unclear, undefined, or confusing. Uncertainty, by contrast, refers to the future: to not knowing what will occur. With uncertainty, you may understand the situation clearly but still not know how it will play itself out.

Let's look at ambiguity first.

As an existential wellness coach, or as someone interested in existential wellness, you hardly need a crash course in the philosophical concept of "ambiguity." But a little grounding in that history will serve you, as "ambiguity" has long played a subtle but powerful role both in the history of philosophy and in our understanding of life's realities. This remains true because "ambiguity" *is* a reality, one that can't be wished away or washed away.

Ambiguity first emerged as a philosophical concern in the dialogues of Plato. Socratic questioning often exposed how seemingly clear concepts like justice, beauty, and virtue dissolved and fractured under scrutiny. The Socratic method of questioning helped us understand that abstract concepts refused to be pinned down because they did not stand for any single thing but rather for many things (or collections of things), often as many things as there were human beings.

Millennia later, philosophers of the Enlightenment championed clarity and reason, and as part of their agenda to elevate rationality to some sovereign pinnacle, they viewed ambiguity as an obstacle. Empiricists like Descartes, Locke, and Hume tried to argue ambiguity away, announcing that it was possible to eliminate all doubt from living. Descartes, for instance, famously announced in Discourse on the Method, Part II, "My first precept is to never accept a thing until I knew it as such without a single doubt." Ah, but this is nothing like life, and so, this attempt at perfect clarity was doomed to fail.

DOI: 10.4324/9781003724971-11

In reaction to the Enlightenment, Romantic and Idealist philosophers reclaimed ambiguity. The German philosopher Hegel, for instance, argued that contradiction and ambiguity were not failures of thought but rather engines of dialectical development. Ambiguity marked the in-between stages of *becoming*, the transitions between what he called "thesis" and "antithesis." Similarly, the Danish existentialist Kierkegaard explored the existential ambiguities of faith, freedom, and selfhood, arguing that ambiguity is intrinsic to the human condition.

Then came the twentieth century, the beginning of what might be called the age of ambiguity. British language philosophers began to explain to us exactly how language works, helping us understand that words do not have set or simple definitions, thus making all communication and conversation ambiguous. At best, the multiple definitions of a word might possess what the linguistic philosopher Wittgenstein called "family resemblances." Similarities, yes; commonalities, yes; but nothing solid enough to allow for communication free from slipperiness.

Then came the existentialists and the postmodernists. In the twentieth century, ambiguity became central to existentialist thought. Jean-Paul Sartre initially sought a clear ontology in *Being and Nothingness*, but, as his work matured, he increasingly acknowledged the role of ambiguity in human affairs. His student and companion, Simone de Beauvoir, elevated ambiguity to a philosophical ideal in *The Ethics of Ambiguity* (1947/2018).

De Beauvoir argued that the human condition is unavoidably ambiguous because we are both subject and object, free and constrained, and individual and universal. Any ethics that denies ambiguity is either overly abstract or dangerously authoritarian. Her existential ethics reject the dream of purity, finality, and total knowledge. Instead, they call for an embrace of ambiguity as a mark of human freedom and responsibility. For her, living authentically means acting within and despite ambiguity, not fleeing from it.

11.1 Postmodern thought and contemporary implications

Postmodernism deepened the philosophical role of ambiguity by challenging foundationalism, binary thinking, and fixed meanings. Jacques Derrida's concept of *différance* emphasized how meaning is always deferred and context-dependent. Language, according to Derrida, is inherently ambiguous—never fully present or stable.

Michel Foucault, too, explored the ambiguity of power and knowledge, showing how systems of classification and discourse shape what we take as truth. Rather than imagining that ideas could be pinned down, Foucault traced the shifting, often contradictory ways in which meaning and identity are constructed.

In contemporary philosophy, ambiguity is no longer just a problem to be solved but a condition to be understood and navigated. Feminist philosophers like Luce Irigaray and Gloria Anzaldúa have explored ambiguity as a site of resistance and multiplicity, especially in gendered and cross-cultural identities.

Phenomenologists, existential therapists, and existential wellness coaches see ambiguity as intrinsic to choosing, perception, and emotional life. Philosophers of language, meanwhile, treat ambiguity not only semantically (as in polysemy or vagueness) but also pragmatically—as something speakers manage contextually and that literature and poetry may intentionally cultivate.

In contemporary existential coaching, ambiguity is not a technical glitch—it's part of the terrain. Coaches like Emmy van Deurzen and Mick Cooper emphasize the multilayered, paradoxical nature of existence. Van Deurzen speaks of clients needing to navigate multiple life dimensions (physical, social, personal, and spiritual), each of which comes with its own tensions and ambiguities.

Rather than aiming for premature resolution, the existential coach accompanies the client in "staying with" their experience. When a client asks, "Should I leave this relationship or stay?", the answer is rarely clear-cut. Existential coaching provides a framework for exploring how both choices can be right, wrong, or necessary in different ways—in other words, ambiguous.

To be human is to be suspended in ambiguity. We live, breathe, strive, suffer, and love within a framework that resists definitive interpretation. Philosophers, mystics, and poets have tried for centuries to decode what it means to exist—but every answer has only led to more questions. This ambiguity is not incidental to life; it *is* life. To exist is not only to occupy space and time but also to dwell in a web of contradictions, polarities, and shifting meanings.

Consider the client who asks, "Am I on the right path?" An existential wellness coach does not reply with a checklist but with questions: *what does* "right" *mean to you? Who are you becoming on this path? What fears are shaping the question itself?* The ambiguity is not an obstacle but the raw material of exploration.

To live existentially is not to eliminate ambiguity but to befriend it. It is to replace the desire for certainty with the courage to choose anyway. It is to accept that meaning, freedom, identity, and truth are not static nouns but dynamic verbs—always in flux, always negotiated.

In a world that pressures us toward quick fixes, binary thinking, and false clarity, honoring the ambiguity of existence is a radical act. It is a stance of maturity, of presence, and of depth. We do not need to solve life to live it meaningfully. We need only to engage it—responsively, honestly, and compassionately. Or, as Maurice Merleau-Ponty put it in *Phenomenology of Perception*, "The ambiguity of reality is not a defect, but the condition of its truth."

11.2 Dancers on the beach or zombie apocalypse?

We say that something is ambiguous when it is unclear or confusing, when it is inexact and open to multiple interpretations, or when it can be understood in more than one way. As human beings, we may crave clarity. But the world is not obliged to supply us with that clarity. Rather, reality is confusing, contradictory, complex, and inevitably ambiguous.

Is that surrealist painter depicting dancers on the beach or a zombie apocalypse? We can't quite tell. The painter has made the matter ambiguous, not to irritate us or to confuse us but to say something about reality, truth, and life. The painter is saying, "You want to know whether those are dancers or zombies? Well, maybe they're neither. Maybe they're both. Welcome to reality!"

The wise coach understands this. Existential wellness coaches alert their clients to the reality that much of life is ambiguous, that craving clarity when clarity is not available is a recipe for distress, and that life does not come with the slogan-sized homily "all will be revealed."

Often, certainty is not only impossible but also not even desirable. Say that your client, Mary, is not sure about the man she is dating, a fellow named Mark. Mark smiles, but is he really smiling? He says the right things, but somehow, it's hard to believe him. He honors his agreements, yet there's always something just a bit off in the way he honors them.

Mary can't put her finger on what's wrong or even how she feels about Mark. It all feels ambiguous . . . and frightening. It would be lovely if you, as her coach, could snap your fingers and grant her clarity. But that quick success would also prove a missed opportunity. This moment is an opportunity for Mary to gain insight into the inevitability of ambiguity in life. She can use that lesson as she deals with Mark, and she can use it throughout her life.

It may be that clarity is coming. But that isn't a coach's first objective. As an existential wellness coach, her main objective here is to help Mary learn an important lesson about the naturalness of ambiguity. Let's accept it, she messages, and let's learn to tolerate it. Because if you find it intolerable, Mary, you're rather likely to jump to conclusions, just for the sake of manufacturing clarity.

If Mary can't tolerate this moment of ambiguity, she might ignore the warning signs and enter into a troubled relationship. Or she might focus on those warning signs, drop Mark, and lose what might have been a fruitful relationship. Yes, sometimes, we meet ambiguity with intuition, and we boldly or tentatively make our decision. But that is different from fleeing from life's ambiguities just because they make us anxious.

What in your own life feels ambiguous? Take a moment and give that question some thought. Then, rather than trying to resolve that ambiguity and force clarity when clarity isn't available, try simply embracing that ambiguity. Frame the matter as one of existential honesty: that, rather than wishing away the contradictions that exist and rather than hoping for a slogan-sized solution, you will tolerate contradiction and make your peace with this aspect of reality.

Sometimes, matters are clear. Sometimes, matters are ambiguous. This is true for you; this is true for your clients. This is such important learning that you might invite your clients to journal on it. If you're a coach who invites clients to journal, either in session or between sessions, picture offering up one of the following prompts to a client.

- What's an area of your life where you long for certainty but know that you must act without it?
- Describe what happens when two truths oppose one another.
- Recall a moment in your life when not knowing for sure led to something unexpectedly beautiful.

Isn't it likely that journaling to one of these prompts would provoke some interesting reflecting, while at the same time deepening your client's understanding of existential reality? Relax into the reality of ambiguity. It isn't going away any time soon.

11.3 Normalizing uncertainty

Next, let's look at uncertainty. To leap to a headline: *you deal with ambiguity by better tolerating paradox; you deal with uncertainty by better tolerating risk.* This amounts to a simple, useful way to "hold" the difference between these two seminal ideas.

Uncertainty is not some modern affliction, nor is it a sign of personal failure. It is, and always has been, a fundamental part of what it means to be human. From ancient times to the present, human beings have had to navigate the unpredictable and the unknowable.

By normalizing uncertainty and by treating it as a given in life, we recognize a truth that philosophers, theologians, scientists, and poets have long accepted: that we live in a world where not everything can be known or controlled.

Socrates, often regarded as the father of Western philosophy, famously declared that his wisdom lay in knowing that he knew nothing. This was not self-deprecation but an existential insight: to be human is to stand on shifting ground, constantly aware of how limited our knowledge is.

Of course, it isn't that we know nothing. But we know so very much less than we wish we knew . . . and so very much less than we need to know in order to make fully informed decisions. That means that all of our decisions, including the most important ones, are going to be edged with anxiety: the anxiety of not really being able to feel certain that we made the right one.

Psychologically and culturally, the modern world has often tried to suppress uncertainty by pursuing control—through technology, data, or productivity. But such efforts often backfire, leaving individuals feeling anxious when life fails to conform to expectations. In contrast, existentialist thinkers like Jean-Paul Sartre and Simone de Beauvoir encouraged a confrontation with uncertainty. To them, the lack of fixed meaning was not a problem to be solved but a condition to be accepted—and even embraced—as the starting point for freedom and authentic living.

Normalizing uncertainty allows us to shift from a stance of fear to one of curiosity. Instead of interpreting uncertainty as failure, we can view it as an invitation to grow, reflect, and adapt. This is especially relevant in times of global upheaval—pandemics, climate crises, and political instability—when the desire for certainty can lead to rigid thinking, polarization, or denial.

By acknowledging that uncertainty is not the exception but the rule, we cultivate resilience and compassion, both for ourselves and for others. In coaching, therapy, education, and leadership, normalizing uncertainty can create safer, more humane spaces. It encourages risk-taking, creativity, and humility. It invites people to say, "I don't know yet," without shame, and to live with open questions rather than rushing to premature answers.

Ultimately, to normalize uncertainty is to befriend reality. Life is unpredictable. Plans change. People evolve. Systems break. And still, we can live with a sense of purpose. Will the sands shift? Yes. But that need not surprise us . . . or disable us.

To not know is deeply human. Yet most of us are raised in cultures that prize certainty, answers, and mastery. From childhood, we are rewarded for knowing things—correctly, quickly, and confidently. But life inevitably confronts us with situations where knowing is impossible.

The discomfort stems not only from uncertainty itself but also from our attempts to resist it. When we can't find answers, we may ruminate, obsess, catastrophize, or numb ourselves. Our nervous system activates, and we are inclined to rush into premature conclusions just to escape unpleasant uncertainty. But these strategies, though understandable, often compound our suffering. They are attempts to avoid a state that is not really avoidable.

In contemporary life, the discomfort of not knowing is exacerbated by a culture that encourages immediate answers. We have Google in our pockets, endless information at our fingertips. But not all questions have factual answers. What should I do with my life? Will this relationship last? Can I make peace with this loss? These are not problems to solve; they are mysteries to live with. And tolerating not-knowing is how we create the space to live them well.

In our coaching work, helping clients build tolerance for not knowing can be transformative. A person facing a major transition may long for clarity, but premature decisions made just to avoid uncertainty can lead to regret. Instead, we can help them develop what some psychologists call *distress tolerance*—the ability to stay with discomfort without reacting impulsively or destructively. This capacity opens space for reflection, insight, and eventual clarity to emerge.

In the end, tolerating the discomfort of not knowing is a skill—and like all skills, it can be practiced and taught. It may never feel easy, but it can become more familiar, more bearable, and even a fertile ground of being. In that quiet space where answers haven't yet formed, something else can arise: patience, humility, curiosity . . . and maybe a path forward.

11.4 Clarity and not-knowing

At first glance, clarity and not-knowing seem like opposites. Clarity suggests insight, decisiveness, and understanding, while not-knowing brings to mind confusion, ambiguity, and doubt. But in practice—and especially in the realm of human experience—these two states often coexist—and must coexist.

Clarity does not always require answers. Clarity can arise from a deeper recognition of what is real, what matters, or what is possible—even in the absence of certainty. Learning to hold clarity in a context of not-knowing is a mark of emotional maturity, creative insight, and existential wisdom.

Not-knowing is not merely ignorance or indecision. It is the honest awareness that some questions do not yet have answers—or may never have them. In the spiritual traditions of Zen Buddhism, "beginner's mind" is celebrated as a state of openness and receptivity. The Zen master Shunryu Suzuki wrote, "In the beginner's mind there are many possibilities, but in the expert's mind there are few." This mindset doesn't seek to close uncertainty with quick conclusions. Instead, it finds clarity in staying present, curious, and undefended in the face of uncertainty.

In Western thought, too, we find this paradox championed. The ancient Greeks used the term *aporia*—a state of puzzlement or impasse—not as a failure but as a fertile ground for inquiry. Socrates, through his method of questioning, led others into this space of not-knowing. His aim was not always to reach a definitive answer but to illuminate assumptions, open space for dialogue, and move closer to wisdom. The clarity came not from having the answers but from a clearer grasp of the limits and shape of one's understanding.

Clarity within not-knowing often takes the form of values clarity. A person may not know what decision to make in a moment of crisis—say, whether to leave a job, end a relationship, or move to a new city—but they may still know what they care about: integrity, connection, creativity, or growth. That clarity can guide action even when outcomes are unclear. As Viktor Frankl wrote in *Man's Search for Meaning*, "Those who have a 'why' to live, can bear with almost any 'how.'" In existential terms, clarity about purpose or commitment can illuminate the path forward, even when the terrain ahead is shrouded in fog.

In the realm of coaching and personal growth, this distinction is vital. Clients often come seeking answers, and it's tempting to try to resolve their dilemmas with logic or strategy. But a skilled coach will often invite a client to sit with the not-knowing and ask, "What feels most true here?" or "What are you clear about, even in the middle of this uncertainty?" The answers may not resolve the situation, but they offer orientation—a compass rather than a map.

Clarity within not-knowing can also manifest as emotional clarity. One may not know what the future holds after a divorce or a loss, but there may be clarity in the grief, in the love that was shared, or in the commitment to healing. Clarity, in this sense, is not about prediction—it is about presence. It is the clear seeing of what *is*, even when what *will be* remains unknown.

This paradox is especially important for creatives, who often operate from a place of deep not-knowing. Creating is in part a surrender to the unknown. And within that surrender, clarity can arise: a feeling, a vision, and a line of poetry. It is not born from certainty but from attention.

Ultimately, clarity within not-knowing is a practice. It invites us to slow down, listen more deeply, and trust that even in the absence of answers, there is something to be known. Sometimes, it is the truth about ourselves. Sometimes, it is the truth about our limits. Sometimes, it is simply the clarity that we don't know—and that that is okay.

11.5 Distinguishing between the knowable and the not knowable

One of the great challenges of being human is learning to live with limits—especially the limits of what we can know.

In a world that prizes information, analysis, and prediction, we often assume that with enough effort or expertise, anything can be known. But this assumption leads to frustration, confusion, and anxiety when we inevitably bump into situations that resist resolution. A core life skill, then, is learning to distinguish between what is knowable and what is not.

This distinction is not always easy or obvious. We live in a time when knowledge is expanding exponentially. We can sequence genomes, map the ocean floor, and predict the weather with remarkable accuracy. In science and technology, many things that were once deemed unknowable have come within reach. But even the most brilliant scientists understand that some phenomena remain inherently uncertain.

Quantum mechanics, for example, teaches us that particles behave unpredictably at a subatomic level. The Heisenberg uncertainty principle shows that we cannot simultaneously know both the position and momentum of a particle with precision. In other words, limits to knowledge are built into the very fabric of reality.

In the realm of human affairs, the line between the knowable and the unknowable becomes even more significant and more personal. We can know the facts of a situation, but not always the motives of others. We can know what happened, but not always why it happened. We can know how we feel today, but not how we'll feel tomorrow. We can plan, but we cannot predict with certainty how things will unfold.

Practically speaking, distinguishing the knowable from the unknowable can bring tremendous relief. In a moment of decision-making, we can ask: what do I truly know? What am I assuming? What remains unclear, no matter how much I think about it?

For example, we may know that a job offer meets our financial needs and interests, but we cannot know whether we'll thrive in the company's culture.

We may know that we love someone deeply, but we cannot know whether the relationship will last. Acknowledging what we *don't* or *can't* know helps us make decisions realistically rather than romantically.

This discernment also cultivates humility, patience, and faith—not necessarily religious faith but a kind of existential trust. Trust in our ability to respond to the unknown. Trust that some truths emerge over time. Trust that not knowing is not a failure but a fact of life. When we stop demanding certainty where none exists, we make room for other kinds of clarity: clarity about what matters, what we value, and what we're willing to risk.

We become better listeners, more honest decision-makers, and less reactive in the face of uncertainty. Ultimately, the line between the knowable and the unknowable is not a wall—it's a threshold. And learning to stand there, eyes open, is a mark of true wisdom.

11.6 Triggered by uncertainty

Uncertainty is a universal part of life—but not everyone responds to it in the same way. For some, uncertainty sparks curiosity or creative energy. For others, it provokes anxiety, irritability, or paralysis. Our reactions to uncertainty are often shaped by deeper beliefs, past experiences, and psychological patterns.

One powerful way to increase resilience and self-awareness is by learning to *track our personal triggers around uncertainty*—to notice what kinds of situations provoke disproportionate stress, what internal stories accompany that stress, and how we habitually react.

A "trigger" is anything that sets off a strong emotional response. When it comes to uncertainty, triggers often appear in moments when the future is unclear, when outcomes are out of our control, or when we're asked to make a decision without having all the information we want.

These situations might include waiting for medical test results, not knowing how someone feels about us, navigating financial instability, or facing career transitions. What's triggering for one person may feel completely manageable to another—so tracking our individual responses becomes a deeply personal process.

The first step is *noticing the pattern.* When uncertainty arises, how does your body respond? Do you feel tightness in your chest? A spike in heart rate? A knot in your stomach? Physiological reactions are often the first clue that something is being triggered.

Then, what thoughts arise? Do you move into worst-case scenarios, judgment, or self-blame? Do you try to take control, seek reassurance, or avoid the situation entirely? These responses are not flaws—they are learned strategies for managing discomfort. But they can become limiting if they're left unchecked.

For example, someone with a childhood history of unpredictability—perhaps due to inconsistent parenting or chaotic environments—may be especially sensitive to uncertainty in adult life. Even small unknowns, like a delayed email or a last-minute schedule change, may set off a cascade of anxious thoughts. The emotional reaction isn't just about the current situation; it's a residue of past experiences. Tracking these moments helps bring that history to light, allowing for healing and growth.

To track your triggers around uncertainty, consider keeping a journal specifically devoted to this inquiry. Each time you notice a stress response, write down:

- *What happened?* (the external event)
- *What did I feel?* (physically and emotionally)
- *What did I think?* (automatic thoughts, assumptions, and fears)
- *What did I do?* (actions taken or avoided)
- *What might this connect to?* (earlier experiences and core beliefs)

Over time, patterns will emerge. You may discover that uncertainty in relationships is more triggering than uncertainty at work—or vice versa. You may see that certain thought loops (e.g., "I should have this figured out by now" or "Something bad is going to happen") consistently amplify your distress. With this insight, you can begin to *interrupt the cycle*—not by forcing yourself to be comfortable with uncertainty overnight but by responding more consciously.

The ultimate goal of tracking triggers is not to eliminate them but to *build a different relationship to them*. Once we understand our reactions, we can choose to pause rather than to panic. We can ground ourselves with self-compassion, remind ourselves of past resilience, or reframe the situation in more helpful ways. We might ask, "What part of me is afraid right now?" or "What would it look like to stay with this question a little longer?"

In existential wellness coaching, helping clients track their triggers around uncertainty can be a key step toward emotional freedom. By shining a light on hidden patterns, we reduce their power. By naming them, we make room for different choices. Over time, what once felt intolerable can become merely uncomfortable—and eventually, just part of the landscape.

Uncertainty may always bring some level of discomfort. But, when we track our triggers, we begin to shift from being controlled by them to being in conversation with them. That shift—from reaction to reflection—is where resilience begins.

11.7 12 tips for coping with uncertainty

Uncertainty is woven into the fabric of life. Whether it's related to health, work, relationships, or global events, the unknown can trigger anxiety and restlessness. While we can't eliminate uncertainty, we can change how we relate to it. These 12 tips offer practical ways to cope more effectively with the unpredictable nature of life. You might offer this list to clients for whom "uncertainty" is an issue.

1. *Acknowledge What You're Feeling*
   The first step in coping with uncertainty is simply naming your emotions. Anxiety, frustration, helplessness, or even grief may surface. Suppressing or denying these feelings only intensifies them. Instead, try saying to yourself, "This is hard, and I feel anxious—and that's okay." Naming the feeling often takes away some of its power.
2. *Focus on What You Can Control*
   When the big picture is unclear, shift your focus to what's within your sphere of influence. You can't control the economy, but you can manage your spending. You can't control someone else's choices, but you can set your boundaries. Making small, grounded decisions helps restore a sense of agency.
3. *Limit Information Overload*
   Endless scrolling for news or updates rarely calms uncertainty—in fact, it often amplifies it. Decide how much and when you'll check news or social media, and stick to it. Curate your sources to include trustworthy, balanced information rather than sensationalism.
4. *Practice Mindfulness and Grounding*
   When uncertainty activates fear, your nervous system can enter a stress response. Mindfulness and grounding techniques bring you back to the present. Try this simple exercise: name five things you can see, four you can touch, three you can hear, two you can smell, and one you can taste. This practice calms the mind and centers attention.
5. *Create Predictable Routines*
   Routines offer stability in uncertain times. Even small rituals—making coffee in the morning, walking at the same time each day, and journaling before bed—can provide structure and reassurance. When much feels unknown, daily rhythms serve as anchors.
6. *Cultivate Flexibility and Curiosity*
   Uncertainty often provokes resistance—"Why is this happening?" or "This shouldn't be happening." Instead, try shifting into a stance of curiosity. Ask, "What's unfolding here?" or "What can I learn from this?" Flexibility doesn't mean passivity; it means staying open to new responses as situations change.
7. *Stay Connected*
   Uncertainty can be isolating. Talking with a friend, coach, or therapist helps you process what you're experiencing and reminds you that you're not alone. Social support doesn't eliminate uncertainty, but it softens its emotional impact.
8. *Take Care of Your Body*
   The mind and body are deeply connected. Sleep, nutrition, movement, and hydration all affect how we respond to stress. When uncertainty hits,

self-care often falls by the wayside—but that's precisely when it's most needed. Even gentle movement or a nourishing meal can shift your internal state.

9. *Give Yourself Permission Not to Know*
   You don't have to figure everything out right now. Some situations simply require time, patience, or more information. Tolerating uncertainty is a skill that grows with practice. Try reminding yourself, "I don't have to know yet. It's okay to be in the middle."
10. *Scenario Planning*
    Imagine several possible futures and sketch out responses to each. If one seems the most plausible, flesh it out as completely as possible. If one seems the most desirable, visualize it happening.
11. *Break Problems into Steps*
    Reduce big unknowns into smaller, manageable decisions. Describe each small step as clearly and concretely as you can.
12. *Reconnect with Meaning and Purpose*
    Uncertainty often invites us to return to what matters most. What values guide you? What kind of person do you want to be, even in this uncertain time? Acting from purpose—whether it's creativity, kindness, service, or growth—gives you stable ground to stand on when outcomes are unclear.

Uncertainty may never feel comfortable, but it can become more manageable. These strategies won't remove the unknown, but they will help you meet it with greater calm, clarity, and resilience. When you learn to cope well with uncertainty, you develop not just a survival skill but a life skill.

11.8 Helping clients deal with ambiguity and uncertainty

Ambiguity and uncertainty are constants in human existence. The future is not fully knowable, choices rarely come with guaranteed outcomes, and meaning is something we must construct rather than discover prepackaged.

For many people, this reality generates anxiety, paralysis, or the desperate search for rigid answers. Existential wellness coaches can play a crucial role in helping clients meet these challenges, not by eliminating ambiguity and uncertainty—which is impossible—but by guiding clients toward more resilient, flexible, and meaning-centered ways of engaging with them.

First, existential wellness coaches normalize ambiguity and uncertainty as conditions of life rather than signs of failure or inadequacy. Many clients mistakenly believe that if they were smarter, more disciplined, or better prepared, they could avoid doubt or confusion. Coaches help dismantle this illusion by reminding clients that ambiguity is intrinsic to relationships, careers, and creative work and that uncertainty accompanies every authentic choice. By naming these conditions as natural, coaches reduce shame and self-blame, making it easier for clients to face them directly.

Second, existential coaches support clients in cultivating tolerance for ambiguity. Tolerance is not passive resignation but an active capacity to remain grounded in situations where answers are partial or evolving. Coaches can use mindfulness practices, reflective journaling, or guided dialogues to help clients sit with discomfort rather than fleeing from it. For example, a client facing a major career shift may learn to hold open multiple possibilities without rushing prematurely into a choice. By practicing this tolerance, clients expand their emotional bandwidth and develop patience with life's unfolding.

Third, existential wellness coaching emphasizes choice and responsibility in the face of uncertainty. While uncertainty cannot be eliminated, clients still must choose, and every choice involves a leap into the unknown. Coaches help clients recognize that not choosing is also a choice and that authentic living requires accepting responsibility for one's decisions, even when outcomes are unpredictable. Rather than offering ready-made advice, existential coaches accompany clients as they clarify values, priorities, and commitments so that choices are guided by personal meaning rather than by fear or external pressure.

Fourth, existential wellness coaches can help clients reframe uncertainty as a space of possibility. The unknown is not only threatening—it is also the source of creativity, transformation, and growth. An uncertain future means that new meanings and identities can emerge. By encouraging clients to approach uncertainty with curiosity rather than dread, existential wellness coaches help shift perspective from "What if I fail?" to "What might I discover?" This reframing can be especially powerful for creative individuals, entrepreneurs, or anyone in transition.

Finally, existential coaches help clients anchor themselves in self-created meaning. When outcomes are unpredictable and life feels unstable, meaning serves as ballast. Through dialogue, existential exploration, and values clarification, coaches assist clients in articulating purposes that matter to them. With this anchor, clients can face ambiguity and uncertainty not as disorienting chaos but as conditions in which they can still live meaningfully.

In short, existential wellness coaches empower clients to meet ambiguity and uncertainty with resilience, courage, and creativity. Rather than seeking premature certainty or rigid answers, clients learn to embrace life's fluidity while grounding themselves in chosen meanings. This stance transforms ambiguity from a source of paralysis into an invitation to live more authentically.

FOOD FOR THOUGHT

1. Describe in your own words the difference(s) between ambiguity and uncertainty.
2. Do you struggle with the challenge of life's ambiguous and uncertain nature in your own life?
3. If you had an important decision to make that was made that much more difficult by the realities of ambiguity and uncertainty, how might you proceed?
4. How might you help clients deal with the ambiguous nature of reality?
5. How might you help clients deal with the uncertain nature of reality?

Chapter 12

The problem of work

Work is a key existential problem. How we make our money, how we construct our lives around a work identity, how we occupy our time, and how we deal with the existential challenges of our work no longer interesting us, no longer feeding us, and even no longer existing, as when whole professions vanish overnight because of technological advances: all of this matters to us.

Helpers like psychiatrists, psychotherapists, and self-help pundits rarely concern themselves with something as mundane as the work that we do. But work is a huge affair in the lives of actual human beings. It takes up our time, it wears us out, it inhabits our mind, it has all sorts of existential ramifications, and it significantly defines who we are.

What, for example, if the work that you do has no connection to your life purpose choices except that it meets the basic life purpose need of sheer survival? Aren't you going to resent that work a lot and continually dream about doing something else?

Or, to take a different sort of example, say that you are doing work that holds meaning for you, but the actual doing of it is an unpleasant experience. You desperately want to write a novel, say, but the writing of it is torture. How difficult will that prove?

Or, as a third example, say that you are a stay-at-home parent raising children and running a household. Even though you work every moment of the day, will it feel like you have "real work"? And will the world credit you with doing "real work"?

Existential wellness coaches need to think about these matters and address them with their clients.

A recent poll put the number of workers who hate their jobs at 85%. Other polls have put the number at "only" 70%. Are all of these workers malcontents? Or is work the problem? It certainly looks like we have another epidemic to go along with our depression epidemic, our addiction epidemic, our anxiety epidemic, our insomnia epidemic, and our loneliness epidemic. But what is the actual problem?

DOI: 10.4324/9781003724971-12

The problem is simply that most work is hard to tolerate, hard to enjoy, and hard to experience as meaningful. It is hard to tolerate even the work that we ourselves dream up. A wise existential wellness coach knows that it has always been like this. They know that work is no innocuous, incidental, or smiley-faced thing. Rather, it is often something brutal.

Work is something that steals away one-third or one-half of our lives. It may pay the rent, but it is also a thief. For some people, the lucky few, this is not the case. For most people, it is. For most people, work is a burden, an albatross, and even a killer.

Why should the work that most people do not actually suit their human needs? Let's try to picture ideal work, work that fits us so well and pleases us so well that we don't even think of it as work. What would work of that sort look like and feel like?

Ideal work would provoke the psychological experience of meaning. It would feel interesting. It would match our moral calculus. It would match our personality and identity. It would pay well enough. And it would not exhaust us or overwhelm us.

It would also come with certain bonuses and benefits, like, for instance, a sense of community. These extras might actually matter a lot. Maybe we need our work to provide us with a sense of prestige. Maybe we need it to make us feel powerful. We may need a lot from it!

Maybe we crave a rock-and-roll lifestyle and need our work to provide it. Maybe we crave respectability and need that from our work. Maybe we need our work to allow us to be our most creative selves. We may need our work to do all of that and more. Is that even remotely possible?

Can any work match this ideal? A teacher may love her work—but not be paid decently. A lawyer may love what she does—except for the ethics of it. A social worker may find her work valuable—but burn out doing it. A poet may never earn a cent.

Let's say that we did miraculously find ideal work. Then, we would need the world not to change, the work not to change, and we ourselves not to change. How likely is that? How likely is it that a Starbucks wouldn't open up right across from our sweet café? If we'd picked a lovely location for our little café, wouldn't someone else consider it an ideal location, too?

The whole nature, currency, and psychological cachet of a profession can change overnight. Consider the difference between delivering the mail when the mail consisted of letters from sweethearts, grandchildren, and faraway friends, rather than what it now consists of, tons and tons of unwanted supermarket ads and almost nothing else. Can such a change really be tolerated?

What are the odds of competitors never appearing? What are the odds of your work interesting you forever? What are the odds of cultural cataclysms not changing everything? What are the odds of you not being transferred or remaindered?

So, for work to feel tolerable, we need it to meet a great many criteria—too many, really. We need nothing to change, no new boss to arrive, no new technology to appear, and no creeping boredom to overtake us. Where did we get the idea that this could be possible?

And work takes up so much time! Maybe we could survive terrible work that lasted just an hour a day. But eight full hours! Or nine! Or ten! Add in those lost hours before and after work, commuting or brooding about the job. Should half a life be spent this way?

Given that work is exactly like this, how ought an existential wellness coach deal with all this as she works with her clients? Are there ways to make work "better"? Is there some way to move work from the albatross side of the ledger to the status of acceptable or even satisfying? Or is there nothing for an existential wellness coach to do but commiserate with her clients?

Unless we are independently wealthy or otherwise supported and provided for, we need to make money in order to survive. Coaches and clients—everyone—must therefore take work seriously, first of all at the level of survival. That is a bedrock reality, and existential wellness coaches pride themselves on being real.

Likewise, human beings need to feel occupied. In a core existential sense, we can't not work. Yes, we can take vacations. Yes, we can spend stretches of time at sea, in transition, or otherwise not quite occupied. But, for the most part, we need occupation.

Occupation and livelihood are bedrock needs. Then, we have our many wants: that the work interests us, that the work feels moral to us, that the work provides us with certain perks, like a sense of community and a chance to be creative. We may not have answers, but these are surely the questions.

12.1 Harry's story

Consider Harry, who finds his corporate job both taxing and meaningless. When a person says, "My job is meaningless," we don't imagine that spending a month in an ashram will do much to change his experience of work when he returns to it. Won't it still be meaningless when he returns?

That month away may help him see that he ought to quit his job. It may help him talk himself into feeling more positive about his job. It may have some other useful consequences. But work will again begin to eat him alive the moment he returns to it, won't it?

The long and the short of it is that Harry hates his job. It strikes him that he's obliged to do something about that, something he's characterizing to himself as "something radical." But what exactly? With the help of his newly hired existential wellness coach, he decides to do all of the following.

First, he creates his list of life purposes. He finds this task grueling, but, as luck would have it, an item on the list sparks his interest. His diabetic sister living in South America has always had trouble procuring her insulin. This gets him thinking.

Next, he mulls over the matter of individuality. He considers his need for it, the challenges associated with it, and who he might want to be from now on. He hears himself say, "I need to be the individual that I really am." This gets him thinking.

Next, he takes to heart the idea of absurd rebellion (which we'll examine in the next chapter). Harry is aware that he has been a "go-along-to-get-along" kind of person. The idea of rebellion ties his stomach in knots. But he finds himself nodding to himself: is it time to take some necessary risks?

He thinks about the phrase "the movement from personality to personhood." In considering it, he senses how his formed personality has aimed him at safe, reliable work that he detests. Can he now make use of his remaining freedom to achieve personhood?

He begins to take to heart the demand that what he does should be moral, worthy, and aligned with the multiple meanings of the phrase "Do the next right thing." His current job is morally neutral at best. He decides that his next work really must be higher-minded.

He enters the "room that is his mind" and takes notice of his indwelling style. He makes a mental note of some needed improvements, like adding windows to let a breeze blow through and installing a safety valve to reduce the constant pressure he feels.

He comes to realize that he has not been authoring his own life. Maybe he's been doing a decent job of accepting his lot. But a life of headaches and stomachaches from attending boring meetings about sales projections really must stop.

He makes a decision. He will start his own business. He does some research and discovers that no one is devoted to providing low-cost insulin internationally. Of course, this may prove fantastically hard to do. But he embraces the challenge.

He starts his day earlier and with a new orientation. His orientation is no longer toward his miserable workday. Now, when he wakes up, he spends a full hour on his new business. Sometimes, he spends two hours, even if that makes him late to his day job.

Building his business is even harder than he imagined it would be. And, so far, it feels less meaningful than he had hoped it would feel. But he knows to align his thoughts with his intentions and to repeat to himself, "I'm building my business."

He attends to the needs of his budding business for that hour with as little drama as possible. He doesn't always love that hour, but he knows that it is the exact right thing for him to be doing from five a.m. to six a.m. each day.

At work, he manifests his chosen personality upgrades. He practices calmness and detachment, he reminds himself not to evaluate life negatively just because he is obliged to work, and he regulates his energy, avoiding gearing up into speediness.

At lunch, which he now takes every day instead of skipping it, he invests meaning in "just being" and goes for a walk to a certain park a quarter mile from his office. There, he eats his sandwich. He uses this time to breathe and to relax, and he doesn't rush back.

In the afternoon, he gets his salaried work done, and at the same time, he makes use of his breaks to do some work on the insulin business, sending out an email, writing some website copy, or learning how nonprofits similar to his have designed themselves.

When he leaves work, he really leaves it behind him. Rather than joining his colleagues and stopping for a few too many drinks, he leisurely strolls to a bus stop a full mile away, enjoying the afternoon bustle, the city sights, and the light of dusk.

When he gets home, he takes a shower and then makes a mindful choice as to whether he will relax by watching a few episodes of the television show he is currently following or whether he will invest an hour in his insulin business.

Was that a splendid day or a perfect day? Perhaps not. But it was certainly an intentional day and a better day than those days that he'd been experiencing before deciding to organize his life around his life purposes. And it was a day that made him feel proud.

Harry's saga underscores why so many people today find themselves becoming solo entrepreneurs. By creating their own work, they better meet their self-obligations and more fully engage in self-authorship. There are existential reasons why so many people today are attempting some version of the one-person business and exploring possibilities that never existed before the advent of the Internet.

12.2 A brief history of my work

Growing up with my mom in Brooklyn, I already had some sense of "my work," which back then had to do with physics and math, on the one hand, and literature and philosophy, on the other hand. I had no job, of course (except for working at my in-laws' antique store for parts of a few summers during high school), but I somehow felt "gainfully employed" reading Newton, Einstein, Sartre, and Camus. All that "felt meaningful."

College did not feel meaningful, and I flunked out. So, I joined the army (during the Vietnam War). After I got out of the army and graduated from college (with a degree in philosophy), I briefly worked for the Veterans Administration as a veterans' benefits counselor. Veterans would come into the office with their concerns and questions, and we counselors tried to help them.

I saw one veteran after another. In my naiveté, I thought that the idea was to help each veteran expeditiously and to then get right on to the next needy veteran. I did this for about a day and a half before I was summoned into my supervisor's office.

He explained to me that I was seeing too many veterans and making everyone else look bad. I had to slow down. I had to slow down a lot. His message was perfectly clear. I would not survive my probationary period if I kept working this fast.

That didn't sit so well with me. Soon, I left.

Next, I talked my way into a job as a proofreader at the American Meteorological Society. I had never previously done any proofreading, but I crammed, learned a few symbols, passed a test, and got hired.

The challenge with this job was that it was stupendously, mind-numbingly boring. It wasn't just dealing with paragraph after paragraph of jargon-drenched minutiae that addled the brain. It was also that, as a double-check, we were to read each line backward to catch any last errors. Can you conceive of that? Backward! Yes, you might indeed discover that a "the" had been spelled "teh." But what sort of salary would it take to allow you to sit there, straining your eyes and your nerves for 40 hours a week, scanning lines backward? More than they were paying. More than anyone could pay.

Then, through a friend of a friend, I got an odd job "judging contests." I would travel around the country to radio stations and "officially" select the winner of the contest that the station was running. The prize was typically some up-and-coming band appearing at a local high school prom.

I'd cover my eyes and pluck a name out of a bowl. I'd show the deejay the prospective "winning" entry, and, as often as not, he'd shut our mikes and whisper something like, "It can't be a junior high school kid. Pick again!"

So, I would pick again. And maybe pick again, until we get to the "perfect" winner. I'm sure that repeated picking wasn't the worst sin the world has ever seen. You and I could both name graver ones. But I couldn't do that job for very long, either.

Then I sold encyclopedias door to door. I memorized the pitch and went out with my trainer. It was instantly clear to me that the poor folks I was pestering shouldn't buy the overpriced encyclopedia set I was hawking. One evening of doing that, and I was done.

Then, through some fortunate connections, I got a writer's dream job. I started ghostwriting. I loved writing, and I loved being paid for writing. Indeed, it met a great many of the criteria for ideal work, except, unfortunately, the ethical.

First, someone else's name would appear on each of these books for hire. Did it matter that readers thought they were getting a book written by Joe or Jane? That probably wasn't such a giant fraud. But weren't readers being duped just a little?

But was it really proper to, for example, write a book about "the best singles' bars in America" without visiting any? (I used Chamber of Commerce handouts.) Well, who was I hurting by sending folks to some well-liked fern bar in Houston? But still.

More tellingly, was it okay to write an arthritis guide when I knew nothing about arthritis? This well-paid one, I just couldn't make myself do. Instead, I handed it off to a friend, who tackled it gleefully, creating a book's worth of made-up arthritis cures.

Then, there was the book about biorhythms. I was asked to confer the mantle of research on some very dubious ideas about human rhythms promulgated by Wilhelm Fliess, an eye-ear-nose-and-throat doctor and Freud's cocaine connection.

I did the research, wrote the book, debunked Fliess, and said some sensible things about biorhythms. The book appeared, carrying the name of a well-known clinical psychologist—and turning around everything that I had said about Fliess.

Well, that was it for ghostwriting. It was perfect work, but dubious. I mourned the loss of that wonderful writer's gig, one that was allowing me to write my novels, and faced once again the need to acquire that ravenous eater of life and time, a job.

So, I went into training to become a psychotherapist. I found it curious that, after not so many classes, very few of which prepared us to do anything in particular, we were supposed to be able to "diagnose and treat mental disorders." Amazing!

It was clear to me that my peers loved calling the folks they saw "patients," as if they, my peers, were surgeons. I knew that something fishy was afoot, and I've spent the last 35 years writing about the serious shortcomings of psychiatry and psychotherapy.

I could go on. And, if I asked you, you could go on, too. It isn't just that work is "hard." It's that so much of the work doesn't sit well with us, psychologically, existentially, or ethically. Work is solidly embedded in a world of tedium, bottom lines, difficult personalities, dubious ethics, and contentious mini-dramas—and who needs that?

But there are those bills to pay . . .

All of this an existential wellness coach knows all too well. And so, how might an existential wellness coach work with clients whose paid work falls far short of serving their meaning needs? Here are ten tactics, presented as mini-vignettes.

12.3 Ten existential wellness coach tactics

12.3.1 Clarify sources of meaning beyond work

Maya, a 34-year-old accountant, told her coach, "I sit at my desk and think, 'None of this matters.' I feel like I'm wasting my life." Her coach acknowledged her despair and then invited her to widen her lens by asking, "What parts of your life do feel alive, or even just slightly meaningful?" Maya mentioned hiking with her kids, cooking for friends, and volunteering at an animal shelter. Her coach gently highlighted how much meaning she was already making outside of work. Together, they discussed how to cherish these dimensions more fully. Maya realized her job could be understood as the platform that funded a meaningful life, rather than its primary source of purpose.

12.3.2 Reframe the nature of work

Darius, a delivery driver, came to coaching saying, "My job is just meaningless busywork." His coach offered up the following reframe: "What if we saw work not as the thing that has to feel meaningful, but as an exchange—your effort for stability or opportunity?" Darius reflected that his job provided health insurance for his ill partner and allowed him the free time to practice guitar. By repositioning work as a transaction, he could relieve himself, at least somewhat, from expecting it to be profound and instead appreciate what it made possible.

12.3.3 Explore values alignment

Angela, a mid-level manager, felt restless: "I don't see how my work connects with who I am." Her coach asked her to list her top five values. She named creativity, fairness, compassion, learning, and autonomy. Comparing these with her current role, she saw little overlap. Together, they explored options, including taking on mentorship duties and considering a transition into nonprofit leadership. This process helped Angela see her work dissatisfaction less as a personal failure and more as a mismatch of values.

12.3.4 Encourage meaning-making within current work

Samuel worked in customer service and confessed, "It's just complaints all day long." His coach asked, "Is there a way to approach your role that could feel meaningful, even in small ways?" Samuel decided he could reframe calls as opportunities to practice patience and compassion. He also began mentoring a new hire, which gave him a sense of contribution. The coach emphasized that while the job itself remained difficult, Samuel's meaning-making within the role did appear to give him a renewed sense of purpose.

12.3.5 Strengthen existential tolerance

Patricia, a paralegal, longed for a deeper purpose but couldn't afford to leave her firm. Her coach said, "Part of existential wellness is living with the fact that not every domain of life will feel meaningful at every moment." They worked on tolerating this "gap" without spiraling into despair. Patricia began journaling about the difference between her job and her broader life. She came to see that she could live authentically even while her work felt flat, so long as she invested in meaning elsewhere.

12.3.6 Connect work to a larger life purpose

Victor worked in IT but was passionate about environmental activism. He told his coach, "My job doesn't matter compared to the climate crisis." The coach asked, "How does your work support your activism?" Victor realized that his salary enabled him to donate, organize, and attend climate marches. His coach helped him craft a life project statement: "I work in IT to fund and fuel my climate activism." This linkage transformed his relationship to his job from meaningless to instrumental.

12.3.7 Examine identity and self-worth

Helen, a marketing professional, confessed, "If my work doesn't feel meaningful, then I feel like I'm meaningless." Her coach helped her disentangle self-worth from occupation, asking, "Who are you besides your role at the office?" Helen named being a mother, a friend, a musician, and a community volunteer. As she spoke, her sense of identity expanded. Over time, she learned to view her marketing job as just one facet of her identity and no longer the sole determinant of her self-worth.

12.3.8 Cultivate agency and choice

Tom, a barista, complained, "I'm stuck here forever." His coach challenged this: "Let's list every possible choice, even if some seem impractical." They brainstormed: staying put, applying for management, starting a side hustle, enrolling in classes, or saving for travel. Seeing these options laid out, Tom felt a shift: he wasn't quite as trapped as he thought. His coach stressed that existential freedom doesn't mean that all choices are easy but that acknowledging agency can itself prove meaningful.

12.3.9 Introduce existential practices

Renee felt invisible in her clerical job. Her coach suggested an existential journaling practice: each day, she would write one reflection about how she experienced meaning or its absence. At first, entries read, "Nothing mattered today." But after weeks, she noticed glimmers: "Helped a colleague find a file—she was grateful." "Took five minutes at lunch to watch the clouds." This practice sharpened her ability to notice small but real meaning moments, even amid monotonous work.

12.3.10 Support career transitions, if desired

Carlos, a 45-year-old project coordinator, finally admitted, "This work drains me. I want something more." His coach didn't rush him into change but asked, "What does 'more' mean to you?" Carlos envisioned teaching. They mapped a gradual transition, including taking night classes and conducting informational interviews. The coach reminded him that no job guarantees eternal meaning but affirmed his freedom to pursue alignment. Carlos felt empowered, rather than reckless—ready to chart a course toward more meaningful work.

12.4 Work as a profession and work as a task

There are many senses of "work." One is the profession we choose. Another is the chore facing us right now. We are obliged to deal with work in the "big" sense, in the sense of our professional choices. But we are also obliged to deal with work in the "small" sense, in the sense of the thing that we are doing next, whether that's cleaning up a spill, struggling with the song we're writing, or the "work" of having a hard conversation with a loved one.

Each of these "small" tasks provides us with the opportunity to feel anxiety, to procrastinate, and to not get on with it. By not doing that bit of work, and by not doing the next bit of work, we can spend a lifetime not getting our work done. We end up passive, unproductive, and not feeling very proud of the effort we are making at living intentionally.

One tactic that can help with this challenge—and one that you can easily teach to clients—is the strategy of dropping a thought into a breath (what I call "creating incantations"). These incantations serve as calmness charms that can help remind you what your work "is" and that you are intending to get that work done "now."

The template or primary incantation is "(I am doing) (my work)." (The parentheses indicate the inhale portion of the phrase and the exhale portion.) Each time you use it, you would insert a new phrase that names some work that you hope to accomplish. There is great centering power in mindfully naming your work. You at once fortify your intentions and create a simple plan. Breathing and thinking "(I am cleaning) (the closet)," "(I am writing) (my novel)," or ("I am paying) (the bills)" has a calming effect, even as it calls you to action.

The work you name can be the work you are about to undertake, like practicing your instrument or cleaning out the garage. You can also use this incantation to announce an intention, for instance, that you will write after work "(I am writing) (after work)" or that you will clean out the closet as soon as you get home from the supermarket "(I am cleaning) (when I get home)."

You can also use it to work on a quality that you want to manifest, like courage or patience, or a state that you want to enter, like a calm, enthusiastic, or receptive state. For example, you might use "(I am waiting) (patiently)" at the dentist's office and "(I feel open) (and receptive)" upon entering a gallery of avant-garde paintings.

You will get better results the more accurately and appropriately you name your work. Let's say that you intend to make a difficult phone call to your mother, one in which you mean to tell her that she can't come to visit you over the holidays. That's the work you plan to name. The obvious phrase to incorporate is "I am calling my mother" or maybe "I am making that difficult phone call."

However, your real work might be to tell your mother what you're feeling or, conversely, to carefully hide what you're feeling. Or your work might be to stay calm as you speak to your mother or to stay strong in the face of her accusations and complaints. Therefore, any one of the following phrases might be the one you actually choose to use:

"(I will speak) (my truth)"
—or—
"(I will stay) (very calm)"
—or—
"(I won't reveal) (very much)"
—or—
"(I will stay) (strong)"

Each of these phrases refers to the same task, calling your mother, but each puts you in a different frame of mind and relates to a different, particular intention.

The process of consciously naming your work may lead you to fruitful self-exploration. You may find that you don't know what your work is, that you have so much work that you don't know where to start, or that you don't feel equal to any of your tasks and therefore don't want to name anything and "pin yourself down." If these have been problems for you for some time, you've been living with plenty of anxiety for a long time already. Trust that, by facing your anxiety now and by learning to name and do your work, some relief and calm will follow.

Here is how two coaching clients reacted to the idea of mindfully naming their work.

From Theresa:

> At first, I found myself naming tasks that were far too daunting. I began to see that I set myself up for failure by doing exactly this all the time. This afternoon, when I returned to my practice, I tried to name little "bites" of something rather than the whole meal. I really like the "bites" idea. I'm going to try to keep the work small, whether it's something I want to do or something I dread doing.

From Lois:

> It's very helpful to focus and make a conscious decision about what I intend to do. It seems so much better than just spreading energy out there in scatter-shot

> fashion. Since I'm dealing with depression, anxiety, and now a possible medical threat, I choose: (I am centered) (whole, well and strong). I'd like to name work like writing, journaling, calligraphy, poetry, or gardening, but right now I think I need to use this step more as a coping strategy. I've used other practices to help with my exhaustion and depression but this is more specific and, I think, better.

Work, in all its many senses—as profession, as day job, as occupation, as identity piece, as task, as chore, and as responsibility—is just too important for any serious helper to ignore.

Existential wellness coaches are alert to these challenges and help their clients come up with their best tactics, strategies, and solutions for dealing with "the problem of work." This is a taxing problem, a vexing problem, and, for many people, a never-ending problem. Existential wellness coaches stand ready to be of some help.

FOOD FOR THOUGHT

1. How would you describe "the problem of work"?
2. What is your own history with regard to "meaningful" and "meaningless" work?
3. In what ways have you effectively and ineffectively handled the problem of work?
4. What two or three tactics might you employ in coaching a client who is having existential problems with work?
5. What two or three suggestions might you make in coaching a client who is having existential problems with work?

Chapter 13

Freedom, resistance, and rebellion

As an existential wellness coach, you support and promote your client's freedom. "Freedom" is a key existential idea, and helping clients feel freer and act more freely matches that existential ideal and increases your client's overall wellness.

We are free in certain senses and not free in other senses. Understanding that truth is one face of wisdom. There is almost nothing that we are completely free to control. By the same token, there is almost nothing that we aren't free to influence at least a little. We may not have the freedom to control, but we may, and likely do, have the freedom to exert some influence.

This difference between control and influence is a vital one. The more you feel that you control nothing, the sadder and more passive you become. The more you see it as your job to exert the influence that is yours to exert, the more likely you are to spend your days actively living your life purposes.

Take the following example. Let's say that you want the book that you've written to be picked up by a major publisher. You are not free to make that happen—you can't control that. But you are completely free to *try* to make that happen, completely free to *keep trying* to make that happen, and completely free to influence the process by creating something that's wanted, by becoming known, by networking, and so on.

You might want more freedom than that, a more pervasive, larger freedom to make things happen in exactly the ways that you want them to happen. That freedom you don't possess. What you do possess is the freedom to positively influence the process. If you give up *that* freedom, then it is you who is giving it up and no one else. To create the life that you want—and for clients to create the life that they want—you and they must figure out what freedom you and they *do* possess and then make intentional, consistent use of that freedom.

Even where we are potentially free to influence the process, we often give that freedom away. This is one of our worst human habits. When we give away the freedom that we do possess, we end up feeling weak and powerless, disappointed in our efforts, and as if we're just going through the motions in life.

DOI: 10.4324/9781003724971-13

So, we invite clients not to give away the limited freedom that they do possess, not to pass up calling someone who might be helpful to them because they are stubbornly resentful that they need help, not to retreat from the marketplace because someone has criticized them, and so on. An existential wellness coach says, "You may only have a limited amount of freedom, but please use the freedom that you do possess!"

We tend to focus on the ways in which we are not free because there are so many of them and because they affect us so profoundly. By focusing there, we get passive and sad. It is our job to focus on the ways in which we are free, even if those ways are more limited and less numerous than the ways in which we aren't free. It is our job to remind ourselves of all of our freedoms—our freedom to try, our freedom to get out of our own way, our freedom to say what we mean, our freedom to advocate for ourselves, and so on.

Both our society and we ourselves pressure us to relinquish our freedom. The pressures that society applies on us to be conventional and unfree—let's call that social censorship—and the pressure that we apply on ourselves not to take risks, not to speak our mind, and so on–let's call that self-censorship—are powerful inhibiting factors in a person's life.

Let's take a simple example in each category. You probably do not feel particularly free to stop in a supermarket aisle while you're shopping and work on a poem that's just come to you—even though you are actually perfectly free to do that. Who stole that freedom from you? Who made it hard, verging on impossible, for you to work like the artist that you are in a conspicuous place like a busy supermarket?

That's a simple example of how we let society make us unfree. Here's a simple example of self-censorship. How many times have you come up against subject matter in your art, if you are an artist, that you know might have been interesting and maybe even brilliant to examine—but somewhere inside of you, you felt that something about the subject matter was better left unsaid? That is self-censorship in action. Maybe we have the desire to tackle some dangerous, fascinating subject—and we ourselves shut that desire down. In such ways, we reduce our own freedom.

We are pressured all the time by unseen forces into censoring ourselves in public and censoring ourselves in private. We must fight back against these pressures, using the freedom that we have available to us and the personality traits that we have available to us. As an existential wellness coach, you recognize that one of your tasks is to support clients in their efforts to be as free as they can be—and to point it out when they are operating from a conditioned place of unfreedom.

People flee from freedom all the time. Many people actively hate freedom as an idea. Millions upon millions of people hate the idea of freedom and want to hand over their freedom to others as quickly and as permanently as they can. There is a large literature on authoritarian submission—that is, on the personality profile of the person who passionately prefers tyranny to freedom. There are a great many of those people!

But there are also many other ways that people flee from freedom, in addition to handing their freedom over to tyrants. Many people let their safety needs dictate to them and live a restricted life based on the concept of safety. Others substitute habitual, reflexive thinking for fresh, in-the-moment thinking so as not to rock their world with the freedom of fresh thought. People flee from freedom all the time. Your clients, being human, are likely in this majority. Help them be freer—they may not know that they need that help and that permission, but they almost certainly do.

13.1 The freedom to make music

What does "talking about freedom" or "working on freedom" look like in an actual coaching session? Consider the following.

Annie, a client of mine, had built up a wall that prevented her from making music. Her stated goal was to play perfectly, and that she did. Every teacher and every reviewer had the same thing to say about her playing: that it was technically perfect . . . but that it had no soul.

Sometimes, they called her playing cold. Sometimes, they called it mechanical. Sometimes, they called it boring. They had different ways of saying the same thing, that she was a violin virtuoso who played notes and not music.

There is nothing the slightest bit rare or unusual about this. Mastering a musical instrument at the level needed to become a world-class soloist requires so much sheer effort, especially if you lack top physical gifts, that just getting the notes right is an immense accomplishment.

It is one of the little jokes of the universe to make it so hard to do the most beautiful things, like sing gorgeously in your upper register, that the hardness overwhelms everything else. Many musicians are consumed by the hardness of the thing they have chosen to do, spending a lifetime worrying about their shortcomings and the difficult passages ahead, which worrying naturally kills off their joy.

Annie, a second-generation Korean-American, came to see me only reluctantly. She made appointments and canceled them. No doubt, she presumed that I had nothing to offer her, even though she "enjoyed my books," as she mentioned in her first email to me. She understood technical help and had worked with many violin teachers and medical specialists during her career. But how could a coach help her with her playing? No doubt, it made very little sense to her.

After the pleasantries were over, I asked her, "What's on your mind? It wasn't so clear from your emails."

She didn't reply immediately. I wondered if she didn't know or if she preferred not to say.

"I'm getting booked less," she finally said. "I had a career that was going up and now it's stagnating. New violinists are getting concerts that I think I should have gotten. I think . . . I thought it was about my repertoire and maybe changing tastes and all of that. Now . . . I don't know."

"What do you now think it is?"

"I don't know," she repeated mournfully.

I paused, then wondered, "What are the two or three things that it might be?"

She considered. "It might be that people don't like me. I don't have all the social graces. I'm not a networker. I'm uncomfortable around people and they know it."

I nodded. "What else?"

"There are certain things that I'm obliged to play that I don't love to play, like the Tchaikovsky and the Mendelssohn. I don't really like anything romantic or schmaltzy or anything that might be considered 'beautiful.' And people like those things."

"You say that people consider them beautiful. You don't?"

She made a face. "I've listened to Oistrakh play the Tchaikovsky about a million times. Why? Not to hear how he handled it technically. Just to hear him play it. I am completely of two minds about a word like 'beautiful.' On the one hand, it rubs me the wrong way. On the other . . . there's Oistrakh."

I let us be silent for a moment. The next question was not an easy one.

"Can you play beautifully?" I said.

It took her a moment to reply.

"People say that I can't," she confessed. "In a way, I'm not even sure what they mean. I know they say that I'm a slave to the notes. But it doesn't feel that way to me. I feel like I'm making music. Sometimes I think they're just making it up, using that language as a way of saying that they prefer somebody else's playing to mine."

I nodded. "That could be. But tell me . . . you do feel free to drop notes and miss notes?"

She raised her head and stared at me. "I do not! Why would anyone feel free to do that? That ridiculous! That's the first thing you need to get right. And" Hesitating, she fell silent.

"Were you going to say, 'And the only thing'?"

She shrugged angrily.

"Many great musicians," I continued, "have said that if you demand that they play all the notes correctly, they can't also make music. You've heard that said?"

"Of course! But I've never taken that seriously. That's not what they mean! They mean, 'If I was a little off tonight, here's my excuse. I was making music.' It's just a kind of excuse! They don't mean it."

I waited. "What if they do mean it?" I said.

"They can't!"

I let the silence be.

"You need to play the notes correctly," she said in a small voice.

"Of course." I paused. "But is that the music?"

"The music is notes in a score. I think about them, I figure them out, I play them, the strings vibrate and move the air—it's notes and sound waves."

"No heart?"

"I keep hearing that! 'No heart!' 'No heart!' I keep hearing that!" Tears came.

"What am I supposed to do at this point? Go see the Wizard of Oz and get a heart? I'm really tired of hearing about this!"

I smiled. "Well, I have a simple solution. Feel free to play in a heartfelt way and the hell with the notes."

Annie stared at me. "Everybody would rip me apart if I did that."

"Would they?"

"They would!"

"If you missed one or two notes in a concerto but brought tears to their eyes?"

That thought startled her. "If that were the trade-off"

"Who knows? We're not talking about terrible playing. We're talking about freer playing. Make a mental calculation. How many notes would it cost you to play more freely?"

She thought about that for a long time. I could see her playing in her mind's eye. Every once in a while, she made a face—there was a missed note! Finally, she sighed.

"I don't know. Just a few. Not that many."

"But you could sense the difference? Between playing correctly and playing freely?"

"In that split second, I could. I don't know if I could with a violin in my hand."

"Agreed!"

"But, of course, I have to try it."

"Agreed."

"You know, I'm not really sure I know what we've been talking about."

I nodded. "Just think Oistrakh. You understand that perfectly, don't you?"

She sighed. "Maybe. Maybe not. Let me see what happens when I try to play something."

"The Tchaikovsky," I laughed.

"No," she said, almost smiling. "But . . . okay . . . maybe something beautiful."

It's odd to say that feeling freer to drop a few notes might transform a person's life. But that's how powerful and important the concept of "freedom" is.

13.2 What "giving away your freedom" looks like

You have as much freedom as you have, and less than that if you give a portion of that freedom away.

What does "giving your freedom away" look like? The following are ten ways that one group of clients, creative and performing artists, regularly give away their freedom with respect to the art marketplace and with respect to their careers.

We could create a similar list for other groups of clients. Indeed, you might like to create your own list for yourself. How do you give away *your* freedom?

Here are ten ways that creatives give away their freedom:

1. By hiding out.
   We are free to show up at places, to learn from people, and to see what is going on—but out of anxiety or stubborn pride, we often give away this important freedom. You are free *not to hide out*—that is your choice.
2. By demonizing marketplace players.
   It is easy and somehow comforting to mentally turn marketplace players into the enemy. But we are free *not* to take that easy route. It is our choice whether to lead with disdain and wounded pride or to freely admit that we need them, want them, and will endeavor to bring them over to our side. We are free *not* to demonize marketplace players.
3. By overinvesting in one plan or tactic.
   We are free to step back and look at our plans and tactics objectively, rather than to keep obsessing about the one plan or the one tactic in which we've invested everything. If you are obsessing about whether to serve cookies or to serve muffins on open studio day, then obsessing in that way is preventing you from doing other things that would much better support your career. You are free *not* to obsess in such ways.
4. By taking silence personally.
   We send things out into the world, and then we wait. While we wait, all we hear is silence. We are free *not* to take that silence personally and not to construe it as impending criticism or rejection. We are free to keep sending things out even as the silence mounts. We are free *not to turn silence into a problem.*
5. By turning problem people who do not really matter into too much of a problem.
   We are free *not* to care too much about or become too affected by difficult folks in the marketplace who do not directly matter to us. If some gallery owner who is not showing our work takes crazy offense at the email we sent him, we are free not to take his crazy offense to heart or to enter into his dramatic little world. We can just smile and delete his rant. We are free *not* to care about people about whom we don't actually care.

6. By failing to notice—and seize—opportunity.
   We are free *not* to ignore the fact that someone we know knows someone who might be of use to us. Too often, we feel embarrassed about reaching out to people who might be of use to us, and therefore, we get in the habit of not even noticing their existence. I've had countless clients who've failed to notice that a marketplace player has actually expressed interest in them or their work—somehow that information got completely missed. You are free *not* to miss noticing the opportunities that arise and free to seize them.
7. By not persisting.
   We are free to keep trying a given contact a dozen times, or we can give away that freedom by stopping the first time we are met with a lukewarm or negative response. If you improve a project, you are free to get back to anyone who passed on it before—unless you give up that freedom. If you receive a bit of attention, you are free to tell folks who have passed on your work that you are better known now or better received now—unless you give up that freedom. You are free to persist and even pester—unless you decide that you are not that free.
8. By saying yes when it doesn't serve you or when you don't mean it.
   We are free to say *no* to a time-consuming, low-paying gig, or we can give away that freedom and say yes just because we want to be seen as nice or helpful. We are free to say no to helping out with a labor-intensive project that provides us with next to nothing, or we can give away that freedom. We are free to think about whether a project really serves us—*or we can give away that freedom.*
9. By taking long vacations from trying to move our career forward.
   You are free to decide that you will *not* skip days and avoid the work necessary to give yourself a chance at a career. Taking days off is the same as giving away your freedom—your freedom to try, your freedom to make an effort, and your freedom to give yourself a chance. You are free *not* to take extensive vacations from building your career.
10. By throwing up our hands.
    We are free to throw up our hands and exclaim that we don't know what to do to move our career forward, that there are just too many things to do to move our career forward, that we are too much of an outsider to move our career forward, that there are too few opportunities to move our career forward, and so on. And you are also free *not* to throw up your hands at marketplace difficulties. Of course, that's exactly what you need to do: *not* throw up your hands at those difficulties.

The art marketplace is hard enough without you giving away your freedom to do natural and useful things on your own behalf. You may be embarrassed to do them; your pride may get in the way; your anxiety may get in the way; and so on.

But all of that is on your shoulders. The freedom is there, and not giving it away should be your agenda.

The above is one version of "giving away our freedom." What might "giving away our freedom" look like with regard to a different group of clients? Try to picture that.

13.3 Free not to be perfect

"Perfectionism" is another face of our loss of freedom. Annie, the client I mentioned above, needed to play perfectly. Her perfectionism, like all perfectionism, was a certain sort of anxiety state mixed with a certain sort of lack of freedom. You can address perfectionism in both ways, as an anxiety state that anxiety management strategies might help or as a "freedom" issue. Either way works!

Not so long ago, I got the following email from a painter in Rhode Island. She wrote,

> I'm a perfectionist and I want my artwork to be perfect. Sometimes this prevents me from getting started on a new project or from finishing the one I'm currently working on. I think to myself: If it's not going to be the best, why bother to do it? How do I move past these feelings?

One way is to move from a purely intellectual understanding that messes are part of the creative process to a visceral understanding of that truth. As an intellectual matter, artists know that some percentage of their work will prove less than stellar, especially if they are taking risks with subject matter or technique. But accepting that obvious truth on a feeling level eludes far too many creative and would-be creative people.

Mistakes and messes are as integral to the creative process as falling down is integral to the process of learning to walk. An infant would never think the thought, "I will not walk until I can walk perfectly." Only adults think such unhappy, paralyzing thoughts. If an infant wants to get from where she is to the toy across the room, she will crawl, walk, tumble, or fly. She will do whatever it takes because she wants that rattle or that ball.

When artists actually want to create because they are excited by the prospect of turning their thoughts and feelings into tangible things, then perfection tends to recede as an issue. They are like that infant who wants the rattle: they become a beautiful vehicle of vitality and desire. First, gain permission in your heart of hearts to make mistakes and messes. Second, grow as excited about some creative project as a baby grows who spies a toy. Those are the twin keys to exorcising perfectionism.

When I begin to write a book, and I've had more than 60 published, I'm excited to see what will emerge. Maybe something beautiful will appear on the first try, maybe the book will need two complete overhauls and three additional revisions, maybe it will never come to life and will need to be abandoned. I am easy with all of those outcomes, including the last. If I were not, I would be asking the creative process to be something that it cannot be: a guarantee that if I show up, excellent things will happen. The showing up is the main thing; the excellence, if it comes, is an earned but unguaranteed blessing.

Help clients eliminate the word "perfection" from their vocabulary. Help them replace it with the word "freedom." Cognitive therapists teach a useful three-step technique that can help. First, you learn to notice if and when the word "perfection" or some word or sentiment like it pops into your mind. Second, you dispute it instantly: you say something like, "No! That's not a word I countenance!" Third, you replace it with a more appropriate suggestion: for instance, "I am free, I am willing to struggle, and I will show up!"

You can easily and quickly teach clients this simple procedure. You can also invite them to engage in the following practice. It's a "morning life purposes check-in." If clients can remind themselves every day what their life purposes are and which of them they intend to attend to on that day, that is the equivalent of them manifesting their freedom and avoiding "freedom theft" pitfalls like perfectionism.

This morning check-in, which takes hardly a minute or two, reminds you of your intentions, focuses your mind, increases your resolve, and helps you live your life more mindfully and more powerfully. The existentialists say that we are contingent—that we are born into a certain family, born into a certain social class, alive at a time of war or of peace, and so on. Those are our contingencies, our facts of existence. But we are also free to adopt our basic attitudes, free to stand up and be counted, and free to announce our life purpose choices and to live them. A morning life purpose check-in can help.

Consider the experience of a client of mine, Barbara. Barbara reported:

> I've been religiously doing the morning practice. It's made a huge difference in my life. With each day's work building on previous days, I've pulled further out of acute depression. The tools that I set up in interpreting the morning practice instructions are: a spiral notebook journal to use each morning to briefly write any thoughts that I wake up with (ideas, issues, dreams) and to write the meaningful and purposeful activities that I'm planning for that day.
>
> I also keep a monthly calendar page with squares large enough to write the daily "life purpose" activities that I've accomplished. The calendar provides an ongoing and cumulative record of the meaningful activities I actually managed to accomplish. In the journal, as I complete a life purpose activity for the day, I put a broad red check mark beside the item and the amount of time I spent on it (if that's important). On the monthly calendar, I write a post-it note with my accomplishments.

This morning practice takes only a few minutes each day, unless I write longer in the journal. So very important is the basic structure and routine, which is what I needed and which I haven't rebelled against, as I have throughout my life when I felt too boxed in. There is a logic and a spaciousness to this morning life purposes practice that really works for me.

13.4 Freedom fighter as existential concept and metaphor

The concept of "freedom" has embedded in it three related ideas: resistance, rebellion, and absurdity.

In order to be free, we must resist those forces intending to restrict our freedom, say when a fascist candidate runs for office, and actually restricting our freedom, say when that fascist candidate wins. Sometimes, that resistance may need to rise to the even higher level and greater stakes of outright rebellion, like, for instance, the French Revolution.

As a backdrop to our resistance and rebellion is the notion of absurdity. How absurd to think that I can affect the course of world events or make the slightest difference in fighting tyranny. Still, we resist and rebel so as to live authentically and to fight for our freedoms, even if this effort strikes us as patently absurd.

The image that likely pops into your mind is that of the freedom fighter. The figure of the "freedom fighter" is most often understood politically: as a person resisting oppression, challenging tyrannies, or risking their life for liberation. From the resistance movements of World War II to the ongoing struggles for human rights across the globe, the freedom fighter has been cast as the hero we need the most, the person fighting for our freedoms.

However, the idea of the freedom fighter can also be approached as an existential concept and metaphor. When seen existentially, the freedom fighter is not just the partisan with a rifle in a forest, or the underground pamphleteer in a city under occupation. They are the ones who confront the givens of existence and resist those forces—internal and external—that threaten human dignity. We can expand the freedom fighter image into a metaphor for every human being engaged in the task of living freely in a world that often conspires against such freedom.

Albert Camus, for one, framed resistance as existential. In his writings for *Combat*, the underground French newspaper, Camus emphasized rebellion as a moral and human necessity. He argued that rebellion not only opposes an external oppressor but also affirms the value of life against the absurdity of death and meaninglessness. The freedom fighter in World War II became the lived embodiment of the existential refusal to surrender to despair or nihilism, even under seemingly hopeless circumstances.

Camus's later essay, *The Rebel*, universalized this stance: to rebel is not only to say "no" to injustice but also to say "yes" to the concept of human dignity.

The absurd confronts us with the silence of the universe, but instead of surrendering to nihilism, the freedom fighter within insists on creating value, dignity, and solidarity. To live as a freedom fighter, existentially, is to resist absurdity by continuously choosing to live, to act, and to create meaning in spite of it.

Today, existential thinkers continue to use metaphors of struggle and resistance. Philosophers like Jonathan Lear speak of "radical hope" as the courage to envision meaning after cultural devastation, much as freedom fighters envisioned liberation while Europe was still under Nazi occupation. Psychologists like Irvin Yalom emphasized "ultimate concerns"—death, freedom, isolation, and meaninglessness—as ever-present conditions that must be faced directly rather than evaded. Facing them requires a stance of defiance, a stance akin to rebellion.

Existential resistance does not necessarily require physical violence; it requires vigilance against internal and external forces that would diminish human dignity. It is rebellion without hatred and courage without cruelty. The existential freedom fighter wages war not primarily on other human beings but on the forces of bad faith, nihilism, conformity, and despair. And if they sometimes must wage actual war, they do.

The freedom fighter as an existential concept and metaphor bridges history and philosophy. It evokes the extraordinary sacrifices of World War II partisans while also illuminating the daily struggles of individuals confronting the givens of existence today. For Sartre, it dramatizes the reality that we are condemned to be free and must act. For Camus, it symbolizes rebellion as affirmation of dignity in the face of absurdity. And for contemporary existential thought, it continues to serve as a reminder that life itself is a struggle for freedom—not a freedom granted once and for all but a freedom won daily through acts of courage, authenticity, and solidarity.

The existential concepts of freedom, absurdity, resistance, and rebellion offer a powerful framework for navigating the complexities of human life. Freedom reminds us that we are not bound to a single path or preordained meaning but are constantly called to choose, to act, and to create. This freedom is both a gift and a burden, for it confronts us with responsibility and the anxiety of decision-making.

Absurdity underscores the tension between our longing for coherence and the world's indifference to that longing. Rather than collapsing under this recognition, we are invited by existential thinkers—and existential wellness coaches—to embrace absurdity as the ground from which authentic living can emerge.

Resistance becomes a primary existential response: the way to push back against despair, conformity, and nihilism and to assert one's capacity to live deliberately, even in the face of meaninglessness. Freedom, absurdity, resistance, and rebellion converge into a call for authenticity: to live with open eyes, to wrestle honestly with existence, and to forge a life that, while never final or fixed, is unmistakably one's own.

Your clients will not come in and say, "I'm looking for a resistance cell to join." They are unlikely to say, "I see myself as a freedom fighter." They may never once utter the word "freedom." But we understand its importance and its vital relationship to existential wellness, so we keep it in mind . . . and lobby for it.

FOOD FOR THOUGHT

1. What is your main takeaway from our discussion about freedom?
2. What do you see as the differences between "control" and "influence"?
3. Do you regularly "give away" your freedom? When? How? And . . . why?
4. Does the idea that we are obliged to "live like a freedom fighter" resonate for you?
5. What two or three tactics might you employ to help clients "grow freer"?

Chapter 14

On authenticity

Many clients come to us plagued by a painful feeling that is different from and separate from the issues they present. Maybe their stated issue is that their work is exhausting, that their primary relationship is failing, or that they can't seem to get their creative work done. But "underneath" or "beside" this presenting issue is the following painful feeling: that they are not living authentically.

They may not have the words to exactly explain what they mean. Who does? And yet, every single day, they find themselves out of sorts and maybe even in despair as they intellectually, emotionally, and viscerally feel this lack, this shortfall, and this failure. What are they after? What are they missing? What is this thing called "authentic living"?

The idea of *authenticity* has long fascinated philosophers, writers, and seekers of wisdom. In existential thought, authenticity refers to the courage and capacity to live in alignment with one's deepest self rather than in conformity with social norms, external pressures, or self-deception.

The history of existential authenticity probably begins with Søren Kierkegaard, often called the first existential philosopher. Writing in nineteenth-century Denmark, Kierkegaard rebelled against the complacency of Christendom, where religion had become more social ritual than inward passion. For Kierkegaard, the authentic individual is one who faces the anxiety of existence and relates directly to God, rather than blending into the crowd or hiding behind socially accepted forms of faith.

Kierkegaard's famous phrase, "subjectivity is truth," captures this stance. Truth is found not in abstract doctrines or objective systems but in how a given individual lives in relation to ultimate concerns. Authenticity, for Kierkegaard, means refusing to lose oneself in the anonymous mass ("the crowd is untruth") and instead embracing a life of inwardness, insight, responsibility, and personal faith.

If Kierkegaard rooted authenticity in faith, Friedrich Nietzsche located it in the radical affirmation of life. Nietzsche's call to "become who you are" expressed a vision of authenticity grounded not in obedience to God but in creative

DOI: 10.4324/9781003724971-14

self-fashioning. Arguing for self-authorship, he criticized "herd morality," conformity, and what he saw as the life-denying values of traditional religion.

For Nietzsche, authenticity required the courage to overcome false ideals and the cultivation of one's own style of existence. This process involved facing nihilism—the recognition that inherited meanings had collapsed—and courageously creating new values. The figure of the *Übermensch* exemplifies the one who lives authentically: an individual who embraces life, the luck of the draw, and personal creativity without retreat into illusions. Where Kierkegaard saw faith as the authentic response to despair, Nietzsche saw self-affirmation and value creation as the right response.

Today, authenticity remains a vital—and, yes, contested—concept. Postmodern and critical theorists have sometimes challenged it, questioning whether any stable "true self" exists or whether authenticity itself has become something of a commodified lifestyle ideal. Charles Taylor, in *The Ethics of Authenticity* (1991), argued that authenticity should not devolve into mere individualism but must take into account the rights and needs of other people. Authenticity, in this view, does not exalt the self over the other: sometimes an authentic action might be to lay down one's life for another or for the greater good.

In contemporary existential and psychological practice, authenticity continues to signify a life lived with awareness, responsibility, and integrity. It means refusing to collapse into conformity or self-deception while also acknowledging the relational, social, and historical contexts that shape existence. And it means facing facts: facing what existentialists call the facts of existence or "facticity."

You have bills to pay. They are sitting there. You don't have enough money to pay them. That is a hard reality. You can think about that any which way you like, you can try to fantasize the bills away, and you can drink to avoid thinking about your bills, but the bills remain. They are a hard reality.

There are philosophies that make the claim that those bills don't really exist, that all that exists is our reaction to them or our thoughts about them. There are philosophies that invite us to turn away from those bills and toward some different or higher reality, toward the path we are traveling, toward peace, toward oblivion, toward acceptance, and toward God.

But those bills remain. They are a hard reality. The reason that existentialism as a philosophy has always felt rather cold is that it demands this kind of reality check. It honors that tropical storms can turn into hurricanes. It honors that two people who come together can also fall apart. To be authentic is not only to take a certain stance toward reality but also to look reality squarely in the eye. Very often, you will not like what you see. Squarely facing some indignity or clearly seeing some horror won't make you feel well, but it can make you feel proud that you are living that authentically.

It is not enough to "get a grip on your mind" if you hate your job, if you find yourself in a loveless marriage, or if you're forced to flee your country because of civil war. What is needed, first of all, is deep, clear-eyed, primary acknowledgment of those hard realities. What is also required is a good understanding of what can change—and what can't.

14.1 Changing what can change

To be authentic means to announce that you have exactly the freedom you in fact have, maybe no more than that but absolutely no less, either. One face of that freedom is asserting that, while this or that may not be in your power to change, something may be.

When our external circumstances can't change—whether due to age, illness, family commitments, financial limitations, or unmovable systems—we often still retain some ability to change, internally or relationally. Here are 20 things that typically *can* still change. Endeavoring to make these changes is a feature of authentic living.

1. *Our perspective*: We can reframe how we see our situation, moving, say, from victimhood to agency or from despair to meaning-making.
2. *Our self-talk:* We can pay attention to and shift the tone and content of our inner dialogue.
3. *Our attention:* We can choose what we focus on: for instance, on beauty, on kindness, on curiosity, and on gratitude.
4. *Our expectations:* We can adjust what we hope for or require of ourselves or others.
5. *Our habits:* Even tiny tweaks in routine can change how we experience a day.
6. *Our boundaries:* We can set new limits to protect our time, energy, or emotional well-being.
7. *Our values:* We can clarify or reaffirm what truly matters and live more aligned with those values.
8. *Our beliefs:* Old, limiting beliefs can be questioned and replaced.
9. *Our instrumentality:* We can demand less passivity and more action from ourselves.
10. *Our communication style:* Shifting how we speak can sometimes change relational dynamics.
11. *The ranking of our life purposes:* We can elevate a background life purpose to a higher place in the order of what we consider important.
12. *Our relationship to acceptance and surrender:* We can let go of attachments and our hungry need to control what we can't control.
13. *Our use of self:* We can decide to use more of ourselves, for instance, by creating, rebelling, or serving.
14. *Our circle:* We can change, and maybe improve, our circle of friends, intimates, peers, and acquaintances.

15. *Our orientation to time:* We can dwell less on the past or the future and experience a richer and more present now.
16. *Our relationship with ourselves:* We can cultivate greater self-compassion and self-respect and reduce our entanglements with addiction, anxiety, and despair.
17. *Our grudges:* We can perhaps release our bitter resentments and handed-down grudges (as between ethnic groups, religions, etc.).
18. *Our distaste for help:* We might reach out for the help that's available that we're currently avoiding out of embarrassment or stubborn pride.
19. *Our learning:* We can engage with new ideas, skills, and bodies of knowledge.
20. *Our pining for meaning:* We can remind ourselves that meaning isn't owed to us and that we are obliged to engage in meaning-making activities if we want the experience of meaning.

You might consider turning the above list into a handout that you use with your clients. Does that seem congruent with the way you coach and maybe feasible?

14.2 From bad faith to authentic living

When Alan, a 42-year-old corporate lawyer, first contacted John, an existential wellness coach, his email was clinical and to the point. "I feel hollow," he wrote. "I'm successful by most measures. I have a good income, a family, and a reputation. Yet I feel like I'm living someone else's life. I'd like to explore this with you." That last sentence hinted at something hopeful: a willingness to inquire into his own existence.

When he walked into John's office, he carried himself like a courtroom professional—pressed suit, measured tone, and careful articulation. But, as they spoke, the controlled surface gave way to flickers of discontent. "I know I'm supposed to be proud of what I've built," Alan said.

> My parents beam when they introduce me as a partner in the firm. My colleagues envy my corner office. But I wake up most mornings with dread. It's like I'm playing a role in a play I never auditioned for.

John recognized in Alan the classic signs of what existentialists call *bad faith*—the denial of one's own freedom by living according to imposed scripts and external validations, rather than according to chosen commitments. John saw his role as helping Alan move toward what existentialists call *authentic living*—a life owned, chosen, and actively embraced.

In their early sessions, John invited Alan to describe his days in detail. John narrated the grind: 80-hour workweeks, endless mergers and acquisitions, congratulatory nods from partners, and exhaustion at home.

"Do you hear yourself in this?" John asked. "Where are you in these descriptions—your desires, your values, your actual voice?"

Alan paused. "I guess I'm not really there. It's more like I'm reporting a weather forecast: corporate climate, stock market winds, client storms. I'm the reporter, not the person."

At a subsequent session, John introduced the idea of radical freedom—not as an abstract philosophy but as a daily reality. "You could resign from your firm tomorrow. You could walk away mid-trial. You could even decide to move to the mountains and herd goats. These are real possibilities."

Alan laughed nervously. "That would be insane."

"Insane, maybe. But possible. And that possibility means something: you are free. You may feel trapped, but you're not literally trapped. You are choosing this life every day, even by refusing to leave it."

Alan looked unsettled. "So, you're saying that all of this is my doing?"

"Yes. And that's the hard truth—and the liberating one. You are not a victim of your career, your parents, or your firm. You are responsible for the life you're living."

That conversation jolted Alan. He began to notice how often he blamed "the system," "the firm," or "expectations." He started catching himself mid-sentence: "I have to go to this dinner . . . well, actually, I'm choosing to go." Naming the choice made the weight of responsibility heavier, but also more real.

To deepen the work, John asked Alan to imagine himself at 70, looking back on his life. "What do you think that Alan would say about how you spent your years?"

Alan grew quiet. After a long silence, he said, "He'd say I wasted them. That I was so busy winning cases that I forgot to live."

This confrontation with finitude—another key element in existential coaching—cracked something open. He began journaling about mortality, writing letters to his future self, and noting each day whether he was living in alignment with what mattered or just rehearsing old performances.

The next step was to clarify what "authentic living" might look like for him. John asked him to name moments when he felt most alive. Alan surprised himself with the answers: coaching junior associates, mentoring law students, spending weekends hiking with his children, and writing essays about justice for obscure legal journals that no one in his firm cared about.

"These are moments where your voice and your values come through," John said. "What themes do you see?"

Alan reflected. "I like teaching. I like fairness more than profit. I like being in nature. I like writing."

For the first time, he looked animated rather than weary.

Rather than urging Alan to quit his job overnight, John invited Alan to experiment with small acts of authenticity. Alan began blocking off one evening a week to write, even if just for himself. He volunteered to lead a pro bono case, something his firm usually shunned. He started having real conversations with his wife about their future, rather than just logistical exchanges about bills and schedules.

Each small act produced anxiety. "I feel guilty skipping a client dinner," Alan admitted. "But then I realize I'm choosing to spend time with my kids instead. That feels right." The guilt, John explained, was part of shedding old scripts. Authenticity often feels uncomfortable at first!

Over time, Alan began crafting a new life narrative. "I used to think I was just a cog in a corporate machine," he confessed. "Now I'm starting to see myself as a lawyer who can choose his commitments. I don't have to be the firm's puppet. I can direct my energy toward what actually matters."

They talked about the existential courage required to sustain authenticity: the courage to disappoint others, to tolerate uncertainty, and to face the possibility of failure. Alan acknowledged the risks but felt more alive than he had in years. "Even the anxiety feels better than the numbness," he said.

As coaching progressed, Alan made concrete changes. He reduced his hours, shifted part of his practice toward advocacy work, and carved out regular time for writing. He spoke openly with his parents about his choices, bracing for their disapproval. To his surprise, they respected him more for his honesty than for his status.

Six months into their work, Alan said, "I feel like I'm finally at the wheel of my life. I may still be on the same highway, but now I'm driving, not being driven."

Alan's journey from bad faith to authenticity was not about abandoning the law or running away from responsibility. It was about facing his freedom squarely, accepting the burden of choice, and aligning his daily actions with his deeper values. He learned that authenticity is not a onetime achievement but a continual practice: choosing, owning, and living his life deliberately.

14.3 20 mini-vignettes

What follows are 20 mini-vignettes featuring an existential wellness coach working with clients on the issue of authenticity.

1. *The New Mother*
   Clara, 31, confessed that she felt trapped by cultural scripts of "good motherhood." She longed to admit that she sometimes resented the role. Her coach reassured her that authenticity often means telling the truth about ambivalence. They worked with journaling prompts such as, "What parts of motherhood feel real? What feels like performance?" Clara realized that she loved reading stories to her child but hated forced playdates. Naming those truths gave her permission to drop what didn't fit. Authenticity, her coach emphasized, didn't mean perfection—it meant honesty. Clara left the session lighter, ready to parent in her own way.

2. *The Retired Executive*
   At 68, Robert felt unmoored after retiring. "I was my job," he confessed. His coach asked, "Who are you when no one's watching?" That question unnerved him. Slowly, Robert recalled his love of woodworking, a passion he had abandoned decades ago. Together, they framed authenticity as rediscovery. The coach suggested small commitments: clearing a space in his garage, buying tools, and setting aside Saturday mornings. Robert realized authenticity wasn't a dramatic reinvention but a return to long-ignored truths. His identity began to shift from "retired executive" to "maker," a title that felt truer.
3. *The University Student*
   Nina, 20, had chosen a premed track because of parental pressure. "I'm suffocating," she told her coach. Together, they explored her fear of disappointing her family versus the cost of living inauthentically. Through values clarification, Nina identified creativity, freedom, and compassion as central. Medicine could serve compassion, but she admitted her heart belonged to the theater. The coach didn't tell her to switch majors but invited her to experiment—auditioning for a play while staying in school. Authenticity, her coach emphasized, often emerged through trial-and-error experimentation. Nina left realizing she could test her truth without immediate rupture.
4. *The Burned-Out Teacher*
   Mark, 39, said, "I'm exhausted from pretending I believe in the system." His coach asked what part of teaching still felt real. Mark said he loved one-on-one moments with students but hated standardized testing. They discussed how authenticity might mean focusing on what he loved rather than fighting every battle. Mark decided to start an after-school philosophy club where he could teach freely. His coach highlighted that even small, authentic acts can reorient a life. Mark realized he didn't have to quit teaching to reclaim his voice.
5. *The Recent Divorcee*
   Susan, 55, described her marriage as "twenty years of walking on eggshells." Now divorced, she felt both free and disoriented. Her coach encouraged her to reflect on who she was before the marriage. Through guided imagery, Susan recalled how alive she felt traveling solo in her twenties. Authenticity, her coach suggested, might mean reclaiming that adventurous self. Susan booked a short solo trip, nervous but excited. For her, authenticity wasn't about proving herself to anyone—it was about rediscovering her core courageous nature.
6. *The Tech Manager*
   Alex, 34, announced that he felt like a chameleon at work, adapting to please every superior. "I don't even know what I think anymore," he admitted. His coach asked him to identify moments when he had spoken up and felt proud, even if it had cost him. Alex remembered challenging a project's

ethics the prior year. That memory became an anchor. They developed a plan: each week, Alex would practice voicing one authentic opinion in meetings. Authenticity, the coach reminded him, had to be exercised like a muscle. Slowly, Alex began to feel less invisible.

7. *The Grieving Widow*
   Maria, 62, had lost her husband the year before but still lived as though he were beside her, following routines he had set. Her coach asked, "What would your day look like if it were yours alone?" The question startled her. She realized she always made coffee the way he liked it, not the way she did. Authenticity, the coach explained, can begin with small choices. Maria tried making her own style of breakfast. That tiny act of self-claiming became a symbol of moving forward authentically, not by erasing her grief but by allowing for her individuality.
8. *The College Dropout*
   Jared, 23, carried shame about leaving college. "I feel like a failure," he said. His coach reframed the matter: "What if leaving was the most authentic thing you've done?" Jared admitted he couldn't stand academia's pretenses and loved working with his hands. He had a knack for landscaping but dismissed it as "not serious." His coach challenged him: "Who says authenticity must look impressive?" Jared began to see his landscape work as artistry, not a fallback. Naming his truth restored dignity, and he began envisioning a full-time landscaping business.
9. *The Overachiever*
   Leah, 29, filled every spare hour with productivity. "If I slow down, I'll feel empty," she confessed. Her coach suggested an experiment: one hour a week of unstructured time. Leah panicked at first but then rediscovered her joy in sketching. Her coach pointed out that authenticity often hides beneath busyness. Leah realized her real self wasn't a machine for accomplishing things but an artist who needed space. That reframing allowed her to embrace idleness not as a waste of time but as incubation and alignment.
10. *The Pastor in Doubt*
    Reverend James, 50, privately admitted that he no longer believed in much of his church's doctrine. "But my whole life is built around it," he said. His coach acknowledged the terror of dismantling one's identity. Together, they explored what he did still believe—in community, in kindness, and in service. His coach suggested that he could lead authentically from those values rather than reciting creeds he no longer held. James realized authenticity didn't necessarily mean leaving the pulpit but rather reshaping his ministry around what felt true.
11. *The Young Activist*
    Maya, 25, confessed that activism had become performative. "I say what social media wants me to say," she admitted. Her coach asked, "What issues break your heart the most?" Maya realized that she felt most alive

working with children, though that wasn't "trendy." Her coach encouraged her to align her activism with her authentic passion, not external approval. Maya decided to volunteer at a literacy nonprofit. Authenticity, her coach explained, is found where conviction and care meet, not where applause is loudest.

12. *The Aging Parent*
    Helen, 72, confessed that she felt invisible, reduced to "grandma duties." Her coach asked her to identify the parts of herself that remained unexpressed. Helen admitted she still longed to paint, a passion she'd buried for decades. Her coach encouraged her to set up a small studio corner and commit to painting weekly. They discussed how authenticity meant, in part, refusing to disappear into roles. By picking up a brush again, Helen reclaimed her identity as more than a grandmother—she was also an artist.
13. *The College Athlete*
    Derrick, 21, struggled with the pressure to perform. "I feel like a brand, not a person," he said. His coach invited him to imagine life without sports. At first, Derrick panicked. Then, he admitted that he loved music, something he rarely shared. Authenticity, his coach explained, didn't necessarily require abandoning sports, but it did perhaps demand allowing hidden dimensions to surface. Derrick decided to join a campus band. For the first time, he felt whole rather than split between public image and private self.
14. *The Blocked Writer*
    Evelyn, 45, hadn't written in years. "Everything I produce feels fake," she told her coach. They explored whether she was writing for herself or for imagined critics. Evelyn admitted she had been chasing market trends. Her coach suggested an authenticity exercise: write one page daily with no audience in mind. At first, Evelyn resisted, but then raw, honest words began to flow. She rediscovered writing as a way of being, not performing. Authenticity returned not as a career move but as a form of self-expression.
15. *The People-Pleasing Artist*
    Clara, a painter, admitted that she painted for approval rather than self-expression. She showed her coach canvases that "sold well" but felt meaningless. The coach asked her, "What would you paint if no one ever saw it?" Clara burst into tears. She spoke about abstract, chaotic images she never dared share. Her coach guided her to create a "hidden studio practice" where she painted purely for herself. Within weeks, Clara rediscovered joy. Authenticity, she realized, meant creating from her center, even if others disapproved.
16. *The Executive Mask*
    David, a high-level executive, confessed that he always wore a mask of confidence. "If they knew how unsure I was, they'd fire me," he said. His coach challenged this belief: "What if authenticity inspires more trust than performance?" David hesitated but agreed to try showing vulnerability in one

meeting. He admitted to his team that he didn't have all the answers. Instead of backlash, he saw relief ripple across the room. His coach helped David see that authenticity didn't mean weakness—it meant human leadership.

17. *The Silent Marriage*
Lila had been married for 20 years but rarely shared her true feelings. "It's easier to keep the peace," she explained. Her coach asked her to imagine what her authentic voice might say if it could speak freely. Lila hesitated, then whispered, "I feel invisible." Her coach encouraged her to start small, practicing authenticity by expressing one honest sentence to her husband each day. Within months, Lila reported that conversations were deepening. For the first time, she felt seen.
18. *The Burned-Out Nurse*
Sofia came to coaching, exhausted and detached. She had become a nurse out of duty, not desire. "I'm living someone else's life," she said. Her coach asked her to recall a moment when she had felt deeply authentic. Sofia remembered traveling alone through Spain at 20, journaling each night. They explored what that memory revealed: that independence, creativity, and curiosity mattered deeply to her. Slowly, Sofia began weaving these elements back into her current life. Authenticity didn't require abandoning nursing immediately, but it did require honoring her own essence daily.
19. *The Tech Entrepreneur*
Ryan had sold his start-up for tens of millions of dollars but confessed to feeling fraudulent. "I built something successful, but it wasn't really me," he said. His coach asked, "Now that money isn't the issue, what might authentic living look like?" Ryan described mentoring young entrepreneurs and advocating for ethical technology. His coach suggested that he test this vision by volunteering with a local incubator. After several months, Ryan lit up in sessions, saying, "This feels real." Authenticity, he realized, was less about success and more about service.
20. *The Retired Teacher*
Margaret, 68, said she felt lost in retirement. "I don't know who I am without the classroom," she admitted. Her coach asked her to write a life review, highlighting moments when she had felt most herself. Margaret discovered a pattern: she thrived when mentoring young people individually. With her coach's encouragement, she began tutoring teens in writing. Soon, Margaret reported, "I feel authentic again—not because I'm teaching formally, but because I'm nurturing the next generation." Authenticity for her was not tied to a role but to a way of being.

These mini-vignettes present what might be called an "easy" authenticity: add a little painting practice to your life, start a philosophy club, mentor some students, etc. But authenticity in the real world, especially in hard times, can make severe demands. If just whispering something in public gets you fired, deported, jailed, or disappeared, what kind of courage is needed to whisper that truth? And is that even the good-faith thing to do if it costs your family everything?

To what extent are we obliged to remain true to our values if it ruins our family and our life? These are among the tremendously difficult, painful choices that real people must make in the real world. Authenticity is no laughing matter and no easy matter—and falling short of authentic action may often prove the wisest course. But then, having chosen discretion over "perfect" authentic action, we may find ourselves confronted by self-recriminations, guilt, and fury at the situation. All of this, an existential wellness coach must be prepared to encounter and handle.

To live authentically in our contemporary moment is both more challenging and more necessary than ever before. On the one hand, modern life offers extraordinary freedoms—opportunities to choose where we live, how we work, whom we love, and what meaning we make of our days. On the other hand, it surrounds us with pressures, distractions, and seductions that make bad faith living almost second nature. And high-risk situations, where acting authentically comes at a very high price, seem to be increasing daily.

Authentic living begins with awareness. We are obliged to cultivate the courage to examine the ways we have surrendered to scripts handed down by family, culture, or marketplace. This requires honest self-reflection: am I pursuing this career, relationship, or lifestyle because it genuinely expresses my values—or because it spares me the anxiety of disappointing others or the rewards of fitting in? Awareness does not guarantee that we will act authentically, but it opens up the possibility of choice—including very hard ones.

Choice lies at the heart of authenticity. Existential thinkers remind us that we are radically free: free to shape our identity, free to make meaning, and free to take responsibility for our lives. This freedom can feel daunting, even unbearable, in a world that tempts us with ready-made answers and confronts us with real dangers. But living authentically means embracing that freedom rather than hiding from it. Each day presents countless opportunities—small and large—to choose to live in alignment with our deepest values, rather than in obedience to convenience, approval, or fear.

To sustain authenticity, we must continually clarify our values. In an age of information overload, it is easy to lose track of what truly matters. Do we value justice, creativity, compassion, presence, or joy? If so, how are those values embodied in our daily choices? Without such clarity, we drift into conformity. With clarity, we gain a compass for decision-making, even amid the uncertainties and dangers of contemporary life.

Authenticity requires courage—the courage to risk failure, to accept uncertainty, and, at its extremities, to lose everything. The contemporary world promises security through conformity: the steady paycheck, the curated online persona, and the polite avoidance of uncomfortable truths. Authentic living refuses such comfort when it comes at the expense of selfhood—or at least puts the question on the table.

There is probably nothing like "perfect authenticity" available to us, since situations may prove too opaque and the consequences of authentic action may prove too dire. But it is still the high bar against which we measure how we are living and the state of being to which our clients, often unconsciously, aspire.

FOOD FOR THOUGHT

1. How would you describe "authenticity" in your own words?
2. What, if anything, regularly gets in the way of you living authentically?
3. Can you identify one of your "bad faith" moments? What happened? Are you still bothered by that memory?
4. Can you identify one of your "good faith" moments? What happened? Are you still bolstered by that memory?
5. What two or three tactics might you employ in working with your clients on "authentic action"?

Chapter 15

Creativity's place in the puzzle

Those with an existential bent tend to feel that there is some significant, even fundamental relationship between creativity and existential wellness. Why is that? As an existential wellness coach, and maybe as a creative yourself, you may harbor this same feeling. But what is that feeling really "about"?

It can't be that writing a novel, even a great one, or producing an abstract painting, even a striking one, really changes the landscape of life, with its indignities, disappointments, and finitude. So, why does "creating" loom so large in many people's lives, including likely just about all of your clients, to such an extent that they are determined to organize their lives around creating—and feel existentially terrible if they aren't creating?

Let's start our discussion with a historical look. The relationship between creativity and existential wellness has deep historical roots, stretching across philosophy, psychology, literature, and the arts. Our most existential writers, dating back thousands of years, have concerned themselves with this connection and felt moved to comment on it.

In Ancient Greece, thinkers like Plato and Aristotle linked creative activity (poetry, drama, and rhetoric) to the flourishing of the human spirit. Aristotle's concept of *eudaimonia* (living in accordance with one's potential) overlaps with what we now call *existential wellness*. Tragedy and comedy in Greek drama were explicitly about confronting fate, mortality, and meaning—core existential concerns. Creativity was seen as a way to engage with life's ultimate questions, whether through myth, ritual, or artistic production.

The Renaissance marked a turning point: human beings were celebrated as creators rather than passive recipients of divine order. Artists like Michelangelo and Leonardo da Vinci exemplified the idea that human creativity could mirror divine creation. Existential wellness here meant embracing individuality, agency, and dignity through acts of creation. Creativity was not just artistry but a way of *being fully human*.

In the late eighteenth and nineteenth centuries, Romanticism connected creativity with inner truth, authenticity, and emotional intensity. Figures like Goethe,

DOI: 10.4324/9781003724971-15

Shelley, and Wordsworth saw poetry and art as ways to wrestle with life's mysteries, the sublime, and mortality. Existential wellness in this period was linked to confronting despair and alienation with creative expression—turning suffering into beauty.

The nineteenth-century and twentieth-century existentialists—Kierkegaard, Nietzsche, Heidegger, Sartre, and Camus—explicitly tied creativity to the existential project of living authentically. Kierkegaard emphasized subjective truth and creativity as a leap of faith toward authentic existence. Nietzsche saw creativity as the ultimate act of affirming life, even in the face of nihilism. Camus emphasized creative revolt—the act of creating as a way of saying "yes" to life despite its absurdity. For existentialists, existential wellness wasn't about comfort or happiness but about *authentic engagement* with freedom and responsibility—more often than not, through creative acts.

Twentieth-century humanistic psychology, with its focus on self-actualization and manifesting human potential, made this link even more explicit. Maslow placed creativity at the top of his hierarchy of needs as part of self-actualization, a key to existential fulfillment. Rollo May saw creativity as central to courageously engaging life and resisting meaninglessness. Carl Rogers connected creativity with openness to experience, authenticity, and the fully functioning person. Creativity here was not limited to the arts—it was about an existential style of living creatively, flexibly, and authentically.

Today, in positive psychology, for instance, creativity is often seen as a pathway to meaning, resilience, and psychological flourishing—concepts overlapping with existential wellness. In coaching, therapy, and wellness practices, creativity is framed as a tool for confronting uncertainty, cultivating authenticity, and building meaning. Many contemporary thinkers describe creativity not only as making art but also as living creatively—a stance toward existence that fosters existential wellness.

15.1 Sartre, *Nausea*, and the existential importance of creativity

This all makes sense—and yet, why is creating *felt* to be so important by so many existential thinkers? Is it because the creative act feels meaningful to them in ways that nothing else really does, including intimate relationships, service, and all the other life purpose choices available to them? Is creating that special? It really appears to be.

Let's take a moment to consider one of the more revealing depictions of the importance of creating ever to appear in the existential literature. That would be the, to many unexpected and unconvincing, conclusion to Jean-Paul Sartre's novel *Nausea*, whose main character seems to solve all of his intractable and unbearable existential challenges in one fell swoop by deciding to write a book.

Sartre's *Nausea* (1943) is often remembered for its bleak depictions of contingency, absurdity, and the unsettling confrontation with the raw "being" of existence. Yet the novel does not end in despair. In its closing pages, the protagonist, Antoine Roquentin, glimpses a path out of nausea—not through religion, politics, or conventional attachments but through the creative act.

This is a controversial conclusion and freights the creative act with a great deal of importance. Can writing a book or singing a song really do that much work, even to the point of sparing the individual the experience of meaninglessness? Well, our creative and performing artist clients do typically hold the creative act as exactly that important, and, as existential wellness coaches, we are wise to acknowledge the pedestal upon which the creative act is regularly put by those who have fallen in love with a creative medium.

Sartre, at the conclusion of *Nausea*, gestures toward what would become a central theme of his existential philosophy: the idea that human beings can reclaim freedom and authenticity through acts of creation.

Throughout the novel, Roquentin suffers from a visceral recognition of contingency: things exist for no reason, stripped of purpose or necessity. The roots of a chestnut tree, the texture of objects, and even his own body appear alien and oppressive.

This encounter with "nausea" reveals the groundless facticity of existence. There is no essence preceding existence, no stable meaning to rely upon. Existence simply *is*, and human consciousness must face this vertiginous recognition. At the novel's end, however, Roquentin contemplates writing a book—not as a factual historical account (like the biography he has been working on) but as an artistic creation.

He imagines a work that will "justify" his life by transforming raw existence into form, by giving shape and necessity to what otherwise appears arbitrary. The thought of composing such a book fills him with a sense of possibility. For the first time, he senses a way to live authentically: not by fleeing from contingency but by engaging it through creation.

What Sartre is suggesting here is not that art abolishes absurdity but that it provides a way of encountering it actively rather than passively. To write is to take responsibility for one's freedom, to impose form upon the chaos without denying the chaos. Art does not prove that existence has inherent meaning; rather, it demonstrates that human beings are capable of *making meaning*. The creative act, thus, becomes an existential affirmation, a choice to live deliberately in the face of contingency.

In this sense, Roquentin's artistic resolution anticipates Sartre's later philosophical formulations. In *Being and Nothingness* (1943), Sartre argues that human beings are "condemned to be free," always responsible for creating values through their choices. In *What is Literature?* (1947), he will frame writing as a paradigmatic act of freedom, where the writer both asserts and invites freedom.

The conclusion of *Nausea* foreshadows these ideas by dramatizing the shift from passive despair to active creation.

Importantly, Sartre does not romanticize art as salvation. Roquentin's imagined novel is not a guarantee of happiness or transcendence. Instead, it represents a way of living authentically with the absurd. By transforming the world through artistic effort, the individual does not escape nausea but learns to work with it, shaping it into something bearable, even beautiful.

The conclusion of *Nausea* announces, affirms, and asserts the existential importance of creativity. It is through creative acts, Sartre argues, that individuals confront the groundlessness of existence, claim their freedom, and construct meaning. Sartre's Roquentin does not find comfort in God, history, or nature but rather in the realization that, by creating, he can live authentically in a contingent world.

You may agree or disagree with this contention. It is quite reasonable to disagree with it. However, as an existential wellness coach, it is wise to recognize the extent to which your clients may agree and, in agreement, tremendously lament not creating.

It isn't just that they aren't working on their novel or not creating performance opportunities. They are failing at what they themselves perceive to be their most important meaning-making activity. If you can help them return to creating or performing, something that matters to them so much, you will have helped them greatly.

15.2 Coaching the struggling writer

When Daniel first sat down across from Mara, an existential wellness coach, he looked as if he were carrying a weight heavier than his own body. A novelist who had published one successful book a decade earlier, he had since been unable to finish another manuscript. His shelves were stacked with abandoned drafts, half-formed characters, and ideas that had once glowed with promise but now seemed to mock him.

"I don't know if I'm still a writer," he confessed in the first session.

> It feels like that identity belonged to someone younger, hungrier, and maybe more naïve. I still have the desire, but when I sit at the desk, everything feels pointless. Why make another book in a world already drowning in words? Why add my voice to the noise?

Mara nodded slowly. She had heard versions of this despair before—not only from writers but also from painters, entrepreneurs, and even people approaching retirement. What linked them was the existential question behind their complaint: *does what I do matter, and if not, do I even matter?*

Rather than leaping in with solutions, Mara began with presence. "For now," she said, "let's sit with the experience of being someone who wants to create and feels unable to. What does it feel like to be in that gap?"

Daniel frowned but then exhaled.

> It's like being half alive. Like I'm surviving but not really living. When I wrote my first book, even on bad days, I felt connected to something—myself, my characters, maybe even the universe. Now I feel severed from that connection.

Mara recognized this language as the vocabulary of existential wellness. Wellness, in this frame, wasn't merely about physical health or stress reduction. It was about forging and maintaining a tolerable, even passionate, relationship with life. For creative people, that often meant a relationship with their own work. To lose that relationship could feel like losing life itself.

Over the next sessions, Mara helped Daniel map the existential terrain of his struggle. Together, they identified several intertwined themes:

- *Meaning and Purpose.* Writing had once provided Daniel with meaning, but now he questioned its value.
- *Freedom and Responsibility.* He felt trapped but also guilty because no one was stopping him from writing; he was stopping himself.
- *Identity.* His self-image as a writer was under siege.
- *Mortality and Time.* At 46, he felt time slipping away. "If I don't write another book soon, maybe I never will," he said.

By making these themes explicit, Mara offered Daniel a framework that was larger than his personal block. This reframing lifted his struggle out of the realm of "writer's block" and into the broader, more dignified landscape of human existence.

Mara knew that existential wellness coaching often hinged on helping clients reclaim a sense of freedom. One afternoon, she asked Daniel to imagine he had absolute permission to write badly, foolishly, and even incomprehensibly.

"What if your next book was meant only for you?" she asked. "Not for critics, not for readers, not even for publication. Just for the experience of writing."

Daniel chuckled. "That sounds like a diary, not a novel."

"Perhaps," Mara said. "But maybe the act of writing is what you're missing, more than the artifact. What would it mean to write only to feel alive again?"

That thought unsettled Daniel, but it also loosened something. That evening, he wrote three messy pages about a man wandering a city of abandoned libraries. He didn't know if it was a story or just an image, but he felt a flicker of aliveness.

As weeks passed, Mara gently brought Daniel's attention to the shadow cast by his first book's success. "It sounds like you're competing with your younger self," she suggested.

Daniel sighed. "Yes. I'm afraid anything new will be compared to that book, and I'll come up short."

Mara invited him to consider whether meaning had to come from *recognition.* "If existential wellness is partly about choosing your relationship with life," she said, "what if you chose to measure success differently—not by acclaim, but by the depth of engagement, the courage to try again?"

This reframing allowed Daniel to see that his paralysis wasn't only about creativity but also about existential courage. To write again was to risk disappointment, yet not writing was a greater risk: the risk of living half a life.

In another session, Mara asked Daniel to reflect on how writing itself could be a meaning-making practice, independent of outcome. "What if creativity is not about producing something valuable for others," she said, "but about actively making meaning for yourself in the face of existence?"

This resonated deeply. Daniel had always thought of writing as a contribution, but he began to see it also as an existential stance. By writing, he was saying, *I am here. I grapple with the world. I shape chaos into a story.*

To reinforce this insight, Mara encouraged him to journal daily—not with the pressure of producing fiction but with the freedom to engage life through words. These journals became a quiet laboratory of meaning. He wrote about his fear of death, his longing for connection, and his memories of childhood. He began to notice how writing restored a sense of coherence to his days.

As his relationship with writing warmed, Daniel realized how isolated he had become. He avoided other writers because their productivity embarrassed him. Mara suggested that existential wellness often flourishes in community, not solitude. "Isolation can make despair feel larger than it is," she said. "What would it mean to share your struggle with others?"

Hesitantly, Daniel joined a small workshop group of mid-career writers. At first, he felt ashamed to admit his decade-long drought. But, when others confessed their own cycles of doubt, he felt relief. The act of sharing normalized his experience and reanchored him in a community of fellow travelers.

By the sixth month of coaching, Daniel had filled several notebooks and drafted 120 pages of a new novel. He didn't yet know if it would cohere, but he no longer measured its worth solely by completion.

In a pivotal session, Mara asked him to articulate what he had learned. Daniel said:

> Writing isn't just a career; it's how I stay in dialogue with existence. Even when the work feels small, the act of creating pushes back against despair. Existential wellness, for me, means choosing to write despite uncertainty, despite fear, because it connects me to life.

Mara smiled. "That's it. Creativity isn't separate from existential wellness—it's one of its most powerful expressions. By choosing to create, you're choosing life, again and again."

Daniel never reclaimed the naive confidence of his younger years. But he discovered something sturdier: a conscious, deliberate commitment to live as a writer, even in the face of doubt. Through Mara's coaching, he came to see creativity not only as producing books but also as practicing existential wellness—crafting meaning, embracing freedom, and cultivating a life in which writing was not optional but essential.

The work of writing remained difficult, but now, Daniel understood it as a chosen struggle, a way of saying yes to life. And in that choice, he rediscovered both his voice and his vitality.

15.3 Coaching the despondent painter

When Sofia entered the small studio where her existential wellness coach, Mara, held sessions, she carried a sketchbook tucked under her arm. Her hands bore faint traces of paint, though she confessed that she hadn't touched a canvas in weeks.

"I used to paint every day," she began, her voice heavy. "It wasn't always good, but it kept me sane. Lately, I can't see the point. The world feels on fire—climate change, politics, violence—and my little canvases of flowers and abstract shapes seem . . . trivial."

Mara recognized this dilemma: the collision between personal creativity and the enormity of the world's suffering. For many artists, existential wellness falters when their art feels insignificant against vast crises.

In their early sessions, Mara encouraged Sofia to name what she was carrying.

"I feel guilty," Sofia admitted. "Like I should be doing something more direct, more useful. Activism, volunteering, *something.* Not painting."

"Guilt is often a sign that you're wrestling with responsibility," Mara reflected. "But responsibility doesn't always mean abandoning what you love. Let's explore what painting *means* to you, beyond the surface of pretty pictures."

Sofia paused. "It's how I breathe. It's how I touch beauty. But is beauty enough when the world is falling apart?"

Here, Mara introduced the idea that existential wellness often lies in reconciling contradictions—accepting that beauty and suffering coexist and that creativity can be both a private refuge and a public act of resistance.

In one session, Mara asked Sofia to imagine a world without paintings, music, or poetry.

"It would be unbearable," Sofia whispered. "Like the soul would have no place to rest."

"Then why assume your contribution is trivial?" Mara asked. "Might painting be precisely what keeps the human spirit alive during difficult times?"

This perspective softened Sofia's guilt. She began to see beauty not as escapism but as nourishment—her canvases could be small acts of existential care for herself and, potentially, for others.

As their work deepened, another theme emerged. Sofia, at 52, had spent decades as a mother and part-time art teacher. Now her children were grown, and she was no longer teaching.

"I think I don't know who I am without those roles," she confessed. "Maybe I used painting to fill the gaps, but it feels thin now."

Mara suggested that existential wellness involved continually rewriting one's identity in response to life's changes. "What if this is an invitation to claim painting not as a filler, but as a core identity?"

That idea startled Sofia. "Could I really be 'a painter,' not just someone who paints?"

"That's your choice," Mara said. "Existence asks us to choose who we will be."

To loosen Sofia's fear of inadequacy, Mara proposed an experiment. "For a month, let painting be a laboratory. Not for finished works, not for galleries, just for exploration. Give yourself the freedom to play."

Sofia reluctantly agreed. She began working on large sheets of butcher paper instead of stretched canvas, using bold gestures with no thought of outcome. To her surprise, she felt exhilarated. The act of moving color around—blue streaks, gold splashes, and black smudges—reminded her of being a child with finger paint.

"This doesn't feel trivial," she told Mara. "It feels raw. It feels alive."

As trust deepened, Sofia admitted another layer of fear: mortality. "I lost a friend to cancer last year. It made me realize how finite our time is. Part of me thinks—why start anything I might not finish?"

Mara nodded. "Mortality often tempts us into paralysis. But it can also remind us that each brushstroke matters because it may be our last. How might painting become your way of saying yes to life, while you still can?"

Sofia was quiet, then said, "Maybe that's the point. Not to leave a legacy, but to live fully now."

Mara also noticed Sofia's isolation. She painted alone, rarely showing her work. "Existential wellness can grow when we let others witness our creations," Mara suggested.

Nervously, Sofia joined a local artist circle. When she unveiled her butcher paper experiments, she expected confusion. Instead, the group applauded her boldness. One woman even said, "Your work makes me want to try again."

This moment shifted something in Sofia. She saw that her painting could ripple outward, encouraging others, even if in small ways.

By the eighth month of coaching, Sofia was painting regularly again but now with a deeper sense of purpose. She no longer dismissed her art as trivial.

Instead, she framed it as both resistance against despair and self-care in the face of life's uncertainties.

In one session, she summarized her learning:

> Beauty isn't an escape—it's a lifeline. My painting is my way of affirming life, even in a broken world. Existential wellness, for me, means choosing to create not because the world is light, but because it is dark—and needs light.

Mara smiled. "You've reclaimed your voice as a painter. Not by denying suffering, but by painting alongside it."

15.4 Coaching the aging dancer

When Aisha entered the coaching space, her movements were graceful even in her small gestures—tucking her hair behind her ear, crossing her legs, and placing her water bottle on the floor with a dancer's instinct for balance. Yet her words were heavy.

"I don't know if I can keep dancing," she said quietly. "I'm thirty-eight. My body hurts more than it used to. My opportunities are shrinking. Sometimes I feel like I've already danced my last real dance."

Mara, her existential wellness coach, had worked with artists of many kinds, but dancers often carried a unique existential challenge: their art was inseparable from their body, and time inevitably changed that body. For Aisha, existential wellness was entangled with aging, identity, and the fear of losing the very medium through which she expressed herself.

In their first sessions, Mara encouraged Aisha to name what was most frightening.

"It isn't just about pain," Aisha admitted. "It's about disappearing. If I'm not a dancer, who am I? My whole identity is wrapped up in movement. Without it, I feel like nothing."

Mara acknowledged the depth of this struggle.

"Existential wellness is partly about choosing a relationship with life that feels bearable, even when life changes. For you, the question may be: can you remain in relationship with dance, even if the form shifts?"

Aisha frowned. "But if I can't leap the way I used to or spin the way I used to . . . is it still dance?"

To help Aisha face her shrinking physical freedom, Mara introduced a reframe: "All of us live with limits—mortality, time, gravity. The existential challenge is whether we can still find freedom inside those limits. What if your art isn't ending, but transforming?"

Aisha was skeptical but intrigued. Mara suggested an experiment: instead of rehearsing full choreography, Aisha would improvise movements that worked with her current body, not against it.

Aisha returned the next week, surprised. "I moved slowly. I let my body choose what it wanted. It was . . . different. But also, powerful. I felt like I was dancing my age, instead of pretending to be younger."

As the coaching deepened, Aisha spoke about her growing awareness of mortality. "I've given my whole life to something ephemeral. A performance happens, and then it vanishes. When I die, it will all vanish with me."

Mara leaned in gently. "That impermanence is at the core of human existence. But could it also be a source of meaning? Dance has always been fleeting—that's what makes it so alive. Every performance is a reminder that life itself is temporary."

This insight struck Aisha deeply. For the first time, she began to see the ephemerality of dance not as a flaw but as a mirror of existence. "Maybe that's what makes it beautiful," she whispered.

In another session, Mara challenged Aisha to imagine an identity beyond performance. "Is being a dancer only about being on stage?"

Aisha hesitated. "I've taught classes, mentored younger dancers. Sometimes I choreograph. But those always felt secondary, like shadows of the real thing."

"What if they're not shadows," Mara asked, "but extensions of your dance identity? What if your existential wellness depends not on clinging to a single form but expanding into new ones?"

This planted a seed. Aisha began experimenting with choreography workshops, where she guided others to move expressively. To her surprise, watching students discover their own voices in movement brought her a new sense of vitality.

A central theme of the coaching was helping Aisha reconnect with meaning. She often asked, "Does it even matter that I dance, when the world is filled with suffering?"

Mara echoed a lesson she had shared with other artists: "Existential wellness isn't about erasing suffering. It's about creating meaning alongside it. Dance may not stop wars, but it can remind people of aliveness, connection, and joy. That matters."

Aisha began to test this idea by performing small improvisations in unconventional spaces—community centers, senior homes, and even a local park. The reactions surprised her: an elderly woman in tears, a child imitating her movements with delight, and strangers pausing to watch in stillness.

"These moments felt truer than the stage," she told Mara. "Like I was giving something essential, not just performing."

As months passed, Aisha's relationship with dance shifted. She no longer framed her life in terms of loss but in terms of choice. "I may not leap as high," she said, "but I can choose how I move, where I move, and who I move with. I can choose to keep dancing as long as I breathe."

Mara reflected back: "That's the heart of existential wellness—acknowledging limits while claiming your freedom to choose. You've chosen dance as your way of affirming life, in whatever form it takes."

By the end of a year of coaching, Aisha had embraced a broader, deeper identity. She was still a dancer but also a choreographer, a mentor, and a living testament to embodied creativity across the lifespan. She no longer feared that her art was trivial or on the verge of vanishing. Instead, she saw each movement as a declaration: *I am alive, and this moment matters.*

15.5 Helping clients reclaim their creative nature

Here are seven tips for existential wellness coaches who are working with clients to help them reclaim their creative nature:

1. *Reframe Creativity as a Birthright*
   Many clients arrive convinced they "aren't creative." They equate creativity only with painting or writing, ignoring the creative ways they already problem-solve, cook, garden, or design their days. As an existential wellness coach, you can help clients see creativity as a birthright rather than a rare talent.
   This reframing reduces the shame and pressure associated with creativity and makes it easier for clients to step into creative living. By emphasizing that creativity is less about producing masterpieces and more about expressing individuality, you create permission for experimentation.
   Invite clients to recall childhood moments of imaginative play—when creativity was spontaneous and free from judgment. By anchoring them in those memories, you help dissolve internalized messages that have stifled their creative impulse. The existential dimension here is profound: reclaiming creativity is reclaiming agency and uniqueness, a way of resisting conformity and affirming the self as a source of newness and possibility.
2. *Address Bad Faith*
   Existentialists warn against *bad faith*—living according to external scripts rather than authentic desire. Many clients suppress creativity because they believe it is "impractical," "childish," or "not what adults do."
   These are forms of bad faith, where social norms override authentic longings. As a coach, you can help clients recognize these internalized voices for what they are: borrowed narratives, not truths.
   Once named, these stories lose their grip. Invite clients to notice every time they say, "I can't," "I shouldn't," or "I'm not good enough," and explore whose voice is speaking. Then, have them shift toward authentic choices: "What would *you* do if no one were watching? What small creative action could you take that feels true, even if it defies practicality?"
   By challenging bad faith, you help clients return to the authenticity of self-expression, reminding them that choosing creativity is an existential declaration of freedom.

3. *Explore the Link Between Meaning and Creativity*
   Many clients feel blocked because they separate creativity from meaning. They may say, "I don't have time for art when I need to focus on real life." As a coach, you can help clients see creativity as a pathway to meaning-making.
   Creative acts allow individuals to shape raw experience into something that reflects their values and identity. Encourage clients to identify what matters most to them—connection, beauty, truth, and justice—and then explore creative forms that embody those values.
   A client who values justice might write essays, create activist art, or design community events. Someone else who treasures beauty might return to photography or gardening. By linking creativity to existential purpose, you shift it from a "luxury" to an existential necessity. The deeper insight is that creativity is not separate from life but one of the richest ways to affirm meaning, stave off despair, and fully engage existence.
4. *Normalize Creative Anxiety*
   Many clients expect creativity to feel effortless. When they encounter fear, doubt, or resistance, they assume they lack talent. An existential wellness coach can normalize creative anxiety as part of the process.
   Creativity always involves risk—the risk of failure, of exposure, and of confronting one's limitations. Anxiety here is not pathology but proof that something significant is at stake. By helping clients accept anxiety as a companion to creativity, you reduce its power to paralyze.
   Offer tools: grounding exercises, journaling prompts about the fear itself, or gentle exposure (sharing work with one trusted person before going public). This approach reframes anxiety as a signpost of authenticity: "You care about this because it matters."
   The existential lesson is clear—living authentically means stepping into uncertainty. Creativity, with all its discomfort, becomes a training ground for embracing freedom, ambiguity, and the courage to bring forth the self.
5. *Encourage Rituals of Creative Renewal*
   Creativity flourishes when it is nurtured through ritual. As a coach, you can help clients develop personal rituals that mark creative time as cherished time. This might mean lighting a candle before journaling, setting aside Sunday mornings for painting, or taking a daily walk to gather impressions.
   Rituals create psychological boundaries that honor creativity as essential rather than optional. They also serve as existential anchors, reminding clients that creative expression is part of their chosen way of being. Encourage clients to experiment until they discover what rituals feel nourishing—some may prefer silence and solitude, while others may need movement or music.

The act of ritual itself reinforces meaning-making, as clients consciously choose to shape their lives around what matters. By cultivating these small, steady practices, you help clients reclaim not only their creative nature but also their power to structure life in alignment with authenticity.

6. *Challenge Perfectionism and Productivity Narratives*
   Perfectionism often kills creativity before it starts. Clients may equate creative worth with recognition, financial success, or flawless outcomes. As an existential wellness coach, you can help clients separate the act of creating from external measures. Invite them to make "bad art" on purpose, to write messy drafts, and to dance clumsily. These exercises loosen the grip of perfectionism and restore joy to the process.

   Equally important is dismantling the productivity narrative—the idea that creativity must justify itself economically or practically. By naming these cultural pressures, you help clients resist them and return to creativity as self-expression, exploration, and play. The existential insight is that meaning does not need external validation. Choosing to create—even imperfectly—is an act of freedom. It declares, "I am more than my utility. I am a being capable of shaping, imagining, and expressing."
7. *Frame Creativity as Resistance to Nihilism*
   In a world often marked by despair, injustice, and meaninglessness, creativity becomes an existential act of resistance. As a coach, you can help clients see their creative efforts not as trivial hobbies but as responses to nihilism.

   Writing a poem, painting a canvas, or crafting a melody asserts that beauty, expression, and imagination matter. This perspective infuses creativity with urgency and dignity. Invite clients to explore how their creativity confronts despair: perhaps through storytelling that preserves memory, art that protests injustice, or music that creates joy.

   Framing creativity this way helps clients understand that reclaiming their creative nature is not self-indulgent but life-affirming. It is a way of saying "yes" to existence, even amid suffering. The existential reward is profound: clients discover that each creative act is a thread in the tapestry of meaning, a lived refusal to surrender to emptiness or despair.

This chapter is a too-brief examination of the connection between creativity and existential wellness. When a person chooses "creating" as a life purpose and a central meaning container, or is chosen by it, that decision or calling is life-organizing. Existential wellness coaches need to recognize and honor creativity's exalted place in the lives of many of our clients.

FOOD FOR THOUGHT

1. What are your thoughts about the relationship(s) between creativity and existential wellness?
2. Do you consider yourself creative? If you do, do you have trouble manifesting your creative nature?
3. If you don't consider yourself creative, why do you think that might be?
4. What do you see as the special issues of your creative clients?
5. What two or three top suggestions might you offer to creatives who are trying to reignite their creative nature or succeed at a creative profession?

Chapter 16

The possibility of existential joy

Our clients come to us with problems, challenges, concerns, goals, and so on. Where in that picture is the possibility of joy?

Existentialism, and by extension existential coaching, has an answer. And thank goodness that it does! Can you imagine only experiencing anxiety, dread, despair, and the other dark sides of existence? But, fortunately, existential joy is also available—to us and to our clients.

16.1 The history of the concept of existential joy

The notion of *existential joy* is not as widely discussed as its cousins, *existential anxiety* and *existential despair*. But it has a long and intriguing history that stretches across the domains of philosophy, religion, literature, and psychology. Existential anxiety and existential despair emphasize dread and alienation in the face of freedom and mortality, whereas existential joy highlights the possibility of affirmation, gratitude, and even delight in living.

The seeds of the concept of "existential joy" can be found in ancient philosophy, particularly in Greek thought. For the Stoics, the human being was a rational creature embedded in an ordered cosmos. To live in harmony with the logos—the rational principle of the universe—was to experience serenity and a kind of joy in accepting one's place in the cosmic order. Epictetus, for instance, urged his students to focus only on what lies within their control. The joy he described was not the fleeting pleasure of good fortune but a resilient affirmation of life that came from aligning one's will with nature.

The Epicureans, in contrast, emphasized pleasure as the highest good, but not in the sense of indulgence. For Epicurus, the deepest joy was the absence of fear—especially the fear of death. His famous dictum, "Death is nothing to us," opened the possibility of existential joy: once we accept mortality, we can experience the sweetness of life without dread.

Religious traditions provided their visions and versions of existential joy. In Christianity, joy was often framed as a gift of grace. Augustine, in his

DOI: 10.4324/9781003724971-16

Confessions, described the restless heart that finds peace only in God. The joy that arises when that restlessness is stilled is deeply existential: it responds to the human condition of longing, uncertainty, and finitude but transforms it into rapture in the divine.

In Buddhism, too, the insight into that life is impermanent and suffused with suffering leads not only to detachment but also to liberation. The joy of nirvana is an existential joy—it comes precisely from awakening to the truths of existence rather than denying them.

The Renaissance and Enlightenment shifted the ground. Human beings began to be conceived not only as fallen creatures or cosmic actors but also as autonomous individuals. With autonomy came exhilaration and dread—the mixture that would later be called the "existential condition." Montaigne, for instance, wrote his *Essays* as an exploration of what it means to live with death always at one's shoulder. His conclusion was not despair but a kind of joyous acceptance: "To philosophize is to learn how to die," he wrote, suggesting that the practice of confronting mortality could lead to lightness in life.

Spinoza carried this further. For him, joy was a central affect—the increase in one's power to act. His rationalist metaphysics identified human freedom not with arbitrary choice but with alignment to necessity. To the extent that one understands the necessity of things, one is free, and this understanding produces joy. In Spinoza, existential joy emerges as a recognition of the self's place within the infinite whole, combined with the expansion of one's power of understanding.

The Enlightenment's faith in reason and progress was not without its shadows, but it also allowed the idea of existential joy to expand. The human being, freed from superstition and external authority, could find joy in freedom itself. Then came the nineteenth century, with its emphasis on existential anxiety, but even there, joy found a place. Kierkegaard, for instance, although he dwelt on despair and anxiety, also articulated a vision of existential joy rooted in faith. For Kierkegaard, to embrace one's individuality before God, to leap into the absurd, was to find a joy that transcended rational calculation.

Nietzsche radicalized the theme. He diagnosed the "death of God" as a cultural crisis but offered the possibility of joy in its wake: *amor fati*, the love of one's fate. Nietzsche's ideal of the *Übermensch* is a figure who says "yes" to existence, affirming even suffering and tragedy as necessary components of life's richness. The doctrine of eternal recurrence dramatized this: could one will to live one's life again, endlessly, exactly as it had been? The joy of the one who can say "yes" to that possibility is Nietzsche's existential joy—the ultimate affirmation of life without appeal to transcendence.

The nineteenth century sharpened the idea of existential joy, identifying it as not naïve happiness but a defiant or paradoxical affirmation of existence in the face of suffering, doubt, and finitude. Then came the twentieth century, where the idea of existential joy experienced further refinement. Heidegger, for instance, emphasized *Gelassenheit* (releasement), a mode of being in which one accepts the openness of existence. While not "joy" in a superficial sense, this acceptance can be seen as an existential serenity or joy: a readiness to dwell poetically in the world.

Sartre, with his stark emphasis on freedom, depicted anguish as the recognition of radical responsibility. Yet Sartre also acknowledged a kind of exhilaration in freedom. To recognize that one is "condemned to be free" is heavy, but it also opens the possibility of joyous self-creation.

Camus articulated a notion of existential joy more explicitly. In *The Myth of Sisyphus*, he portrays Sisyphus, endlessly pushing his boulder, as the emblem of the human condition. Yet Camus concludes with a stunning reversal: "One must imagine Sisyphus happy." The joy is not in escaping absurdity but in embracing it: the joy is in the act of rebellion, in the act of saying "yes" to life even when it has no ultimate meaning.

Later, existential and phenomenological thinkers like Merleau-Ponty and Levinas emphasized intersubjectivity and responsibility, suggesting that joy can arise in relation to others. The joy of ethical responsibility, of responding to the face of the other, deepens the existential tradition by linking joy not only to solitude but also to community.

In contemporary psychology, especially existential therapy, the theme of joy gained renewed attention. Viktor Frankl, survivor of the concentration camps, argued in *Man's Search for Meaning* that even in the most terrible conditions, human beings can find meaning. And in finding meaning, they can experience a kind of existential joy—a joy grounded not in circumstances but in attitude. His famous line, "Those who have a 'why' to live, can bear almost any 'how,'" captures the paradoxical resilience of existential joy.

Positive psychology, though not always explicitly existential, has explored related concepts. The idea of "tragic optimism" echoes the existential tradition: the capacity to affirm life despite pain and loss. Existential joy here is framed as gratitude, resilience, and the ability to savor existence even under the shadow of mortality.

Spiritual movements outside of traditional religion have also embraced existential joy. Practices like mindfulness and secular meditation encourage acceptance of impermanence and the cultivation of joy in the present moment. This joy is existential in the deepest sense: it arises not from escaping mortality and freedom but from embracing them.

The history of existential joy reveals it as a counterpoint to existential anxiety, but not its negation. Anxiety arises from the confrontation with freedom, death, and meaninglessness; joy arises from affirming those very conditions. From the Stoics' acceptance of fate to Nietzsche's *amor fati*, from Kierkegaard's leap of faith to Camus' happy Sisyphus, and from Frankl's search for meaning to mindfulness practices today, existential joy has been articulated as the paradoxical affirmation of life in the face of its limits.

Existential joy is thus not mere happiness or optimism. It is certainly not denial. Rather, it is a profound orientation toward existence itself—a saying "yes" to life, to freedom, to mortality, and to uncertainty. It is the recognition that even in suffering, even in absurdity, there is the possibility of affirmation. In a world marked by uncertainty, crisis, and fragmentation, existential joy offers not a cure but a stance: a way of being that affirms life as it is.

16.2 Opportunities for joy

Life allows for joy, pleasure, satisfaction, happiness, amazement, grandeur, ecstasy, and elation—it allows for all of that! Not every moment, not every time, not in every season, but to discount its availability would be to make a mistake.

Existential joy is that special joy that reminds us of mortality, humanity, and possibility all at once. It is the way that seeing a child at play produces a joy that is all mixed up with amazement at the species, fear for the species, new beginnings, inevitable death, and much more. That smile that we smile as we watch a child at play is a complicated smile, with pleasure, wistfulness, and wonder all mixed together.

What can produce existential joy? There are many candidates and many opportunities. One candidate is beauty. "Beauty" is both a suspect word, as we can be seduced by beautiful things, for instance, by a glorious sunset caused by air pollution, and it is also as pure a word as we possess, as when some pigments on a canvas bring us unadulterated joy. Beauty has that special power, and encountering beauty is an opportunity to experience joy.

Another candidate is love. Aren't love and joy natural partners? If we opt to love, as opposed to standing back at arm's length and stonily observing the universe, won't we feel that warmth circulating all through our body?

Another candidate is service. When, as a volunteer, we care for an infant brought to an emergency care nursery and see that infant smile after all her crying, the joy we feel is immense. For one split second, we experience a warmth that is indescribable.

Another candidate is mastery. It can bring us joy that we have excelled at something. It can bring us joy that we did a hard thing well. If we both do the next right thing and do it well, what more can we ask of ourselves? And some joy is likely to follow!

Another candidate is creativity. "Creativity" is the word we use to stand for manifesting loves like writing, painting, singing, crafting, and inventing. Spinning a yarn or spinning yarn are age-old joys that remain available to us today.

Another candidate is intimacy. There is no joy like the joy of chatting quietly with an intimate. In that secure space, the world seems safer and saner. And then, there is family. Maybe it isn't our birth family: maybe they are too difficult and not to our liking. If that's the case, then we go about creating our own family, and we lavish friendship, loyalty, and caring there.

And what if a given moment of joy is brief? So be it! Say that your child marries. The ceremony may be quite brief. But those few minutes can be as rich as any other minutes can be. And, somewhere within us, they likely last forever. How can you calculate the value of something that takes only a second but that also lasts forever?

Moments of joy, suddenly here and suddenly gone, are not just passing moments. They are momentous. So, we covet them, we prize them, and we angle for them. And if, sadly, we happen to rarely or never experience them, we step to the side (a metaphor for taking a moment to reflect) and try to figure out why.

We have available to us that step to the side, that step that we take to provide ourselves with time and space to practice awareness. How many more joys and pleasures might we experience if we stepped to the side and took careful stock?

16.3 Angling for some joy

Say that you've been living one of your life purposes, for instance, writing your novel. You stop to make yourself a cup of tea. As the water boils, you might worry that what you've just written was terrible—or, you could "decide" to experience joy at having honorably worked. Imagine what a difference that could make!

Imagine! There you are, standing in the kitchen, waiting for the water to boil, and instead of beating yourself up about your last few paragraphs or shaking your fist at the publishing gods, you allow yourself a moment of joy at having written. You got that precious moment of joy by allowing for it, by angling for it, and by wanting it.

A little joy is surely better than no joy. A client who can't point to a single thing that brings her joy is in crisis, and therefore, we listen carefully for that joylessness in the stories that our clients tell us. We listen, and we look for opportunities to suggest a tactic or a strategy that might bring a little joy into our client's life.

Say that your client finds himself in a joyless marriage. Well, maybe he should leave that marriage. But, perhaps, he has his reasons for staying. If so, then he's obliged to invest in the marriage, including looking for ways for the two of them to experience some joy. What might the two of them enjoy?

Maybe, on your invitation, he'll make a list of possibilities—most of which will maybe strike him as implausible or unavailable. There, far down the list, is a weekend away. That strikes him as just barely possible. Further down the list is walking side-by-side holding hands. That strikes him as a little weird and awkward feeling, but also possible. As he sits with his list, he can feel those two becoming actual candidates. A weekend away? Walking side-by-side, holding hands? Worth an investment?

So, your client proposes that weekend away, including painting a picture of the two of them holding hands. His partner is surprised, skeptical, and pleased all at once. Already, your client may be feeling a slight tingle of joy, pleasure, and excitement. No, the universe has not magically shifted on its axis. But suddenly, a bit more joy exists than did the second before!

You can't count on that weekend working some magic for your client. It is merely an opportunity. Are you confident that it will bring joy? Maybe it will, maybe it won't. Has anything changed? Maybe it hasn't—but maybe it has. Surely your client is now standing more open to some pleasure, some joy, and some happiness! And while nothing joyful may happen, something joyful maybe will. And if it does? Well, you hope that your client will repeat the experience!

16.4 The many faces of joy

Existential joy comes in many guises. Here is a small collection of those guises. You might want to add to this list. The more sources of existential joy you can identify, the more equipped you are to invite clients to find joy in life. And the more equipped you yourself will be! As you read this list, and once you are done with this list, consider what you might add. I hope that many things come to mind!

1. *The joy of being what we are*
   "To be what we are, and to become what we are capable of becoming, is the only end of life."—Robert Louis Stevenson
2. *The joy of walking your walk*
   "I have always known that at last I would take this road, but yesterday I did not know that it would be today."—Natsume Soseki
3. *The joy of aiming high*
   "The greatest danger for most of us is not that our aim is too high and we miss it, but that it is too low and we reach it."—Michelangelo
4. *The joy of not wasting today*
   "Let him who would enjoy a good future waste none of his present."—Roger Babson
5. *The joy of amazement*
   "To live is so startling it leaves little time for anything else."—Emily Dickinson
6. *The joy of creating yourself*
   "Life isn't about finding yourself. Life is about creating yourself."—George Bernard Shaw
7. *The joy of engagement*
   "You must be the change you wish to see in the world."—Mahatma Gandhi

16.5 The joy of meaning returning

Meaninglessness feels awful. But meaning returning feels great! One source of genuine existential joy for human beings is the realization that meaning, which can vanish, can and likely will return. It's right around the corner! A second source of genuine existential joy, in addition to that realization, is the corollary reality: the experience of it returning. Here is meaning again! How excellent!

Meaning is a deep, inexhaustible wellspring and an infinitely renewable resource. Today, it may not seem meaningful to you to sit by the pond and feed the ducks, as you have too much you want to do and too much on your mind. But 60 years from now—or even as soon as tomorrow, for that matter—you may experience sitting by that pond for an hour or two as abundantly meaningful. Now that sojourn and that interlude bring you joy. How lovely!

As your client learns how to "invest meaning" and how to "seize meaning opportunities," she creates more and more possibilities for existential joy. At nine in the morning, she fights an injustice, and that brings her existential joy that she showed up in that way. At ten in the morning, she sends her daughter at college a sweet note, and that brings her existential joy. At 11, she turns to the song she's been writing: paying attention to it and feeling its beauty and its possibilities brings her existential joy. At noon, she pays some bills, and even that feels meaningful, even that brings her a bit of joy, as she senses that she is living her day exactly correctly, exactly as she intends to live it, doing one right thing after another.

To think of meaning as something to find—something like a lost wallet or a lost ring—is to picture meaning as a very paltry thing. In that mental model, meaning is so small a commodity that you can acquire it by taking in a guru's lecture or by sitting cross-legged in a darkroom. You weren't sure what was meaningful; a guru speaks; and now you know. Really? How much existential joy can you experience if you construe meaning that way?

But, if you can help your client get clear that meaning must, by its very nature as a feeling, come and go—then, when it returns, like a lover back from the war or a child coming home from school, how wonderful! You might even throw a party!

Meaning comes in every color, singing every sort of tune. It arises one day one way because today you are valuing this; it arises tomorrow in another way because you are valuing that. Meaning is a renewable resource: you coax it into existence out of nothing but your own decision to represent yourself well and play the hero in your own story. And while it arises from nothing, just like that, it becomes like iron, at least for a moment. You wake up each morning because nature renews you that way; you arise, you consider your next meaning decision, and you make your next meaning investment. What joy!

My client Bob explained:

> I know nothing about ultimate reality and I'm certain that no one else does either. But I recognize that some things feel meaningful to me and even consistently meaningful. If this is true, that is the same thing as saying that

meaning is available to me. It may not be available to me at all times, in all moods, or in all weather, but I embrace the idea that meaning is a renewable human resource.

More than that, I can take charge of it bubbling up: that geyser is in my control. Somewhere I control the valve. If the valve gets turned off—if a meaning crisis strikes—I can turn it back on and cause meaning to flow again. This may sound strange in words but I know what I mean. I know how to accomplish this feat of restoring the meaning flow in my life. To be flowery about it, I am the garden and also the gardener. If nothing is growing, I know an existential cultivation trick or two. And that feels really good!

My client Marcia explained:

As I began to really see that meaning is a wellspring, I felt more connected, hopeful, empowered. I felt a sense of not only connecting to a particular meaning-making choice, but to a deeper awareness of the limitlessness of possible meanings and choices. I found myself at times visualizing journeying into a wellspring deep in the earth, traveling through time, traveling and shape-shifting into the awareness and viewpoints of other people, of animals, of trees, of energies that had taken a drink from the wellspring.

They were like little vignettes of creation stories. I realized that I was previously equating meaning-making with something heavy, demanding, responsible, but as soon as I internally agreed that meaning was a wellspring it not only shifted my understanding of meaning-making but brought on a lightness as well. Lightness and joy!

My client Frank put it this way:

Conceptualizing meaning as a wellspring changed my relationship to meaning. Like Old Faithful, the famous Yellowstone geyser, I began arriving at my desk with a bubbling up of energy. I experienced a building sense of creativity during the days when, because of my other responsibilities, I couldn't get to my writing; then, on the days when I could, I found myself able to stay put for much longer periods of time.

The image of an inexhaustible wellspring helped me maintain meaning on the days when I couldn't get to the computer and it helped me make meaning on the days when I could. It seemed to work on many levels, to deepen my connection to my creative work, to banish existential depression, and to help me do the ordinary, everyday things more lightly and effortlessly. I can't say why it worked that way—but the change is amazing!

Like everyone, I have to decide on a daily basis where to invest my capital, what to care about, and whether anything is worth caring about. On most days, I decide to care, and I figure out where I want to invest meaning.

16.6 The experience of grandeur

Existential joy and the experience of grandeur are related feelings. Both connect us to something not only positive but also to something with a whiff of ineffable mystery, with the sense that life, for all of its undeniable downside, also has an undeniable upside. Grandeur is a feeling to prize, but how often do we or our clients experience it?

We tend to associate the word "grandeur" with events like royal weddings and sights like the Grand Canyon. Hotels are grand, canals are grand, and cruise ships are grand. But something about that way of thinking prevents us from feeling a sense of grandeur from the other stuff of existence, like an image that we craft, a jam that we jar, or a kiss that we give. For more reasons than we can count, grandeur isn't very present in our daily lives.

In all the meetings that I've ever attended—faculty meetings, business meetings, meetings of therapists, and meetings of artists—I've never heard anyone say, "What's wanted is a little more grandeur." Have you? On the long list of things discussed when people gather, grandeur never appears. There are no parties honoring it, no organizations devoted to it, and no lobbyists buttonholing members of Congress and whispering, "Support the grandeur bill, and we'll make it worth your while!"

I remember sitting in a sterile coffee-break room in a suite of offices, writing by hand before the class I taught was to begin. In a corner of the room were some boxes of computer parts. There was a soda machine, a microwave, a copy machine, a fire extinguisher, a sink, a wastepaper basket, and a metal cabinet for office supplies. The walls were a dull blue-gray, the round table at which I sat was the same dull blue-gray, and so were the chairs and the floor.

But on the wall across from me was a poster of a Manuel Neri oil-on-paper called *Alberica No. 1*. It portrayed a woman with a blue face, a yellow torso, and burgundy legs. The top half of the background was a brilliant yellow, and the bottom half was a striking blue. If I hadn't had it or something like it on the wall to look at, I would surely have fainted from grandeur deprivation in a room like that.

Think about your own life. What last stirred feelings of grandeur in you? Was it something you saw on the commute to your day job, some reality show episode, or something you experienced at a meeting? Probably not. My hunch is that you were last stirred by a piece of music, a film, a passage in a book, or a piece of art. You stopped, listened to the music, and said to yourself, "How beautiful!" or "How powerful!" or "This is good stuff!" You were transported. In the back of your mind, you maybe whispered, "I should be creating and doing work this strong." Maybe you said to yourself, but not in such a way that you could hear the message clearly, "Without this beauty, I would die."

The painter Max Beckmann once said, "All important things in art have always originated from the deepest feeling about the mystery of Being." I think that this sentiment comes close to capturing the origins of our sense of grandeur. We are built to appreciate mystery, to harbor deep feelings, and to contemplate the universe with its marvelous quirks and distinguishing features. To bring less than all of this to life is to bring only a shadow of our inheritance. Without a Neri on the wall, Mozart in the air, or Dostoevsky in our hands, we would wither away, no matter how good the benefits and stock options at our day job. We need grandeur to survive.

You can remind yourself of this necessity by installing a grandeur corner in the room that is your mind. Picture your mind as a room that you're able to redesign and redecorate. Inhabiting that grandeur corner, you freely and deeply hold the intention to contemplate or create something powerful, beautiful, admirable, meaningful, resonant, and grand. You remind yourself that grandeur is available and that you can create it yourself.

What is actually in that corner? That's for you to decide. Maybe it's filled with music. Maybe on a chalkboard is the scientific formula that always stirs you. Maybe you'll choose items that evoke feelings of awe and mystery. Maybe nothing in your grandeur corner will look grand in any traditional sense. I'd be surprised if you installed marble staircases and velvet drapes. You might even find very homey objects there: a stone from a riverbed and a whimsical doll. Visit the room that is your mind, pick a suitable corner, and fill it in such a way that being there evokes the feeling of grandeur.

I wanted to end on a note of grandeur. We've looked at many of the challenges that human beings face and how existential wellness coaches can help clients meet those challenges and rise to the occasion of being human. We paint a picture of authentic living, of making meaning, of living our life purposes, of giving life a thumbs-up, and of confronting life as an absurd rebel. And we help clients find opportunities for joy and ways to smile. This is great and good work, and I invite you to participate.

FOOD FOR THOUGHT

1. What, for you, are sources of existential joy?
2. What might you try in order to increase the amount of existential joy in your own life?
3. How might you help clients increase the amount of existential joy in their lives?
4. If you have the desire to become an existential wellness coach, how might you proceed?
5. What are your concluding thoughts about existential wellness coaching?

Postscript

This . . . and so much more

The phrase “a healthy adult” does not conjure up a clear picture. We feel inclined to ask, “healthy in what ways?” A person with everything can still feel suicidal, and a person with nothing can still laugh and smile. A person in chronic pain can still feel alive, and a person in perfect health can feel dull and apathetic. Is there any one thing we are trying to suggest when we say, “Look, there’s a healthy adult!”?

These are among the many complexities about human nature and human existence that existential wellness coaches honor and accept. We do not know why a cloud passing in front of the sun can ruin a week, existentially speaking, but we know that it can. We know that life can feel meaningful—and the next moment, not. We know that we can feel full of purpose one moment and drained of purpose the next. All of this happens—and it is the territory in which we work.

The need for existential wellness coaches can only grow. We can name all of the reasons, from AI to political unrest, from battles over scarce resources to intrusions on our privacy. The list of reasons is very long, longer than we can tolerate. More and more people will be asking, “Why bother?” and coming up with fewer and fewer good reasons. Existential wellness coaches are there on the frontlines of existence, helping clients cope with what is absolutely most important to them: how to live, given life’s realities.

I hope you will embrace this profession and go on what is bound to prove an amazing journey, helping your fellow human beings who are bravely dealing with life’s joys and hardships. If you’d like to participate in the trainings I’ve created in collaboration with Noble-Manhattan Coaching, you can find information on them here:

Existential Wellness Coaching: https://wellnesscoachtraining.online/

Creativity Coaching: https://creativitycoaching.online/

DOI: 10.4324/9781003724971-17

Relationship Coaching: https://relationshipcoach.training/

I also invite you to visit my website: https://ericmaisel.com/

And feel free to be in touch: ericmaisel@hotmail.com

Good luck on your journey!

References

Archer, A. (2022). *Existential coaching: A handbook for working with meaning and purpose*. Routledge. https://doi.org/10.4324/9781003198864

Beckett, S. (1954). *Waiting for Godot* (G. Mcdonald, Trans.). Grove Press.

Binswanger, L. (1963). *Being-in-the-world: Selected papers of Ludwig Binswanger*. Basic Books.

Boss, M. (1963). *Existential foundations of medicine and psychology*. Holt, Rinehart and Winston.

Bugental, J. F. T. (1965). *The search for authenticity: An existential-analytic approach to psychotherapy*. Holt, Rinehart and Winston.

Camus, A. (1991). *The myth of Sisyphus* (J. O'Brien, Trans.). Vintage International. (Original work published 1942)

Chatto and Windus., C. (1991). *The ethics of authenticity*. Harvard University Press.

de Beauvoir, S. (2011). *The second sex* (Borde & Malovany-Chevallier, Trans.). Vintage. (Original work published 1949).

de Beauvoir, S. (2018). *The ethics of ambiguity* (Schwartz, Trans.). Open Road. (Original work published 1947).

Frankl, V. E. (1963). *Man's search for meaning: An introduction to logotherapy*. Beacon Press.

Frankl, V. E. (1967). *The doctor and the soul: From psychotherapy to logotherapy*. Vintage Books.

Heidegger, M. (1962). *Being and time* (J. Macquarrie & E. Robinson, Trans.). Harper & Row. (Original work published 1927)

Kierkegaard, S. (1944). *The concept of anxiety: A simple psychologically orienting deliberation on the dogmatic issue of hereditary sin* (R. Thomte, Trans.). Princeton University Press. (Original work published 1844)

Kierkegaard, S. (1983a). *Fear and trembling* (H. V. Hong & E. H. Hong, Eds. and Trans.). Princeton University Press. (Original work published 1843)

Kierkegaard, S. (1983b). *The sickness unto death* (H. V. Hong & E. H. Hong, Trans.). Princeton. (Original work published 1849).

Maslow, A. H. (1968). *Toward a psychology of being* (2nd ed.). Van Nostrand.

Maslow, A. H. (1971). *The farther reaches of human nature*. Viking.

May, R. (1950). *The meaning of anxiety*. W. W. Norton.

May, R. (1953). *Man's search for himself*. W. W. Norton.

Nietzsche, F. (1967). *Thus spoke Zarathustra* (W. Kaufmann, Trans.). Vintage Books.

Nietzsche, F. (2003). *Beyond good and evil* (J. Norman, Trans.). Cambridge University Press.

Nietzsche, F. (2006). *The birth of tragedy* (D. Breazeale, Ed., W. Kaufmann, Trans.). Vintage Books.
Rogers, C. R. (1957). The necessary and sufficient conditions of therapeutic personality change. *Journal of Consulting Psychology, 21*(2), 95–103.
Rogers, C. R. (1961). *On becoming a person.* Houghton Mifflin.
Sartre, J.-P. (1943). *Nausea* (L. Emmons, Trans.). New Directions.
Sartre, J.-P. (1944). *No exit* (S. Gilbert, Trans.). Vintage Books.
Sartre, J.-P. (1992). *Being and nothingness* (H. E. Barnes, Trans.). Washington Square Press. (Original work published 1943)
Stevenson, R. L. (1882). *Familiar studies of men and books* (p. 36).
Wong, P. T. P. (2011). Positive psychology 2.0. *Canadian Psychology, 52*(2), 69–81.
Wong, P. T. P. (2016a). *Meaning-centered counseling & therapy: New directions in logotherapy and existential positive psychology*. Canadian Scholars Press.
Wong, P. T. P. (2016b). *The human quest for meaning* (2nd ed.). Routledge.
Wong, P. T. P. (2021). Made for resilience and happiness. *International Journal of Existential Positive Psychology, 10*(1), 1–22.
Yalom, I. D. (1980). *Existential psychotherapy*. Basic Books.
Yalom, I. D. (2008). *Staring at the sun: Overcoming the terror of death.*

Index

actions 61
aftermath 42–43
agency 138
aging dancer 38, 57, 109–110, 162, 174–176
ambiguity 116–117, 118–120, 127–128; clarity and not-knowing 122–123; ethics of 15; helping clients deal with 127–128; the knowable and the not knowable 123–124; normalizing uncertainty 120–121; postmodern thought 117–118; tips for coping with uncertainty 125–127; triggered by uncertainty 124–125
American existential–humanistic therapy 13, 15–16
analysis, existential 15–16
anxiety 14; creative 177; of individuality 55–56; *see also* existential anxiety
authenticity 14–15, 154–156; bad faith 157–159; changing what can change 156–157; as commodity 18; decision-making 56; "good enough" 17; vignettes 159–165
avoidance 34

bad faith 15, 57, 157–159, 176
belonging 17
body: healthy body 24, 110–111
boundary clarification 44–45
breakthrough 35
Buddhism 16
Bugental, J. 15

career transitions 139
change 156–157
check-in, life purposes 68
choice 138
clarity 122–123
classical sources 14–15
classical therapies of the self 13–14
client scenarios 35–46
clinical practice 16
coaching *see* coaching meaning; existential wellness coaching
coaching meaning 71–73; meaning investments 73–80; meaninglessness 73
commodity, authenticity as 18
community mapping 45–46
complexity 93
conformity 49–52, 55
Confucian traditions 16
constraint 18
creativity 166–167; aging dancer 174–176; creative expression 57creative personality 52–55; despondent painter 172–174; existential importance of 167–169; reclaim creative nature 176–178; struggling writer 169–172
crisis of meaning 33, 81–90
critical interventions 16
critique 16–17, 18
cross-cultural dialogs 16–17

daily steadiness 25, 114
dancers 118–120, 174–176
death awareness 17
debates 18
de Beauvoir, S. 15

decision-making: authentic 56; ownership 41–42
denial of reality 93
depression 94–96
despair 14
despondent painter 172–174
dialogs 16–17
digital life 17
DSM 11; and medicalization 16–17

emotional acknowledgment 41
emptiness 35
energy management 69
engagement 35
ethics of ambiguity 15
evidence 18
existential analysis 15–16
existential anxiety 104–105; history of concept of 105–109; and twelve pillars of wellness 109–115
existential concept, freedom fighter as 151–153
existential–humanistic therapy, American 12, 13, 15–16
existential importance of creativity 167–169
existentialism 59–60, 106–108, 117, 155, 157, 167; as ambitious philosophy 1–3; need for 3–6; theme of individuality 47–49
existential joy: angling for joy 184–185; experience of grandeur 188–189; history of concept of 180–183; joy of meaning returning 186–187; many faces of joy 185; opportunities for joy 183–184
existential–phenomenological turn 14–15
existential practices 138
existential psychotherapy 16
existential questioning 43
existential reality, marginalization of 12
existential sadness 92–93; choosing and living life purposes 94–103; complexity 93; mistakes and challenges 93–94
existential suffering 12
existential thought 1–9
existential tolerance 137–138
existential wellness: concept of 13–17; core dimensions 18; and existential thought 1, 6–9; and psychiatry 10
existential wellness coaching 1, 6, 13, 20–23, 32–33; client scenarios 35–46; four questions 26–31; hard questions 46; struggling with purpose 33–35; tactics 136–139; three paths 27–31; twelve pillars of wellness 23–26

fear 34
feminist interventions 16
Frankl, V. 15
freedom 15, 142–144; concepts embedded in 151–153; free not to be perfect 149–151; giving away your freedom 147–149; to make music 144–147
freedom fighter 151–153
future visioning 42–43

"good enough" authenticity 17
grandeur 188–189
guaranteed measure of sorrow 96–98

healthy body 24, 110–111
Heidegger, M. 14–15
helpful thoughts 24, 111–112
history: concept of existential anxiety 105–109; concept of existential joy 180–183; concept of existential wellness 10–19; of work 134–136
humanism: American existential–humanistic therapy 13, 15–16
human potential movement 15–16

icon, life purposes 64–65
identity 138
Indigenous traditions 16
individualism 18
individuality 58; and conformity 49–52; existential theme of 47–49; helping clients 55–57; and rebellion 52–55
integrated personality 24–25, 112
integration 18

journal, life purposes 66–68
joy: angling for 184–185; many faces of 185; of meaning 186–187; opportunities for 183–184; *see also* existential joy

Kierkegaard, S. 14
knowable, the 123–124

life-affirmation 14
life inventory 44
life philosophy 24, 35, 109–110
life purposes 59–60, 69, 94–103; align thoughts with life purpose choices 61–62; check-in 68; connecting work to 138; important things as life purpose choices 61; life purposes icon 64–65; life purposes journal 66–68; life purposes mantra 65–66; life purposes practices 68–69; life purposes statement 62–63; live life purpose choices 62; love as 69; practices that support life purpose choices 62; step-by-step process 60–62; vocabulary 68
logotherapy 15–16
loneliness 17
love 69

mantra, life purposes 65–66
mapping *see* community mapping
marginalization of existential reality 12
Maslow, A. 15–16
May, R. 15, 107–108, 167
meaning 17, 61, 177; clarify sources of 136–137; coaching meaning 71–80; crisis of 81–90; daily acts of meaning-making 35; and the *DSM* 11; love as meaning opportunity 69; meaning-centered reframing 40; meaning investments 73–80; normalizing crisis of meaning 33; return of 17; social 17; sustainable 25, 113; as vital need 15; work 137
meaninglessness 73
measurement 17
medicalization 16–17
metaphor, freedom fighter as 151–153
mind: peaceful mind 24, 110; redesign your mind 69
mistakes 93–94
mood 101–103
moral philosophy 13–14
mortality 14–15
multicultural interventions 16
music 144–147

narrative: narrative reconstruction 41; productivity narratives 178
narrow-frame medical model 10–11
nature of the task 60–61
nature of work 137
Nausea 167–169
Nietzsche, F. 14
nihilism, creativity as resistance to 178
normalization: creative anxiety 177; crisis of meaning 33; uncertainty 120–121
not knowable, the 123–124
not knowing 69, 122–123

occupation, purposeful 25, 112–113
outlook, positive 24, 111

painter 172–174
paradox exploration 44
paths 26–31
peaceful mind 24, 110
perfectionism 149–151, 178
personal philosophy of life 35
pharmacology 11–12
phenomenology: existential–phenomenological turn 14–15
philosophy 15–16; life philosophy 24, 35, 109–110; *see also* existentialism; moral philosophy
pluralization 16–17
positive outlook 24, 111
positive psychology 17
postmodern thought 117–118
practice/practices 17, 62; existential 138; life purpose practices 68–69, 68
presence 44
productivity narratives 178
profession, work as 139–141
psychiatry 10
psychology, positive 17
psychotherapy, existential 16
purpose 33–35, 59–60, 69; life purposes icon 64–65; life purposes journal 66–68; life purposes mantra 65–66; life purposes practices 68–69; life purposes statement 62–63; purposeful living 25, 114–115; purposeful occupation 25, 112–113; step-by-step process 60–62; through service 34; work as platform for 34

questioning, existential 43
questions 26–31; tactics for hardest questions 46

reality: denial of 93; marginalization of 12
rebellion 52–55, 151–152
reflection 57
reframing: meaning-centered 40; nature of call 137; work 34
relationships: addressing role of 56–57; valuable 25, 113–114
resistance 151–153; creativity as resistance to nihilism 178
retention 57
ritual creation 45
rituals of creative renewal 177–178
Rogers, C. 15–16

sadness *see* existential sadness
safe environment 24, 112
Sartre, J.-P. 15, 167–169
self, the: choosing the self 14; classical therapies of 13–14; self-creation 14; self-worth 138
service, purpose through 34
silence 44
simplicity 93
social meaning 17
social structure 18
sorrow 94–96; guaranteed measure of 96–98
spiritual care 13–14
statement, life purposes 62–63
steadiness 25, 114
stories 59–60, 69, 132–134; clarifying values through 33–34; life purposes icon 64–65; life purposes journal 66–68; life purposes mantra 65–66; life purposes practices 68–69; life purposes statement 62–63; step-by-step process 60–62
struggling writer 169–172
suffering, existential 12
surrendering to not knowing 69
sustainable meaning 25, 113

tactics 32–33, 136–139; client scenarios 35–46; hard questions 46; struggling with purpose 33–35
task, work as 139–141
therapy 15–16; therapies of the self 13–14
thought: align with life purpose choices 61–62; existential thought 1–9; helpful thoughts 24, 111–112; postmodern thought 117–118
tolerance: existential 137–138; of uncertainty 42

uncertainty 116–117, 118–120, 127–128; clarity and not-knowing 122–123; helping clients deal with 127–128; the knowable and the not knowable 123–124; normalizing 120–121; postmodern thought 117–118; tips for coping with 125–127; tolerance of 42; triggered by 124–125

valuable relationships 25, 113–114
values: alignment 137; clarification 33–34, 40; value creation 56
vignette 49–52, 98–101, 159–165
visioning *see* future visioning
vocabulary, life purposes 68

well-being science 17
wellness: broader vision of 12–13; twelve pillars of 23–26, 109–115; *see also* existential wellness
work 130–134; existential wellness coach tactics 136–139; history 134–136; as platform for purpose 34; as profession 139–141; as task 139–141
writer 169–172

Yalom, I. 16

For Product Safety Concerns and Information please contact our EU
representative GPSR@taylorandfrancis.com
Taylor & Francis Verlag GmbH, Kaufingerstraße 24, 80331 München, Germany

www.ingramcontent.com/pod-product-compliance
Ingram Content Group UK Ltd.
Pitfield, Milton Keynes, MK11 3LW, UK
UKHW022353190926
475702UK00015B/2275
* 9 7 8 1 0 4 1 2 0 9 2 7 0 *